Keep Calm and Fanny On

KEEP CALM
AND
FANNY ON!

The many careers of

Fanny Cradock

by

Kevin Geddes

fantom
publishing

First published in 2019 by Fantom Publishing, an imprint of Fantom Films
www.fantompublishing.co.uk

A catalogue record for this book is available from the British Library.

Hardback edition ISBN: 978-1-78196-339-5

Typeset by Phil Reynolds Media Services, Leamington Spa
Printed and bound by CPI Group (UK) Ltd, Croydon, CR0 4YY
Jacket design by Will Brooks
Front cover image © Allan Warren

All photographs not specifically credited are from the author's own collection.

To Mum, with special thanks for that blue birthday cake all those years ago
in our orange kitchen with flowery wallpaper…

To Callum for endless patience and for not rolling your eyes (too much)
when yet another Fanny Fact was revealed…

Especially for Suzanne, for being a super-number-one-Fanny-Fan…
Hope you enjoy it!

CONTENTS

FOREWORD

I HAVE FOND MEMORIES of my time with Fanny. I remember the positive things. Fanny was knowledgeable, she was an interesting woman, she was well informed. She certainly knew all about cuisine, there was no doubt about that. She was also an incredibly intelligent person. She really was a great entertainer. She was extremely hospitable and generous as well. When she had switched off, when she was not 'on show', she was the most charming, engaging woman.

In private life she was quite laid back. I remember one time she came to stay with us when we lived in the country. After settling in, she came down, kicked her shoes off and sat round the fire, engaging in lively conversation. She was delightful with the children, warm and charismatic. She brought them little presents and clearly adored their company. Fanny was used to being around young minds. She tutored young people, she took them in and was like a surrogate mother to them.

Johnnie, her husband, came into his own in private too; he contributed equally. On television, the impression was that Johnnie was a bit of a hen-pecked husband, but he was not. Johnnie was her rock. Without him, Fanny would have been lost. He was strong and secure. Fanny depended upon him. He supported her professionally and personally, which helped her carry on, with confidence, in public and private life.

Surprisingly, the Fanny I knew was quite a muddled lady. She had the most difficult start in life. She did not have a good relationship with her children, which was sad, strange and never resolved. I did not understand that side to her personality at all. It just was not what I saw when we were in her company.

Watching her during her performances on television, she appeared to be rather aggressive and forceful. Everything was filmed 'live' in those days, which made a tremendous difference. Like a lot of performers, when Fanny was going out to entertain, she became a little tense. We all have nerves, we all get tense, it pumps the adrenalin. When you are a beginner, at times your nerves work against you and you are not as good as you should be. When you are more mature, you still get nervous. If you do not, you are in the wrong profession. You find a way to make your nerves work for you. It seems that Fanny's nerves worked against her and she came across a little combative, which was not her true nature.

Fanny completely changed the way that cooking was seen on television. When she started, cooking was fairly new on television. Television itself was still relatively new. We had Philip Harben and then Fanny Cradock. They proved to be popular personalities, and cooking on television became more widespread. Now, nearly every other programme is either about cooking or they have a cooking item in the programme. A lot of this is due to Fanny. She cooked on TV for twenty years. She led the way, setting the mould for others to emulate.

Fanny introduced a whole lot of different ideas and originality into preparing a meal, not the usual simple dishes. Fanny introduced us all to new products and often strange ingredients that we would probably never have thought of using before. Nowadays, you can buy almost anything; we never had this when we were young.

Fanny had a great intelligence. She could write quite well. She seemed always to be writing. She wrote more books than even she could remember, not all of them cookery books. She especially loved to write children's books. She was proud of those.

When you have known someone for a long time you do not always remember the first meeting. It was like that with Fanny. I appeared on one of her early television shows for the BBC, *Kitchen Party*. It was around 1965 or thereabouts. She was always introducing new ideas. She cooked sensational food for a small group of invited celebrities in a dinner-party setting. That was towards the end of my partnership with Arthur Haynes, and our shows were high-profile then. She had no doubt seen it and that would be the reason I was invited along.

Fanny herself was often called upon to appear on quiz shows on TV, light entertainment shows really. She seemed to thoroughly enjoy those. Some of those were with me, discussion shows like *Look Who's Talking* and *Password*. She was a big personality; she had that show-off element which you needed to shine. Although she enjoyed cooking and was brilliant at it, she realised that people also enjoyed her for the personality. She was a natural show-off. She could talk well, refreshingly so, and was quite striking to watch.

When I hosted a television panel quiz show about food and drink, *Know Your Onions*, on BBC a few years later, I knew that Fanny would make a perfect guest. She returned several times; we got on well. It was perhaps then that I was elevated to her 'friendly' invitation list.

Fanny's 'social list' was the absolute talk of the town. To be invited to one of her legendary parties at the Dower House in Watford was the social highlight in London at that time. Her parties were always great fun. She invited people from all walks of life, from showbusiness to politics. She knew us, so we were asked. On one particular occasion Gyles Brandreth was there; that was where I first met him, and we have remained friends ever since.

Fanny liked to make a grand entrance at her own parties. She was a personality, and naturally took the opportunity to shine. We would all have been somewhat disappointed had she not. She never wore an apron. She believed that aprons marked women out as 'domestic slaves'. She knew that cooking for others should be fun with an added illusion of glamour, so Fanny was always ready to present herself to her guests. She always wore a smart dress and I never saw her spill any of her fabulous food down it.

Fanny enjoyed being the hostess so very much. She ran it all a certain way. All the guests would be ushered into the kitchen, where she would, of course, be thoroughly prepared. She went to a great deal of trouble, preparing all kind of dishes. They were all laid out on her huge kitchen table. She was always testing new ideas. She would say, 'You must try that one over there… This is a new thing I've been trying… This is a wonderful pudding. Try this one. Try this.' All the dishes were, as we came to expect, marvellous. She wanted to please, to show off.

Gyles recalls a very particular story, which was typical of these nights. He delights in telling it. It is somewhat against me, but it makes me smile to think of it still. He was President of the Oxford Union and had met Fanny when he had invited her there to speak. In return, he was invited to the party. We had finished the amazing food. Then suddenly Fanny, out of the blue, for no apparent reason said, 'Right now darlings, everyone quiet, Nicholas is going to entertain us! Nicholas, do a turn!' She never warned me, nor thought to ask me.

When Fanny requested, you followed. So, I stepped forward and did a part of one of my cabaret routines. I used to do a lot of cabaret in those days, in places like Quaglino's, the Allegro, the Blue Angel and at the famous Café de Paris, so I had a lot of cabaret material to call on. It was a routine about foreign films with subtitles. It was different, original, and it went rather well with the party crowd. Gyles could not get over the way Fanny suddenly said, 'Right, Nicholas is going to entertain us,' but that was how she was. Very autocratic and yet somehow, like a lot of people with strong personalities, you responded favourably.

Although we enjoyed the hospitality that Fanny and Johnnie offered, we never stayed the night there. We had been warned if we did to be prepared for something very peculiar. Fanny was a great gardener; she grew her own vegetables. She was quite frugal. According to the rumour which was spread around, she would say to her guests if they were staying the night: 'Do not use the lavatory, use the pisspot under the bed because I like to put it on my brassicas, it does them the power of good!'

I think in many ways Fanny was a sad woman, despite her huge talent and success. Of course, there was the unfortunate moment on television in 1976, *The Big Time* with Esther Rantzen, when she was asked to comment on some beginner's work. I can only presume she was trying to be entirely professional, but again appeared to be tense, coming across instead as rude. I am sure that was her final major appearance on television; people did not see her much after that. She seemed to lack the sensitivity to be tactful to somebody who was trying to cook something for the first time, someone who was not in showbusiness.

She became increasingly known as a difficult woman and has remained as such in people's minds ever since. People remember the negatives. Her last days were rather sad. She had lost her rock in Johnnie, and, like a lot of people who are a little eccentric, she obviously became more so when she was by herself.

I tried to keep in touch. I recall speaking with Mary Malcolm, the television announcer, who knew her well. She said, 'Fanny is suffering; do contact her if you can, talk to her. I fear she is not herself. I wondered if you could reach out to her, maybe cheer her up or help her in some way?' I tried to, but she seemed to disappear. Perhaps she did not want to be found towards the end. I asked around, but it seems she was not in touch with anyone. I think her last days were not happy ones.

When she sadly died, she attracted a lot of criticism in the press. People started to tell very different stories about her. When she was alive, people had a lot of time for her. In her later years she became a little 'difficult', overly critical, and people are inclined to remember that. A hundred positive things about someone will be forgotten if they start to do one thing which is not very positive.

I heard that Fanny died in a nursing home. Some friends, possibly some of those young people that she took in, found her living, sadly, in a terrible state. The word was that they made sure she was looked after and that her affairs were in order. Without Johnnie, things had become a terrible muddle. When Johnnie died, she did not attend his funeral. She found it too difficult to think about. She slightly went to pieces.

I hang on to my positive memories. I know it was sad at the end, and, knowing her well, I put a great deal of it down to the loss of Johnnie. She had a wonderful and varied career, full of all the usual highs and lows, most of which have been tragically overshadowed by the repetition of negative memories. I hope that in some way the wonderful Fanny Cradock that I knew will be reinstated in people's minds once more. She did, indeed, have many careers, and many sides to her character. She was a good friend whom I remember with great fondness.

Nicholas Parsons
July 2019

INTRODUCTION

Mention the name 'Fanny Cradock' to anyone, young or old, and they tend to simply snigger, make an innuendo-heavy reference to doughnuts or squirm at the thought of long-forgotten meals disguised under layer upon layer of ever-increasingly bizarre food colourings and flourishes of garnish. She is, at least, remembered. She was hard to forget.

Her legacy collapsed faster than you could say 'freshly baked soufflé' when she died twenty-five years ago. It became popular to talk her down: laughing at her appearance captured as if in aspic on YouTube; discussing the 'shocking' way she treated her assistants and husband-come-sidekick, Johnnie; repeating rumours that she 'couldn't cook anyway', was rude to everyone she ever met and spent her days swanning around her kitchen in elaborate ballgowns barking orders as she went.

However, there is much more to Fanny Cradock than even the most elaborately pencilled-in eyebrow might suggest. The 'real' story is just as weird, wonderful and wacky as the myths that persist.

Fanny Cradock had many careers; she was the mistress of reinvention before Madonna had even considered it. She was an entrepreneur, business-woman, activist, journalist, food critic, travel guru, food demonstrator, fiction writer, children's author, cookbook creator, media personality and, as she is most remembered, a television cook – often called the first 'celebrity chef'. Fanny deliberately created the over-the-top persona which catapulted her into the living rooms of millions of British viewers in the 1950s, riding high as *the* 'television celebrity chef' until the 1970s, enabling her to remain in the hearts and minds of the public to this day.

Most people connect 'Fanny' to 'Johnnie' in their thoughts. They go together like a force of marriage – even though for most of their life together, including most of their time in the spotlight, they were not married to each other. Johnnie was seen as the 'sidekick' to Fanny's stage and screen persona, loyally by her side to help when things in the kitchen got a little troublesome. In the public's mind, Johnnie was there to support Fanny in whatever endeavour she was embarking upon. Ask people about Fanny Cradock on television and (mostly) they will tell you that about Johnnie sharing the screen with her. Almost as if he always did.

People further connect Johnnie to being fond of a tipple or two, in vision and off. In reality, Fanny was the star beamed into homes around the country. Johnnie seldom appeared alongside her. He did occasionally pop up to provide expert opinion about wine and other drinks, complementing Fanny's choice of food perfectly. They, of course, were professionally known together as 'Bon Viveur', the gastronomic couple interested in only the finest food. They did appear together almost everywhere else, however: in magazines, in the headlines, on game shows. They were *the* celebrity couple. It was this celebrity that ensured that, in the memories of even those who may never really have seen them, they were joined forever.

Just as people recall 'Johnnie' being 'Johnny', the most common mistake to follow them both around was their surname. Forever mistakenly credited as 'Craddock' instead of 'Cradock', Fanny in particular tried her very hardest to correct each and every person who got it wrong. Her typewriter would be brought almost to flame-inducing levels each evening as she typed 'furious letters' to newspaper editors who dared to spell their surname incorrectly, demanding that they issue an apology as well as making sure the almighty slip-up never occurred again. Producers at the BBC, where she filmed her most famous television programmes, were also guilty. Contracts, letters and memos would duplicate the double 'd' with alarming regularity, matched with the same amount of frenzied correspondence from the Cradock household. No one was immune to correction. No one would escape the wrath of Fanny. No one would forget any interaction with her. The mistaken spellings would continue to flow long after both Fanny and Johnnie died. They are not forgotten, but sadly now there is no one to write the incensed letters.

Fanny herself is often remembered for her appearance, either positively or less so. Almost sixty-five years after she first appeared on stage, and screen, wearing an elaborate ballgown to cook an even more elaborate 'bill of fare', that image is scorched into the collective retina of the nation. She always cooked in a ballgown, didn't she? The reality, again, is very different from the memory. Fanny herself continued to connect herself to 'cooking in ballgowns' as it was her unique selling point, regardless of the fact that she updated her fashions and appearance, matching the trends of the time effortlessly to define each decade. The fifties were glamorous. The sixties were fun and playful. The seventies were bold. The eighties were colourful and powerful. Her eyebrows headed ever north on her forehead as each decade rolled past, but her 'look' adapted, changed and evolved as much as her careers did. Ballgowns remained in the past, but would forever define Fanny's future.

It can be hard to erase the images of some of Fanny's food from your mind. This is what she planned all along. She invented mashed potatoes luridly coloured green (with harmless vegetable dyes) knowing that 'once seen, never forgotten', even if they were only 'seen' in monochrome by readers, listeners and viewers at first. She associated herself with flashes of colour, flushes of fun and façades of flamboyance in food from day one. She never explained 'why'; she just steamrolled through with ever-increasingly eye-watering hues, tones and presentation, insisting that 'above all, garnish and presentation' was the key to culinary success. Over time, she didn't need to justify a thing, it was just 'her thing', something that people thought strange at the time, but still copied. The colours may have dimmed (a little) today, but retro fashions for bright, clashing creations still remain.

People remember the food, too. 'She invented the prawn cocktail' is a line often associated with Fanny Cradock, even though she actually held the dish in disdain. She called it 'one of the most sordid little affairs', normally featuring a 'tired prawn drooping disconsolately over the edge of the glass like a debutante at the end of her first ball', made with severely inferior mayonnaise and tomato sauce, 'bottled stuff', that should be consigned to the bin. The solution, of course, was to make it according to her recipe. She preferred shrimps. She made 'real' mayonnaise. She added Tabasco, cream and sherry. She gave the dish a flourish with paprika, cucumber rounds arranged in overlapping lines and a garnish of a basket made from lemon. She never claimed to invent the dish. Similarly, she never denied it. If people wanted to connect her with it, she would not correct them. Only their methods.

A similar myth has formed as the years have passed, forever entwinned with Fanny and Johnnie. Doughnuts. People claim to remember hearing Johnnie say to the adoring audience at the end of a television demonstration: 'May all your doughnuts turn out like Fanny's!' Others believed it to be a continuity announcer between programmes. Regardless, it became an innuendo-laden catchphrase for impersonators and comedians to latch on to. No doubt Fanny and Johnnie laughed about it too, but they were not responsible for it. Many people have claimed responsibility for the phrase. Many people have claimed to have heard it being broadcast. Many people have claimed to have laughed like a drain at the time, and indeed since. The truth is that only a few people really heard it happen at the time. Only people watching Scottish Television as Bill Tennant, a leading personality in the early years of STV, allegedly said the immortal line as Fanny finished making her famous doughnuts. Whatever the truth, Fanny will be forever linked to doughnuts, and doughnuts linked to Fanny.

Doughnuts, green mashed potatoes and prawn cocktails are not the only foods to be associated with Fanny. Hardly a surprise, given her reign as 'queen of television cuisine' for over two decades. Her food legacy is just as bizarre as her life. People imagine a Fanny Cradock dining table to be groaning with rather suggestive-looking banana candles, overly moist mincemeat omelettes and indeed anything other than a bramble sauce, regarding which she famously claimed to have no idea of what a 'bramble' was. People remember her food as 'snobby' as well as playful, which probably sums her up nicely in reality. She had her own distinct style, a creation designed to ensure she was never forgotten, even if for all the wrong reasons.

It can be hard to conjure up an image of Fanny and to not see a trembling assistant at her side. The most-played clips on the most-watched television retro shows play into this memory. She was nasty to them, wasn't she? She treated them as badly as she treated Johnnie, didn't she? She surely force-fed them green potatoes, prawn cocktails and doughnuts day and night. They must have been kept captive in her home, only allowed out to perform basic tasks on television in response to her booming, and often hurtful, instructions. Again, the reality may veer off the accepted and acceptable memory that has been preserved of Fanny Cradock.

Whether Fanny is being remembered as a pioneer of television cooking, or as an ogre who 'abandoned her own children' in pursuit of fame and fortune, she is still being remembered. Recreations of aspects and carefully curated memories of her dramatic life have appeared in biographical films like *Fear of Fanny* starring Julia Davis and Mark Gatiss, which met with mixed reviews from those who knew her, worked with her and remembered her. Not always the figure people 'love to hate', more positive memories are portrayed by leading figures of food television, whether it be Annie Gray recreating some of her best foil-cooked dishes or Nigella Lawson referencing her as part of her Christmas specials; her name at least is still on the tip of the tongue where food is concerned.

The story of Fanny Cradock is hard to tell in simple, straightforward chronology. She did not live a linear life. She was always on the go, always thinking of 'what next', always dreaming up another cunning plan to cement herself in the history books. In many ways, this was her greatest success. She is remembered.

However, her real life story and in particular the many, many careers that she successfully navigated are lost in the mists of time. In the chapters that follow, an attempt is made to remedy this. Each chapter will look at one particular 'career' in detail (with distinct chapters dedicated to each decade of her most famous career, as a television cook), with some overlap in time and place. There is no other way to lay out her complicated, intertwined and ultimately amazing story.

The Britain in which Fanny grew up and worked was not as open a society as it is today. Ideas of 'mental health' were not discussed. Traumatic events in anyone's life were often hushed, with those in pain and agony encouraged to have a 'stiff upper lip' approach to battling on regardless. No one talked of abusive, unloving, un-nurturing childhoods. Life was tougher, and as a result, people developed a tougher exterior, hiding true feelings and impacts from the world where they could. It wasn't commonplace to discuss conditions like dementia, fearful of the stigma that surrounded them. Today, things have changed, and we recognise the effect of actions in our past on our mental health. We recognise and support deteriorating conditions in later life, making allowances through our increased understanding.

As Fanny became older, her outwardly bizarre, and at times unpleasant, behaviour could be hard for some to bear. None of this makes any excuse for some of the behaviours displayed by Fanny. She could be mean to anyone who crossed her. She could be mean to people she had only just met. She could be mean to lifelong friends. However, her meanness was taken literally during her life, and in particular directly after her death, in a way that perhaps would be more respectfully acknowledged (perhaps) with a veil of understanding around some of the issues she faced, caused and dealt with during her life.

It does, however, throw a shadow over her achievements, achievements that would otherwise be hiding in plain sight. With a somewhat more sensitive understanding of her life, maybe, just maybe, we can re-evaluate her contribution more favourably. She had many careers, took many twists and turns, made many mistakes along the way.

Ultimately, should she be remembered as a batty old woman, bumbling around in a battered old ballgown, beastly to anyone and everyone, belting out bizarre culinary creations all day and every day…?

Or…

Early Life

Fanny Cradock spent most of her entire professional life trying to convince us that the version of her past she had created was true. Every interview would feature a 'fact' or two dropped into the conversation to reinforce the image of 'young Fanny's early life'. The problem was, perhaps, that very little of it was based on reality. The more research into Fanny's early years that is undertaken, the less is known with any certainty. This is maybe not the best thing to admit early on in a book devoted to her life; however, it is the backdrop to her whole story. It may all have been made up.

Family history, however, was important to Fanny, or at least to the created version of Fanny that we were presented with. She portrayed herself, at times, as a loving mother and even grandmother. She was, she told us, a doting wife. She had had a privileged upbringing, although she admitted it had been rocky at times, which had enabled her to learn all about the grander things in life. She had always been 'special' and had been treated as such by her proud parents, and her own grandmother.

Wendy Colvin, who later became an actress in her own right as Wendy Danvers, appearing as Amazonia in the *Doctor Who* story 'The Curse of Peladon' and alongside Russell Brand in 'My Old Tart?', an episode of his *Re: Brand* television series, worked with Fanny as her assistant, planning and delivering events in the 1950s and 1960s. Wendy believes that Fanny fabricated every detail of her 'story' to match the vision that she presented as the real 'Fanny Cradock'. 'I don't know about her when she was younger,' Wendy said. 'She wanted people to not know the truth.' Although Wendy was close to Fanny and crossed the line between 'assistant' and 'friend' (at least for a while), even she can't say with any certainty what the truth to her background is. All that Wendy is really sure of is that nothing was true. Perhaps nothing was *entirely* true? Surely everything had to have some basis in fact before it was embellished beyond belief? The issue remains that as soon as you begin to doubt things, everything is thrown into question.

Wendy believes that Fanny also spent as much time producing a suitable backstory for her husband and professional sidekick, Johnnie. 'Johnnie was frightened of her,' she said. 'He never really stood up to her. I only ever heard him one time, when we were driving down to the South of France. Fanny was shouting instructions. Johnnie told her to shut up. She went bananas. She told him, "You will be gone. Fanny can live without Johnnie, but Johnnie cannot live without Fanny. You will be back in the gutter!" She was furious.'

Fanny's imagination and flair for exaggeration were put to good use. If only she could remember what her version of the truth had been. She evaded any in-depth questions about her background (or indeed her personal life at all) throughout her life, preferring instead to repeat snippets of 'fact' from her portfolio of the past.

'She was a good cook though,' Wendy insists. 'I would defy anyone to say otherwise. Her omelettes were brilliant. I do not know where she learnt to cook; she used to say it was from her Gran. It was glamorous to say it had been in France. She really did test recipes time and time again. Nothing went in a book or on television before she tested it. Cooking with her was honest: she did not cheat. I gave her many recipes. I was not very clever in those days; I just gave them to her. She told me she could never find a good recipe for gingerbread. I had a good one from my mother. She said it was the best she had ever tasted. It then appeared in one of her books as *her* grandmother's recipe.'

Lifelong friend Evangeline Evans agreed, to some extent. Evangeline is an actress and was married to British actor Tenniel Evans. Evangeline's father was the English stage and screen actor, director and producer Leslie Banks, who was awarded a CBE for his services to the theatre in 1950. 'Her cooking was extraordinary, and pretty disgusting actually. Elizabeth David was god at the time, she taught us all about foreign cookery. Fanny said that all her culinary teaching came from France. With Fanny, nothing was ever left to be itself; she insisted on everything being covered in something or given another colour, like her green potatoes. She was a great snob, she had a thing about things being grand, but in reality the surprising thing was that her food was incredibly common. Embellished. Never the same. Had she grown up in a household where food was disgusting? Fanny was a marvellous baker, especially her bread and croissants. Her other food though was dreadful.'

Evangeline continued, 'She wasn't real, she did not seem real. You were not being presented with the real person. She didn't know who she was. She made herself up while she went along. I don't think she even knew the truth herself. Whatever the truth was, it was probably far too dreary; she had to make it up to be more colourful. She didn't look like a real person. She always thought she had huge sex appeal, but she was mannish. Odd. Strange. Endearing though!'

It will never be clear whether Fanny was cleverly leading us all to believe her version of the truth or if she indeed came to believe it herself. Something, or perhaps a combination of many things, in the past led her to lie about it. She kept things close to her chest and, with hindsight, appeared to be very guarded about every aspect of her private life. Did she have something to hide, or was the truth simply too hard to bear repeating, remembering and reliving?

'She could be incredibly cruel,' Evangeline recalls, 'but she had this enormous charisma. I don't know whether she invented herself in a way. She was a very complicated person. The persona of Fanny Cradock made her feel so unreal in a way. You never knew what the actual person was. She was very, very made-up. She was also incredibly dirty; she thought to be clean was very bourgeois. She decided she was going to be this grubby person.'

Fanny was born on the 26th of February 1909 in a large family-owned house called 'Apthorp', located at 33 Fairlop Road, Leytonstone, in the East London borough of Waltham Forest. She would later say that she had been born in the Channel Islands. Her mother, known as Bijou, was reputed to be eighteen years old at the time. Her father, Archibald, was thirty-two. The family home was owned by Fanny's grandmother, Emily Francis Hancock, and her husband, Charles James Sortain Hancock. Bijou and Archibald were married around eight months earlier, in June 1908, in West Ham. Perhaps as a result of their situation, with a child on the way, they moved in with Bijou's parents.

The site where the house was now sits on the corner of a suburban street in the heart of Leytonstone, an area about five miles north-east of London between the river Lea and Epping Forest. Leytonstone is now mainly a commuter suburb of small houses built between 1870 and 1910, interspersed with modern block and tower housing. The ancient parish was known as Low Leyton, because part of it lay low by the Lea.

A controversial 'blue plaque', part of the Waltham Forest heritage trail, marks the spot where the house once stood, noting that it had been there until 1930. Visitors may be mistaken in thinking that Fanny herself lived in the four-storey block of flats that occupies the site today, on the corner of a residential street, which no doubt Fanny would not be pleased about. She would indeed be furious that her name is misspelled on the plaque in the same way that enraged her throughout her life: a double 'D', causing it to read as Craddock instead of Cradock.

The plaque commemorates her years of birth and death, names the house that previously stood there as 'Apthorp', marks Fanny as 'the famous TV cookery expert' and records her name at birth as Phyllis Pechey, so at least her basic history is preserved in some way. She is joined on the Waltham Forest blue plaque trail by the infamous Damon Albarn, lead singer from Blur, and the illustrious Alfred Hitchcock, legendary film director.

Bijou and Archibald named their new daughter with a flourish, lifting her out of the ordinary, as Phyllis Nan Sortain Pechey, combining elements of both family histories in one. Before their marriage, Bijou was Bijou Sortain Hancock. It's not clear from any records if the 'Sortain' was a middle name, or indeed a double-barrelled addition. Her father was Charles James Sortain Hancock, and both connected and separated versions of the surname pervade today.

Fanny famously told and retold the story throughout her life of being 'gifted' to her grandmother at the age of one by her mother, supposedly unable to cope with a young and unexpected child. Bijou is reputed to have left her on the billiards table as a birthday present; allegedly she could think of nothing else more suitable for her own mother. Fanny's grandmother, Emily Francis, declared that Bijou was not fit to be a mother and accepted her gift. Fanny remained with her grandmother until she was ten years old. At this time, she was sent off to a boarding school.

Bijou and Archibald had been staying at Apthorp when Fanny was born, yet presumably had found a home of their own in the following twelve months. According to Fanny's recollections, Bijou was intent on becoming a mother again, dreaming of holding a baby son in her arms. That dream was realised only a few months later, when a brother for Fanny was born: Charles John Pechey. Perhaps the arrangement for Fanny to stay with her grandmother was born out of logistics rather than neglect, we will never be able to tell, but certainly Bijou and Archibald seemed to feel that bringing up both of their offspring together was not a good idea.

Whichever way it came about, Fanny held the memory of her grandmother very dearly. In her autobiography, *Something's Burning*, Fanny chooses to dedicate a chapter to her Gran ahead of her mother in the rundown of 'the people who have played the largest part' in her life. Fanny says she was raised by her grandmother with 'grandfather-clock stability' until she was ten.

A small lady, at five feet 'in her buckled slippers', Fanny also described her Gran as talented and immensely powerful. Fanny claimed that if she had been able to choose, she would have approved of her 'adoption'. She felt a rapport with her Gran: they were two of a kind. Fanny said they both preferred an intelligent sinner to a foolish saint. She went further, saying that they both put knowledge above virtue and talent above social position, which doesn't really chime with the version of Fanny she went on to portray. It was all part of the revisionist persona she created, and would continue to create for the rest of her life.

Fanny and her Gran were similar in spirit and soul. Fanny wondered if it was because she was brought up by her or whether she had been born that way. We don't know when Phyllis was first known as Fanny, short for Frances, which she said was her grandmother's middle name (although this was unlikely, given that her surname was Francis before she married). Perhaps it was the name she was known by? Phyllis appears to have mostly been referred to as Phyl when she was younger, and actually for the rest of her life she insisted upon some close friends calling her Phyl. Fanny was the 'creation'. Emily had an elder sister (nine years her senior) called Fanny, whom she may have reminded her of.

Fanny attributed all of her education to her Gran. She herself had been educated, which was not a given for young girls at the time she was born. Her own mother had worked as a tailoress, in what appeared to be a family business. Emily taught Fanny to read, with resources such as *The Times* and Darwin, naturally. As if mastering English at a young age was not enough, the leader from *The Times* had to be translated by Fanny into both French and German each and every morning. Emily also taught her deportment, instilling in her the inherent social value in being able to 'make an entrance' which Fanny would go on to use wherever she went. Others were drafted in to teach her violin and ballet, but it was her Gran herself who taught young Phyllis to play the piano.

However, it was food that became the main lesson for life in Phyllis's education plan. Fanny reported that her Gran adored cooking: so much so that she used to cook for her own social events and parties, a secret which had to remain undercover for fear of the guests finding out. They would be appalled to realise that the domestic staff had not been involved, you see. Fanny painted a picture of high society, dropping in references to her Gran throwing parties while they lived in India and then recreating scaled-down versions of the sumptuous soirées in semi-retirement in Essex.

In her autobiography, Fanny tells of times when her Gran was preparing food for these parties. Fanny would be installed in her 'high chair' so that she might view the proceedings well, and of course ask pertinent questions. These were not cookery lessons; Fanny learnt her culinary skills only by absorption. Emily spoke of great chefs and the origins of dishes with tremendous excitement. It was here that Fanny learnt her methods and started her lifelong passion for food. Later, Fanny would recount a similar tale, but this time the scene had moved from Essex to some of the finest kitchens in France. Again, she was placed in a 'high chair', or perched on the counter top. In the later telling of the same history, she had sneaked into the kitchen when she found herself bored while staying in fancy hotels on the continent as a child and watched in awe as the chefs prepared dish after dish. Again, she learnt how to do this simply by sight, absorbing everything around her.

Regardless of the elusive 'truth', Fanny's grandmother was undoubtedly the most influential adult in her formative years. Her descriptions of her character and life at times read like the life Fanny would have liked us to believe her own was. Her Gran loved a colour scheme for any party, insisting that everything in view was pink for a 'pink luncheon'. Flowers, tables, lampshades, candles and napkins would all fill the room with pinkness beyond belief, only to be offset with an entire menu of pink food. Even the wine, which a young Fanny was introduced to, was pink. All part of her education. Pale pink wine at age five, deep pink by eight and then, naturally, straight from the bottle by age ten, ready for school.

Fanny lays down the 'fact' in her autobiography that she had French blood running through her veins, from both sides of her family. Again, she would often repeat this notion as her career progressed. She maintained on the *Parkinson* television show during her appearance in 1972 that she was, after all, 'half French'. Perhaps she believed it herself. She claimed that her surname had been anglicised to 'Pechey' from 'de Peche', but it's not clear where her information came from. At the time of writing her autobiography she wrote to various members of her family, including her Aunt Mabel Pechey, a speech therapist living in Woking, Surrey, to try and get the history straight in her mind, or perhaps to ensure that everyone then had the same version in their minds. Mabel wrote several times to Fanny with snippets of alleged family history she had uncovered in dusty library volumes. Mabel drew a rough estimation of a family coat of arms and a crest for Fanny to use. In January 1958 she wrote to Fanny saying, 'I enclose some news of Peches – whether the Peach or Pechey or Peachie etc were related I do not know – I guess Peche and Pechey are the same.' Fanny welcomed the information, paying little regard to any accuracy. She said, 'A memoir of this kind is only written once in a lifetime.' At least never corrected.

The Pechey family actually can be traced back to 1777 when William Pechey was born in Isleham, near Cambridge. He married Ann Sharpe, and had a son called Richard in 1811, also born in Isleham. Richard married Charlotte Primrose and they named one of their sons John Thomas Primrose Pechey in 1837. He was Fanny's paternal grandfather and married Alice Emily Vallentin in 1865. Alice came from the aristocratic Vallentin family of distillers, based in London. Her brother, Grimble Vallentin, married Lucy Ann Fillis and had several children. One of their daughters, Florence Dorothea Vallentin, went on to marry into the Fearnley-Whittingstall family in 1905, providing Fanny with an albeit distant connection with cooking and television, which she would never know.

Fanny discusses her Gran's time in colonial India, and briefly mentions her maternal grandfather's career in the British Indian Army. He had in fact been an army doctor: Surgeon Major Charles Hancock of the Assam Valley Light Horse. This regiment, part of the Indian Volunteer Force, had its headquarters at Dibrugarh in the north-eastern state of Assam; Charles had been awarded his regimental long service medal in 1904. He was a very tall gentleman with two distinguishing features: a rather splendid set of white whiskers, and, as Fanny put it, 'a Bit of a Reputation'. Her Gran seemed in on the indiscretions, merely raising her eyebrows and murmuring 'At his age?' when secret dalliances were uncovered. Her Grandpa taught Fanny how to eat Stilton with good grace, the joys of pipe and cigar smoking, and the pleasures to be gained from sipping a fine Madeira. Again, all skills that Fanny would put to good use as her life developed.

Charles died in 1924 when Fanny was fifteen. He was buried in the family vault, according to Fanny. Fanny's Gran was not keeping in the best of health either by this stage. Following Charles's death, the contents of the house were sold off, and then presumably the house too. Emily was transported to live with Archibald and Bijou, who by this time had moved out of London. Emily died the following year.

Bijou had been born during the time the family lived in India, presumably giving rise to her grand name and matching view of herself. When Fanny thought about her mother, she always saw her in Technicolor. Bijou was slim with, according to Fanny, 'snow-white breasts'. She lit up the room when she entered. She never just went into a room. Her entrances stopped all talk and turned every head. She threw spectacular parties, was a divine dressmaker, had an eye for interior decoration and could cook rather well. Fanny, however, felt that the only similarity they had was in their deep, gravelly voices. No one could tell them apart on the telephone, which gave them endless opportunities for fun. Later, Johnnie remembered her quite differently, drawing many likenesses between her and Fanny, saying she was 'just as mad'.

Bijou loved her father, Charles, and seemed to take relish in being able to get away with almost anything in his eyes. The adoration she felt was passed to her son, whom she named Charles in his honour, although he was often referred to as John, especially by Fanny. Bijou bestowed all her love upon him, with Fanny watching from the sidelines. Her brother Charles had inherited Bijou's good looks, sense of style and desire for the limelight. Fanny, on the other hand, had inherited her father's large feet. She seemed to take great delight in how Charles turned out, however: fat. Very fat. Fanny claimed that a great surgeon once said, 'This feller doesn't want a surgeon, he wants a cooper,' with reference to his barrel-like status.

Bijou appears to have been supportive to her husband's budding career as a writer, encouraging him to enter a literary contest. No doubt the prize money of one thousand pounds would have been encouragement in itself. Archibald had only three weeks in which to write his entry, and somehow managed it. Bijou saw no reason that it could not be possible. She became the inspiration, in some way, for some of the best lines contained within the work. She was forever mixing up words and phrases to comic effect. Fanny said she had little regard for the English language and never read a book herself. The inspiration clearly helped: Archibald actually won the prize.

Bijou was in love with herself by all accounts, and Archibald was besotted by her too. Where Bijou loved a late night and a party, Archibald preferred reading and rising early for the morning papers. Bijou enjoyed the finest of foods. Archibald ate practically anything that was put in front of him. He hinted at a wilder life before he met, and became entranced by, Bijou. Gambling was his downfall. As soon as he met Bijou he allegedly sent a telegram to his then fiancée simply stating, 'Engagement off – letter follows.' He fell in love with Bijou and was never submerged by her eccentricities. Fanny recalled that the marriage was, from her eyes at least, 'as restful as an atomic explosion'.

Archibald began his writing career proper with poetry. Bijou convinced him to make a go of it, writing for newspapers and magazines. He wrote lyrics, pantomime books, short stories and plays. His play *Tons of Money* was turned down by almost everyone who considered it, until, after nine years of trying, it was staged in London in 1922. Archibald had ploughed all the family savings into the play, ending up so broke that he even had to pawn his gold cigarette case to pay for a dress for Bijou to wear on opening night. It paid off, with the play running for three years solidly and making everyone involved exactly that – tons of money.

Bijou convinced Archibald to celebrate their new-found financial success with a spending spree. They wintered abroad, stayed in the best hotels, frequented many casinos and generally spent the money sooner than it had been accumulated. A successful follow-up for *Tons of Money* never materialised. His next two plays, *Compromising Daphne* and *Ring Off, Please*, were somewhat anti-climactic and failed to replenish the bank balance. The bankruptcy courts loomed, and it seems as if Bijou also ran for the hills. The marriage did not survive, with Bijou eventually trying again for a happier home life. She went on to marry a successful estate agent in Berkshire.

Archibald continued to write and write. He wrote three novels a year in steady stream. Seemingly in a bid to outsmart the taxman, the bailiffs and the bankruptcy courts, and perhaps his divorce settlement too, he chose the pseudonym 'Valentine' (sometimes expanded as Arthur Valentine), a corruption of his mother's family name Vallentin, to launch his seemingly never-ending series of light romances about a group of amateur crime fighters, known as the Adjusters. Often billed as 'novels with real humour' filled with 'breezy and bracing wit', Valentine was said (at least by his publicity department) to have 'a comedy touch', a capacity for blending humour with pathos. He wrote 'clean' stories which promised to leave no bad taste behind. Newspaper reviews described him as 'good-natured yet candid', 'rambling easily and pleasantly' with 'modesty and not the vestige of a frill'.

His first books, with titles like *One Good Turn*, *The Blue Pool* and *Flight to the Finish*, traded on his connections to *Tons of Money*, attempting to connect him in readers' minds with P. G. Wodehouse as a national humorist. His tag line remained 'Author, Lyricist, Dramatist' in print.

Once Archibald had repaid his debtors, he switched pseudonyms again, this time taking the name of Mark Cross. Continuing to write an endless series of novels with more of a thrilling pace, his crime series also featured the exploits of the Adjusters, led by Daphne Wrayne. As Mark Cross, he was described as an ingenious 'creator of excitement and suspense', placing Miss Wrayne in lively, thrilling tales with a 'touch of Sherlock Holmes with just a suggestion of Raffles' that Edgar Wallace allegedly may have been proud of.

Although published by the same publisher, Ward Lock & Co, no connection was made between Valentine and Mark Cross. Titles reflected the shift from romance to thriller, with *Murder in Black*, *Not Long to Live* and *Perilous Hazard* among the series. Reviews played into the supposed mystery surrounding the true identity of the author, suggesting that 'Mark Cross has made himself (or herself) familiar to the reading public by good work' which always made the Adjusters books 'worth reading'.

By the time Archibald had reached eighty, Fanny claimed he had also neatly published eighty novels. Archibald died five years after that, in 1961. His final tally of published works stretched to a mighty one hundred, with forty-six alone in his Adjuster series. He lived his last days alone, Fanny referring to him as 'Our Father who art in Shepton Mallet', enjoying the tranquillity afforded to him, in contrast to what Fanny referred to as the 'shambles of a life' he had led with Bijou.

Bijou had died many years before, in 1949, the same year that Fanny's own career really took off. Fanny mentioned her often throughout her work, continuing the usual vague references to a glamorous creature who had played a significant role in her life. Many of the recipes Fanny presented in books and on television were attributed to 'Mum' who had been a great stage actress.

Fanny also had a colourful personal life prior to meeting her most well-remembered husband, John Whitby Cradock. In future interviews and her autobiography, Fanny would make light of her life 'before Johnnie', reducing it to often inconsequential significance and dismissing any deeper intrusion. Whether cagey or carefully crafted, Fanny wanted to be in control of the version of herself that was projected.

Her first marriage, at the tender age of seventeen, was to Sidney Arthur Vernon Evans, five years her senior, on the 10th of October 1926. They had met when Fanny was a flighty but feisty fifteen-year-old. Sidney had been to public school, was well educated, enjoyed sports and had joined the Royal Air Force. Fanny had just been sent home from the boarding school she had attended. In proper wild-child mode, she attached herself to several hopeful 'new flames' that might rescue her from her teenage misery, even boasting that, at the age of just fourteen, the year before meeting Sidney, she had accepted a proposal by an unnamed millionaire. Whether Sidney tamed her a little, or the unnamed millionaire (should he have indeed existed) fled for the hills, we will never know.

Fanny tells the rather romantic tale of their wedding in her autobiography, which she writes as if it happened directly following her Gran's funeral. It had been arranged for some reason that Fanny should go to live with her mother's sister, Aunt Cecile, in Bath, but Fanny recalled that she had other plans. She says that she gave her aunt the slip at Paddington Station and fled to be with Sidney instead on the Isle of Sheppey, where he quickly arranged a marriage licence. Fanny was just seventeen at the time but gave her age on the licence application as twenty-one, avoiding the need for parental consent. She did, however, retain her full name as Phyllis Nan Sortain Pechey.

Two weeks later, enough time to establish local residency, on the 10th of October, they were married in a small church at eight o'clock in the morning, with only two fellow RAF officers for witnesses. Fanny said they quickly 'sailed away', presumably on their honeymoon. She added in an extra nugget of embellished drama to the story: their vessel ran into trouble 'off the Goodwins' and they both narrowly avoided drowning.

Three weeks later, still alive and well, they called Fanny's parents, now living in Norfolk, to break the news of their wedded bliss. The good news was not received as such by Bijou, who felt cheated out of a big wedding for her one and only daughter. After much ranting and raving it was decided that a ball would be thrown to celebrate the wedding, as if it had happily just happened, in an attempt to mask the truth.

Fanny remembered that at the ball, for some inexplicable reason, the band played *Auld Lang Syne*, despite Bijou allegedly having an aversion to that particular tune. It was not that she was overly sentimental, or in any way connected to Scotland; rather, it seems she had developed a phobia after realising that each and every man next to whom she stood while that song played went on to die at some stage in the next few months. If she were to hear the song at any time, she would run away rather than face the conseq-uences. Everyone knew about this, and everyone assumed that someone else had told the band not to play the song. When it was played, Bijou ran as usual. Unexpectedly, however, Sidney had also slipped away from the ball, meeting her head on in a corridor.

And so it seemed that Sidney's fate had been sealed. Four months after the celebratory ball, just as Fanny approached her eighteenth birthday, the family doctor confirmed that Fanny was pregnant. Two days of excitement followed, with the happy couple making glorious plans for the child that they had already decided to call Peter, sure as they were that it would be a boy. On that second day, Sidney left for work as usual, nothing out of the ordinary. Fanny recalled seeing his plane fly over the house at around eleven, with Sidney giving her a quick wave as he passed. He did not return as expected, or as usual, for lunch.

Later that afternoon, Fanny was visited by a Royal Air Force commanding officer, looking white and hopeless. He had been dispatched to break the news that Sidney's plane had hit bad weather while on a routine map-reading exercise, leading to Sidney losing his bearings and, eventually, control of the plane. He had attempted to parachute to safety but was not quick enough and perished in the flames as the plane crashed. Fanny said as soon as the officer arrived at her door, she knew what had happened.

What she was not prepared for was the military funeral. Her state of shock was seemingly compounded by lack of knowledge or awareness of what this would entail. A startled Fanny was taken aback as a gunfire salute began as the coffin was lowered into the ground. She had no idea that this was about to happen, and later told Jane Chapman, who at that time was the daughter of a family friend, that she very nearly jumped into the ground with Sidney's coffin herself through fright.

Jane recalls the day Fanny told her about the funeral. 'I was engaged to a boy in the Royal Air Force, Mark, and he was a navigator. He was in a plane crash, and he died. I had to go to a military funeral. At the same age, Fanny had done the same, she had to go. I was living with her at the time when Mark died; she came up to my room and pleaded with me not to go to the military funeral. She told me it was different for her as they were husband and wife, but what a miserable funeral. You don't want to do it. She was so sweet to me, she told me what she'd been through. She explained it all. "They will fire a salute as they put the coffin in the ground," she said. Even then, I jumped, and I knew. She had no idea it was going to happen and nearly jumped in the coffin with Sidney. She helped me through it and put me on the train home afterwards. She was really lovely to me then.'

Fanny herself said that, if anything ever went wrong in life, she preferred to cope alone. Losing her beloved Gran, marrying her sweetheart, realising she was pregnant and then losing her husband all in such a short space of time would certainly have been difficult for any eighteen-year-old, no matter how brash or brazen they appeared to be. She wrote in her autobiography: 'Coping with any form of acute discomfort always seems to use up all my concentration, so that I do not have any to spare for talking. Getting down inside myself seems, still, to be the only way I know of getting out from under difficulties at the greatest possible speed.'

Fanny, left with a small service widow's pension of twenty-four pounds a year, moved back to live with her parents, who by all accounts did exactly as she wished – they left her alone and did not try to 'interfere' with her plans, nor pregnancy. Peter was born in October 1927, a year after his mother and father had been married.

Fanny continued to live in Norfolk, where she soon met civil engineer and surveyor Arthur William Chapman, who was to become her second husband, when Peter was just six months old. Arthur was three years older than the now nineteen-year-old Fanny, and the couple began a short courtship. This led to a swift wedding when it was discovered that Fanny was again pregnant. Fanny and Arthur married on the 23rd of July 1928, and their son, Christopher, was born eight months later in 1929. That summer, Fanny packed her bags and fled the marriage, and Christopher, taking her firstborn son Peter with her.

Fanny makes only a fleeting mention of the marriage in her autobiography. She wrote that the marriage had not been 'a happy one' and therefore 'Christopher, John and I have decided it shall have no place in this story.' Despite later claims that Arthur was devoted to her, Fanny had decided that he was not for her, leaving Arthur to live a quiet and simple life.

She also left her new son, Christopher, with his father, and would not see him again until he was an adult. She dedicated her autobiography, published in 1960, to him in his rechristened name of 'Christopher De Peche Cradock' – adding 'although he is a lousy cook' in a typically whimsical touch.

Christopher grew up with his father, his aunt and his grandmother in Norfolk. He was educated at Harrow, where Johnnie had also been, and worked for a while at Marshall's Airport in Cambridge, before reconnecting with Fanny. Christopher was married to Nikki Watson, and they had a child together called Julian, who had been born in 1956. The marriage did not last, and Nikki emigrated to Australia with Julian. Christopher went on to marry Rosemary Jane Cornelius, the daughter of family friends of Fanny, George and Joan Cornelius, and to have two children, Christopher and Karen. They ran pubs together in Devon, before Christopher sadly died in 2015.

Fanny made her way back to London with Peter, eventually living in a 'hole in the wall' in West Kensington that Fanny declared would have brought them before some authority or other in the era of the Welfare State. She clearly did not think it to be suitable for herself, nor for her growing child. Much later, when all the stories came out about Fanny 'abandoning' her children, this was never discussed. It certainly would have been an extremely challenging environment in which to bring up a toddler, never mind a newborn baby also, had she brought Christopher with them.

Not much has been recorded about their lives in those first few years back in London. Peter and Fanny lived together until Peter was five years old. He was then sent to live with his paternal grandparents in 1932. They adopted him and gave him a secure, steady and stable life. As part of the adoption agreement, Fanny had to consent not to see her son again until he was twenty-one. He grew up blissfully unaware of her existence, not remembering his time with her at all, nor that he had a brother.

Peter was educated at Wellington College, a public school in Berkshire, England which was also the place of education, at later dates, for the likes of impressionist Rory Bremner, author George Orwell, broadcaster Peter Snow, racing driver James Hunt and entertainer Will Young. Now providing an education for both boys and girls, during Peter's time it was boys only. The school had strong links with the Royal Navy, Royal Air Force and the Royal Marines, which Peter would go on to join in 1944. After his service career, he became an underwriter with Lloyds of London, before reconnecting with Fanny and pursuing various ventures with, and without her, with just as much variation in success. He joined the Kenyan Police in 1955, moving there with his wife, Pamela, whom he met when she was working with Fanny, and went on to have three boys of his own: Christopher, David and Jeremy. Peter sadly died in August 2017, in Kenya.

Fanny kept her third marriage a secret, almost until the day she died. Husband number three was never mentioned, and indeed Fanny herself only admitted to being married three times in total, Johnnie being the third in the tale she told. However, in the seventies, it came to light that there had been another marriage. Her attempts to airbrush him from her life and history had almost been successful. Gregory Holden-Dye had been a firefighter in Fulham when he met Fanny, in 1939. Gregory was by all accounts a fun-loving, handsome, motor-racing daredevil. Gregory was two years younger than Fanny.

Their marriage intentions were posted in accordance with the law. Fanny had no contact with Arthur Chapman, although they were still married. Arthur had converted to Catholicism following his time with Fanny, and by all accounts had refused to consider a divorce. Her marriage to Gregory Holden-Dye went ahead on the 26th of September 1939 in Fulham, with the bride being recorded as Phyllis Nan Sortain Chapman. Fanny was clearly attracted to him, although they enjoyed different ideas of 'society'. Cracks in their marriage emerged quickly. Fanny was prone to embarrassing him; Gregory was prone to having a fiery temper.

A mere six weeks following their marriage, Fanny would meet Johnnie. Fanny returned home to Gregory one night and simply said, out of the blue, 'I am sorry, I have met someone else.' Gregory was reportedly devastated. He struggled with the news but moved on with life. Eventually he met Helen Gibson and the pair were keen to marry. Gregory contacted Fanny to attempt to clarify the situation. She told him she had met up with Arthur in London, and, as he was alive and well, her marriage to Gregory had been null and void all along. Gregory and Helen married in 1954 in Staffordshire. They had a son, Jonathan, whom Fanny was keen to meet and even suggested becoming his godmother, a suggestion which was declined by both Gregory and Helen. Gregory died in 1974 after a period of senile dementia. Helen went on to marry again, and their son, Jonathan, married Linda Lloyd in 1978 in the New Forest.

John Whitby Cradock was born five years before Fanny on the 17th of May 1904, in the leafy green South London area of West Dulwich. Henry

Whitby Cradock, John's father, and his wife, Katie Minnie Groves, lived at 77 South Croxted Road, a property which is worth today in excess of a million pounds, in the heart of what is now a fashionable part of London. Henry and Katie had married in 1903. Henry was twenty-five, and Katie twenty-three.

Henry had been born in New Brighton in Cheshire, a popular location for merchants and tourists with easy access to the Irish Sea, situated by the River Mersey. His father, Sheldon, was the youngest of four children, although his brother had died shortly after birth. He grew up with his two sisters, Eliza and Mary. Sheldon married Harriet Ackerley in 1875 in Prescot, Lancashire, bringing up a large family of five. They eventually made their home on the Isle of Wight where they died – Harriet in 1924 and Sheldon in 1927.

By the time of his marriage to Katie, Henry was the owner of a successful wool and fabric business. Katie had been born in Plaistow in the West Ham area of London, where she had lived with her parents, John and Emily, and one brother called Sidney. Henry and Katie employed a servant and a nurse at home to help run the household.

Henry and Katie's family was complete when John was joined by a sister, Dorothy Whitby Cradock, in 1908. Dorothy went on to marry when she was twenty-one, to a Charles Bowie Findlay, who was five years her senior. John himself married in his early twenties.

The Whitby Cradocks were a well-to-do family. Both arms of the family tree had prestigious beginnings, known to be part of the upper classes of British society – the landed gentry. Landowners and landlords, they would have derived their incomes from rent across their country estates and as such would have been at one time among the richest people in the country.

The Cradocks can be traced back to 1685 when the 'Cradocks of Leicestershire' lived at Quorn Court in the village of Quorn in Richmond, Yorkshire. Their pedigree stretched back to the House of Plantagenet, a royal house originating in the lands of Anjou in France. The Plantagenets held the English throne, transforming the constitution of England forever, from 1154 with the accession of Henry II, until 1485, when Richard III died in battle. Henry Tudor claimed the throne, as Henry VII, bringing the Plantagenet line of Kings to an end and heralding the beginning of the Tudor dynasty.

Further royal connections can be uncovered deep in the family tree when, in 1792, John Cradock, a third-generation Cradock of Leicestershire, married Mary Alleyne, daughter of the Reverend John Alleyne, a direct descendant of King Henry III. The family motto, used on their coat of arms, was *Nec Temere, Nec Timide*, the Latin form of 'neither rashly nor timidly'.

The Whitbys too were of a similar class. Mentioned in *Burke's Peerage* and lists of the landed gentry, the Whitbys lived in Creswell Hall, the family mansion and estate consisting of four hundred and sixty acres in Staffordshire in the late eighteenth and early nineteenth century, before it was sold to the Meakin family of pottery manufacturers. Creswell Hall was severely damaged by fire in 1914 and the Hall was all but demolished, with only a small part of the service buildings remaining today. The Whitbys originally hailed from Great Heywood and were descended from Thomas Whitby who had been appointed to a peerage by Queen Elizabeth. Their family motto was *Virtus Vitium Fugere*, a corruption of the Latin meaning 'to flee vice is the beginning of virtue'.

Whether or not the young John Whitby Cradock was in any way aware of his esteemed genealogy, we will never know. He was an unremarkable, middle-class student at the local preparatory school. This continued when he attended Harrow, an independent boarding school for boys near to London. Boys who attended the school wore a uniform which consisted of straw hats, morning suits, top hats and canes. Harrow has spawned several Prime Ministers and other politicians, and been home to royalty, future Nobel Prize winners and notable figures of the arts and sciences. Harrow was famous for allegedly inventing the game of squash, and for a long-standing love affair with cricket. John claimed to be a proficient sportsman, enjoying cricket, rugby and a game or two of golf along the way.

Scholarly achievements were not essential to secure a place in his father's wool merchants' business, however. Henry Whitby Cradock and his business had some connections that led him to Aberdeen in Scotland, which in turn brought him into contact with many local dignitaries. This gave rise to a suggestion that John should marry the daughter of Sir John Hannett Irvin KBE and his late wife, Lady Mary Ann Boak. Sir John was President of the Aberdeen Liberal Association and a local fishing magnate, campaigning for social and political change amongst the fishing communities of the North East.

John's summer marriage to Ethel May Irvin, two years older than he, on the 24th of July 1928 was quite the social occasion for Aberdeen, bringing the two successful families together with a fanfare. John and Ethel appeared to settle down to married life well, with their first son, who carried on the John Whitby Cradock name, being born the next year. Three other children followed: Pamela Dorothy in 1931, Richard Henry a year later and finally Sheila Margaret in 1934.

John's mother, Katie Minnie, lived to see all four grandchildren born before she herself died in 1935. Henry, now a widower at the age of 59, married again. He too chose an Aberdeen wife in Jeanetta Davidson Mackie, twelve years his junior, who had never been married before. John was witness to the marriage, and his address is given as Deepe Dell, The Park, Beckenham, near to where his father lived. The impressive mansion house, which still stands today in Beckenham Place Park, was presumably home to John, Ethel and their four children.

By all accounts when John left his family in 1939 for a new life with Fanny, it came as a bolt from the blue for Ethel. The divorce in 1940 was costly for John (he would later tell people it had cost him seventy-five thousand pounds) and emotionally devastating for Ethel. John's father, Henry, barely spoke to him afterwards. John went on to have little or no relationship with his four children, who all moved back to Aberdeen. However, Ethel and the children maintained the Cradock name and, it can be assumed, were more than well aware of John's future career as the infamous husband of Fanny Cradock as it played out across the media. The Cradocks of Aberdeen did not venture far across Scotland. Ethel died in 1983 in Aberdeen; Pamela in Dundee. They were followed by Richard in 2006, John in 2010, also in Aberdeen, and then Sheila in 2017 in Perth.

Fanny would later offer a suggestion that she had met Johnnie previously, in a past life. 'The moment we first met, years ago, we recognised each other. It was because we have known each other in previous lives.'

Neither Fanny nor Johnnie appear to have been fully aware of, or bothered by, the accuracy of the truth of their past generations. Fanny worked so hard to find the prestigious past that she craved deeply, that she may have overlooked the true genealogy which would have provided her with the links to 'high society' that she was so desperate to have. A version of the family lineage was all she required to construct her heritage to weave a story that she would use time and time again as her life and career developed, returning to this 'family tree' which had grown overnight.

Regardless of the facts, Fanny continued to create her own version of the truth of her life, and of Johnnie's, rarely wavering from the story she told in her autobiography. Both Fanny and Johnnie, however, left their 'real' past lives and families behind in search of a new life together.

Prolific Publishing

Fanny had become somewhat accustomed to living life 'at a gay rate' during her short marriage to Sidney. His death left her without much of an income, and without much of a clue as to how to support herself. Her young days had been fast-living and fast-paced, and now she had to face life in a much slower lane. Although Fanny had experienced so many things in the so few years of her early existence, earning a living had not been at the top of her agenda. She realised that she was quite incapable herself of earning a living at anything.

Living in a basement room in West Kensington, with barely a penny to her name, Fanny found a job in the City of London, on Lower Thames Street, in a Roman Catholic canteen. They needed someone to do the washing up, and she needed the half a crown they offered. Fanny says she walked from her room to the canteen and back again, which would have taken two hours each way in itself. With no option other than to leave Peter (presumably alone) during the day, she walked across London, worked from eleven in the morning until three in the afternoon and walked back to her Kensington basement afterwards. Once there she would clean Peter up and then head out again in search of work, hoping to find something, anything, a little closer to home.

Growing up she recalled being rewarded for her ingenuity at being able to turn her hand to almost anything, in typical future Fanny Cradock style. Her sense of initiative was particularly keen during times of adversity, and she certainly found herself deep in difficulty as she struggled to look after herself and Peter, secure in the knowledge that Christopher was being cared for with his father. Deciding that she must take control of the situation for herself, Fanny hit upon the bold idea to become a dressmaker.

This did not come entirely out the blue. Fanny claimed to have made dresses from *Vogue* patterns in her younger days, while living with her parents. She remembered making dresses out of 'almost nothing', including cleaned-up ducks' feathers sewn onto an old petticoat with her brother, Charles, which wasn't fit for sale following the discovery that the feathers were flea-ridden. Dressmaking was also in her family history, on her mother's side, whether she had been aware of it or not. Still, she had the confidence to give things a bash, coupled with some basic ability to carry it off. Desperate times called for desperate measures. All she lacked was the wherewithal to make it happen.

In true entrepreneurial fashion, Fanny placed cards in local newsagents' windows claiming to be an 'Experienced Dressmaker', which was not entirely untrue, able to take in alterations. A few days later, she had acquired her very first customers. The only thing she had overlooked, however, was the essential equipment to make her new trade a success – a sewing machine. Fanny searched out old beaus in the hope that they might be inclined to support her new venture; but in the end she said that an old, and unnamed, flame from Norwich found her, by way of a private detective, offering to loan her the funds required to secure the deposit on a sewing machine on hire purchase. She used the rest of his gesture on her rent.

Whichever way the money came her way, she quickly set to work, somewhat unsuccessfully. With only limited skills, but a fair amount of bravado, she hoped that her new customers would pay for their alterations without trying on their returned garments. Somehow, she managed to save up the princely sum of nine pounds, which would have meant a great deal of West Kensington's ladies wandering around in ill-fitting garments. With the realisation that perhaps her future was not destined to be as a dressmaker after all, she somehow managed to persuade a skilled, professional dressmaker, Elsa Waters, to enter into business with her. Fanny would get the orders rolling in, Elsa would initially do the work. Fanny would learn to do things 'properly' by her side. After six months their little enterprise had swollen to accommodate four of them.

Fanny, however, was always looking for the next thing. She had ambition to be a writer, just like her father. She had seen him earn, and lose, vast amounts of money by pumping out words, stories and collections which required only his imagination to conceive, in his own time. This notion must have been appealing to Fanny. She quickly sent off twelve poems she had written to the editor of the *Argosy* magazine, a London-based publication which specialised in reprinting short stories and serials by leading authors of the time. Fanny may have known that they required other submissions to fill their pages from her father, who was already a published writer. Eleven of the poems were returned, together with a payment of one guinea for the twelfth. Encouraged, Fanny continued to submit, sending in a novel she had somehow managed to find the time to write. However, this was rejected, along with all her other submissions around this time.

A series of jobs were obtained in the coming months. Fanny worked in a grocery shop in Clapham, South London, selling produce outside to passers-by. Fanny found herself selling packets of Swiss Rolls for a well-known manufacturer at an exhibition held at the Alexandra Palace. Her job was to bake the Swiss Rolls using the company's pre-made mix, adding only eggs, roll them with jam when they were fresh from the oven and present them to the audience. This must have been essential training for Fanny in the future. At other times, she sold cures for tired feet at the same exhibition.

During Christmas, Fanny worked in the bargain basement at Selfridges, the famous department store on Oxford Street. She also sold vacuum cleaners door to door. It was here that she learnt a valuable lesson in persistence, and quickly. The art of selling involved knocking on as many doors as possible in the hope that at least one door which opened would lead to a sale. Fanny's motivation remained that Peter was locked in her room at home, during her normal working day of ten until ten, waiting for her to return so he could eat.

Fanny reflected years later than the whole pitiful situation had led her to appreciate, and strive for, the finer things in life that she simply could not afford at that time, no matter how hard she worked in any number of jobs. She had faced starvation herself, alone in London with a young child she was increasingly incapable of looking after while being surrounded by temptation and aspiration to a better life all around her. She became far more interested in the problems of the ambitious housewife who is poor than those with plenty of money at their disposal. She developed an understanding of how wearying life could be, scrimping and scraping, never being able to splash out on luxuries. But always dreaming. She would hold on to these memories as her own career developed.

In 1932, perhaps considering that her dual task of survival and providing a suitable home was insurmountable, she reluctantly sent Peter back to his grandparents' care, where he remained. Fanny carried on lurching from dead-end job to dead-end job, eating hand to mouth and trying to establish a better life in harsh conditions. She says in her autobiography that she accepted any and every invitation to parties or social events. This was where, not long after her third marriage (to Gregory Holden-Dye), she was to encounter the person who would enable her to change her life forever – Johnnie – while also changing his.

The first time the pair met, officially, was the 19th of November 1939. Fanny was tasked with staging some entertainment for the air troops stationed just outside London, a role fitting for the newly married Mrs Holden-Dye, as she was at the time. The Second World War had only just begun in September of that year, so the troops would have been unaware of what lay ahead. Bored and restless, they were keen for a night of fun and frivolity. Fanny recalled the evening being far from it, describing it as 'an evening of almost unrelieved gloom'. Her escort for the evening, the fun-loving Gregory most likely, was late, leaving Fanny in a foul temper. The gloom lifted in some small way because Johnnie Cradock was there. In Fanny's version of events, he had caught the eye of almost every woman in attendance initially, but not including hers. They spoke briefly at the bar later that night, and Fanny seemed more inclined to be interested in him than she had been all evening.

The next day, while she was working with Elsa at the dressmaking business, Johnnie called for her, persuading Fanny to accompany him to lunch. Accustomed to accepting any invitation that involved food, she did so, albeit with low expectations. However, Johnnie took her to lunch at the allegedly rather impressive Luigi's in the West End on Jermyn Street, still a popular location for Italian restaurants in the city today. Fanny was certainly impressed. The lunch ended at 5.45 that evening, seemingly only coming to an end with Luigi himself enquiring if they were staying on for dinner? It's not known if it was that night, or following one of their subsequent dates, that Fanny returned home to tell Gregory bluntly that she had met someone else.

Johnnie continued to woo her with trips into the country. Fanny responded with invitations to dine with her at home, an opportunity for her to show off her best food and wine knowledge. From the account Fanny chooses to tell, they were instantly besotted with each other, and bound together for ever more, 'permanently entangled' in each other's lives.

They survived the ravages of war together, seeing each other through the trauma and uncertainty of the Blitz in London. Fanny recalls spending the evening of the 7th of September 1940 in some trepidation. With Johnnie 'doing the rounds', she was left at home, wondering yet again if her husband would return home safely. Of course, Fanny and Johnnie were not married but lived together as if they had been. Fanny even changed her name by deed poll to Cradock to solidify the illusion for the outside world.

As London erupted in the 'swishes and the thuds of falling bombs; the grunting and the roar of the guns; the drumming of aircraft and the crackling of fire', Fanny fell asleep waiting for Johnnie to return to her. He did, with the only casualty of the night being his wristwatch. Johnnie went on, Fanny said, to attend a six-week senior officers' course, where he returned, as all others in the regiment also appeared to do, sparkling in a monocle. He'd be forevermore referred to by Fanny as 'Major' as they adopted their own moniker of 'Major and Mrs Whitby Cradock'. The arrival of the monocle seemed to coincide with Johnnie being diagnosed with a painful inflammation of the iris known as iritis, which left him temporarily blind in one eye. His vision recovered slightly, but his monocle was required to increase in strength to support his failing vision. The monocle remained in place for the rest of his life.

The once-rejected novel which Fanny had continued to work on, *Scorpion's Suicide*, was picked up by a small, enterprising and ambitious publisher, Hurst and Blackett Ltd, based in London. Their logo proudly stated that they had been publishers since 1812, although in reality they began in 1852. They expanded rapidly, continuing to publish throughout the nineteenth and twentieth centuries. In 1922 they published Charlie Chaplin's *My Wonderful Visit* which included his recollections of meeting H. G. Wells among others. Early in the 1930s, Hurst and Blackett acquired the British rights to Adolf Hitler's *Mein Kampf*, and also published the less contentious, perhaps, Inspector Maigret series of novels by Georges Simenon. Later, they were taken over by the larger publishing house, Hutchinson, who themselves were later taken over by Penguin Random House, said to be the largest general interest paperback publisher in the world.

Fanny mentions Hutchinson as the publisher, perhaps to connect her literary heritage to a more well-known company. At the same time as her own books, Hutchinson were publishing seemingly endless novels by Barbara

Cartland, which may have been a parallel Fanny would have liked to draw. Whichever way, Hurst and Blackett were keen to publish her first novel, and Fanny was, quite rightly, delighted.

She was less delighted with their suggestion of publishing it under the name 'Phyllis Valentine', linking Fanny to her father's published pen name. She point-blank refused, holding her nerve until they called an end to the stalemate. Hurst and Blackett called to say they had changed their mind after all and agreed to publish *Scorpion's Suicide* under the name 'Frances Dale', which Fanny felt more comfortable with. Frances was close to her grandmother's surname of Francis at least.

The novel was published conforming to the Book Production War Economy Standard of the time, brought in to conserve paper as a result of rationing, which reduced paper availability by forty per cent during World War II. The agreement covered strict guidelines over print size, words per page and any blank pages. Publication was consequently limited during the war, despite an increased demand for books, so getting a first novel to the printing press was even more of a feat during that time. Paper rationing in Britain continued until 1949.

Dedicated 'To John', *Scorpion's Suicide* earned Fanny an advance of thirty pounds for the British Empire volume rights. With her agent, Curtis Brown, receiving a customary ten per cent, the initial cheque for twenty-seven pounds must have been extremely welcome in the Cradock household as it arrived in July of 1942. Despite her not adopting his name for the publication, Fanny's father wrote to her when the book was announced for publication, with the approval she perhaps had so badly sought.

> Darling daughter, delighted to see your name in the Hurst and Blackett advertisement in the *Times Literary Supplement*; and heading the list too. You can take it as a compliment. Publishers have bunches of authors and only the selected few appear in the ads. So, you have made another step and will soon no doubt make many more and outstrip your old father. May it be so. But you do hop about don't you? What's the next book going to deal with – bimetallism, body-lines, bowling, banshees, Bolshevism or birth control? But I am a bad one to talk, after all, and it took me more than ten years to find my eventual direction. So, go on, my dear, and good…

The *Times Literary Supplement*, in the third week of August 1942, described *Scorpion's Suicide* in the following terms:

> A promising first novel is *Scorpion's Suicide* by Frances Dale, where the heroine, hedged round by people she despised and surroundings that she hated, thought to escape them by plunging into a hasty marriage. This ended disastrously a few years later, and after a series of adventures she married again, this time a charming weakling who proved to be much more worry than he was worth. Then, when war is about to overshadow the whole of human happiness, Mary Grey meets the man who had always been intended for her. Miss Dale brings her heroine by slow and painful stages to the realisation that there is no escape from the grim realities of life and that self-knowledge is an essential step to any kind of spiritual progress.

Fanny herself drew the comparison with her own life as she recalled the review in her autobiography, *Something's Burning*. 'After all, most first novels are partly autobiographical,' she said. Delving deeper into the story it is surprising just how accurate that statement might be. Far from 'partly', it may indeed be entirely more autobiographical than the autobiography itself.

Scorpion's Suicide centres upon a strong female character named 'Mary Catherine Hamilton Greville' who was born in 1909 in Essex. Her mother was 'as beautiful as a princess' and her father, Napier, was a dramatist. Mary was brought up by her Gran but 'hates nearly everything since then'. Mary despised her messy home life, and was desperate to escape her sad, lonely childhood. She is described by Fanny as a 'dark child' with 'dark hair and eyes and the beginnings of dark corners in a mind singularly active and already over-sensitised by the seclusion of her upbringing beneath the protective petticoats of tired old age.'

Her Gran was her saviour. Mary told her own father that 'Gran was my mother'. Mary's father explains that, as he sees it, 'There is no wrong in your mother. She is a child herself in many ways.' Napier admits to being a 'rotten father' to Mary and her angelic-looking brother. Her father entered bankruptcy, after being unable to sell a few of his latest works.

Mary spent six years at boarding school, reluctantly. Aged sixteen, she met a dashing, uniformed, Bentley-driving fellow, Hugh. Hugh became besotted with Mary. They married but all did not end well. Mary's heart had not been in it; however, she was ultimately left a widow seeking solace in the arms of Charles, even though she knew again he was not right for her. They lived together in a small flat in Kensington.

The story also plots the tale of a young man named Simon, who is married to Judy. They had four children together, and he had a good job, in his father's firm, despite not having a head for business himself or a desire to learn. None of this made him happy.

Through a series of coincidences, Mary and Simon met and fell head over heels in love. Mary discovered in Simon a contentment that she had only previously felt with her Gran. They agonised over their feelings for one another, and the impact that being together would have on their families, in particular Simon's own children.

Simon eventually faced his future and asked Judy for 'his freedom'. In return she only asked for 'the respectability we have always had', fearing the scandal that would ensue if Simon left her and the children. Not content with the blessing of continuing his affair with Mary alongside his marriage, Simon left his life with them behind to be with Mary. Judy refused a divorce, mindful of the scandal, so Mary and Simon had no option other than to set up home together living as the husband and wife that they were not. They lived together from the 7th of September 1940, thus realising their desire to be together without the shame of divorce and scandal looming. They created a new life for themselves, a new story to match their new future.

A further review in the *Queen* magazine highlights the sheer length of the text – running to over two hundred and thirty pages tightly packed with over six hundred words on each – as well as the 'curious naïveté' of the earnest, and not very attractive, female lead, aged thirty-one (Fanny was thirty-three herself at the time of publication) who has lost two husbands and a lover. It could indeed have been Fanny they were referring to.

This review offers some critical feedback which Fanny seemed determined to take on board, suggesting that when she had 'learned restraint and mastered her style (and punctuation), Miss Dale might one day write a really good novel, for she has a sense of values and observes well'. In her normal dismissive style, Fanny, during the writing of her autobiography, hoped that 'one day' this would happen.

Fanny took the advice to heart and spent the next few years trying to perfect her craft as a writer. Johnnie, 'blinded' in one eye with iritis, was sent to work in Warwick Castle – a role that Fanny felt was most unsuitable, for him and herself. They moved to a huge, rambling house near to Stratford-upon-Avon and continued their mock-married life together, throwing themselves into the local community with gusto. They participated in amateur dramatics, hosted weekends away for London pals and generally hunkered down to life in the country.

Without much else to do, Fanny concentrated on making the most out of next to nothing. She made fabulous meals from very little and began a lifelong obsession against wasting any food. So successful was she in transforming the scraped-together produce they could find that friends and neighbours assumed that they were 'deep in the black market'. The truth was that Fanny became skilful at using what she could get hold of, by legitimate means, as well as making full use of all that the countryside offered her. They reared rabbits for the pots, grew mushrooms for soups and even baked hedgehogs in clay. Despite their lack of finances, Fanny maintained that the time they spent 'in exile' in the country was full of contentment.

Fanny spent a great deal of time at the typewriter, bashing out more words than she cared to recall, shaping most of them into novels. However, she felt an early desire to diversify her writing portfolio, which would become a theme of her entire life. In July of 1942, she wrote to a literary agent, David Davidson, enclosing three short stories which she thought would be sensational for magazine publication. Despite only handling plays, novels and non-fiction books, he did feel that at least one of the stories, *Our Bruvver*, was good enough to share with colleagues from three of the leading magazines in Britain. Ultimately, none of them was interested enough to consider it for publication, however.

Mr Davidson provided more valuable feedback for Fanny, noting that things in the world of publication were moving 'with such dreadful rapidity' that Fanny's stories, which seemingly continued to draw on her own experiences of living in London during the Blitz, were already considered by editors to be 'outdated'.

Fanny took the critique on the chin and made it her mission to react favourably to the feedback. She wrote back to Mr Davidson outlining her ambitions to 'make the grade in America'. In the same letter, she gives a glimpse of the marketing and promotion skills she would later display throughout her career. She informed him that she was currently writing a play based on her own life story, which she admitted was so far fairly brief. Meanwhile she had completed her second novel *Women Must Wait* which, she lamented, touched on the war. She let Mr Davidson know that she was unable to send it his way at present, as it was currently being considered 'for film', whether it truly was or not.

It would be two years before *Women Must Wait* was published, again by Hurst and Blackett, and again under the pseudonym Frances Dale. Proudly billed as 'by the author of *Scorpion's Suicide*', and once again drawing on her own life experiences, the reviews were good despite Fanny claiming that it caused no great stir, as indicated by this one in the *Buxton Advertiser*:

> There is, in the mind of Frances Dale's heroine, the belief that one's decisions are largely influenced by circumstances over which we have no control. It gives an interesting twist to the main theme of the story. As a minor basis for the course of Gabrielle de Travenne's life prior to and during the early years of the present war, it plays an important part. Always, when any great decision had to be made between her wealthy dressmaking business and the matrimonial offers which she received, certain conditions at the moment always weighed the scales in favour of business.

By the time her third Frances Dale novel, *The Rags of Time* (again plundering Fanny's own experiences, this time of life in Stratford-upon-Avon, a 'merciless novel of provincial theatre life, written evidently from first-hand experience'), was published, also in 1944, the glowing reviews were pouring in: '*The Rags of Time* has considerable merits'; 'The author has steered clear of the obvious and the story ends with an unexpected and strange denouement'; 'Frances Dale shows her literary ability... Characterisation is excellent... Miss Dale is to be warmly complimented on writing so illustrative a story. A fine piece of work'; 'Sharply memorable portraits among its many characters... excellence of its local colour... Miss Dale has so many good gifts and has written so interesting a novel, obviously influenced by Dickens.'

For her fourth novel, *The Land is in Good Heart*, published the next year, Fanny set out to tell the tale of the Lowndes family. The novel raised awareness of the farmer's plight in troubled times. The Lowndeses lived on farm land which had been passed down through the generations, but the plot focused on the years between the wars which had been particularly difficult and complex for farmers. Intended to be the first in a saga series, the book sets the scene. The Lowndeses were once gentlemen farmers, living in a mansion. Now they were working farmers, but their gentleness remained. Life was hard for the Lowndeses – they were tired and shabby. They worked hard. They were forced to eat margarine as wartime regulations did not permit them to eat the butter made from their own cows' milk.

The book was described as being 'rich in humour' and in hindsight can be seen as prophetic of Fanny's life to come, as well as the semi-autobiographical novels it followed. The Lowndes's life is interrupted by the arrival of a couple 'from another world', Londoners Gillian and Anthony. Gillian is charming and just happens to be a famous cook. Anthony is shrewd and comedic. They arrive just in time to help with Christmas. They somehow manage to find wonderful food to prepare and dazzle, even managing to cook for a healthy twenty-three people, including twelve young men from the nearby aerodrome.

Fanny left the saga idea behind her once this novel was published, or at least put it on hold. She had an urge to write books for children, having written one for the village doctor's grandson, Michael Sutcliffe. In the book, Michael lived with his Grandpa and his mother in a house at the top of the hill. The story unfolds that he had a friend, Johnnie, who lived in the valley nearby. Johnnie was a large man who kept a lot of rabbits, a big fat pig and liked hedgehogs.

The trick now was to persuade a publisher to take it on. *When Michael Was Three* told the story of Michael's nursery toys, who came to life and had their own adventures in Fairyland once Michael went to sleep, returning to their original spots just before the 'Moon's accommodating beams give out'. An early *Toy Story* perhaps, if it were to be reimagined as *The Wind in the Willows*. Fanny's agent, Jean Curtis Brown, managed to interest Hutchinson, the parent company of Fanny's original publisher, Hurst and Blackett. Hutchinson had tested the book out with some readers, however, and had some constructive criticism to pass to Fanny in the hope that she could make one or two revisions:

> This story embodies a pretty idea. The toys, animals and fairies are attractive, and the story is pleasantly written. I venture to think, however, that it could with advantage be shortened in length and perhaps, since it is obviously intended for quite young readers, both sentences and paragraphs might be made more crisp here and there. The humour, too, might be toned down a little in some places and 'grown-up' turns of speech eliminated. Personally, I like the idea of James the young buck-rabbit dancing 'intimately' with a lady chinchilla, but perhaps this is slightly sophisticated for very young readers.

With the 'grown-up' aspects toned down and 'delightful' illustrations from Ernest Noble added, the book was published by Hutchinson in 1945 through their Books for Young People imprint. Ernest had been born in Stoke Newington, London in 1881, the son of a Quaker minister. He gained notoriety as a comical postcard artist in the 1910s and 1920s. Prior to illustrating *When Michael Was Three*, Ernest brought the Larry the Lamb comics to life, and went on to illustrate a number of children's books.

Fanny quickly followed up her surprise children's hit with a sequel, which saw Michael age at an alarming rate. *When Michael Was Six* was published barely a year later; it again featured a range of illustrations from Ernest Noble including nine in full colour. Fanny dedicated this follow-up with the rather cutting inscription 'To Mother, the nicest child of all', going one step further in her autobiography with the elaboration: 'At last we had found a book that she could read.'

Fanny, as Frances Dale, added a preface and a tailpiece to this volume, which seem to have been designed as an early attempt to connect and engage with her audience, more than likely to convince her publishers that subsequent books were 'in demand' and should of course be commissioned. The preface read:

> Children, I do hope that you will like this story. I think you will, but you must have a lot of ideas of your own that you would like to see in print with pictures like these. Why not send your ideas to me (with your name and address)? I shall be writing more of these stories and will see if I can include your suggestions in some of them.

Gaining feedback and acting upon it was becoming the norm for Fanny. She had no interest in writing (or otherwise producing) anything that people did not want, or would not buy from her. As well as the bald sales figures, she often showed the feedback she had received to publishers and other professionals she would go on to work with as evidence of her popularity. It seems perfectly normal now and became standard for Fanny. Another aspect of her life would become the non-stop writing of letters, which she alludes to in the tailpiece:

> Well you did like it, didn't you? Don't forget to write to me and tell me your idea, and I promise I will answer all your letters.

It's hard to imagine that Fanny had been running out of ideas; however, it is more than probable that she did write back to each and every child who took the time to put pencil to paper and send in their stories. The preface and tailpiece were repeated in her next children's book, *Always – The Enchanted*

Land. Always told the humorous story of Peter, possibly based on Fanny's own son, and his adventures in the enchanted land that lies at the bottom of everyone's garden, if they are young enough at heart. Peter had a stoat for a best friend and companion, and wore rose-coloured spectacles to enter the enchanted land at the bottom of his own particular garden.

This time, *Always* was illustrated by Nigel Mould, who would become a long-time collaborator. He would eventually go on to illustrate a number of Sooty books also. By this stage Fanny, still as Frances Dale, was writing several books each year, switching happily between fiction for adults, and illustrated stories for children. Titles such as *My Seed Thy Harvest*, *O Daughter of Babylon*, *Echo in the Cup*, *The Shadow of Heaven* and *Dark Reflection* kept her fantasy readers fulfilled with regular releases of dark tales and complicated family dynamics. *The Shadow of Heaven*, for example, wove together the theory of reincarnation with the romance of 'lost Atlantis' to tell its story of a recovering schizophrenic. Younger readers were satisfied with stories to stoke their imaginations such as *The Dryad and the Toad*, *Brigadier Gooseyplum Goes to War* (which became a series of books to feature the Gooseyplums), *Fish Knight and Sea Maiden* and even educational, historical, biblical volumes dealing with subjects such as *The Story of Joseph and the Pharaoh.*

In 1947, Fanny published a book for slightly older children, with a new publisher and a new name. This book was published using the pseudonym of Susan Leigh, which Fanny would only use once, for this title. Hodder and Stoughton, who published this new title, *Naughty Red Lion, Beware*, had previously published Lewis Carroll's *Alice's Adventures in Wonderland* and had just published the fifth in Enid Blyton's 'Famous Five' series. Fanny maintained a professional relationship with her original publisher, who continued to release new titles by Frances Dale over the coming years, but perhaps they simply were not interested in this tale.

Naughty Red Lion, Beware told the by-now familiar story: 'Something special happened when the queer, lovable, laughable animals pictured on the shields of the Knights of Castle Gallantry came alive to go adventuring!' The reviews for *Naughty Red Lion, Beware* were strong, noting that due to its 'air of gaiety and humour' it would not only be the children who enjoyed reading it. Fanny enlisted the illustrations of Nigel Mould again, but the marketing message included in the book appeared to try to suggest that Susan Leigh was someone quite different:

> Note for Parents and Others – This book is for children, but take your chance. You will enjoy it too. It is Susan Leigh's first story, full of gay inventiveness, humour and zest, and the artist, Nigel Mould, has caught the spirit of the thing to perfection. The Shield Animals come fresh from Heraldry and take the field. They are individual and delightful, in the best tradition of strange creatures.

Fanny included reference to a second volume, or more technically a prequel, simply titled *Naughty Red Lion*, in the 'by the same author' section of her books in the future. No catalogue entry for this title exists. It would seem that even Fanny wasn't sure which, and how many, books she had published, such was her prolific output. No further stories were written or published as Susan Leigh, and the book lay all but forgotten (expect perhaps by the children, and parents, who had read it) for several decades.

In 1983 the publisher, now part of BPC Publishing Ltd, received an enquiry from a company that produced animated films who wished to acquire the rights for *Naughty Red Lion, Beware*. Correspondence went back and forth as the producer, Antionette Moses, attempted to find suitable financing. Fanny was asked to send a copy of the book to show to prospective motion-picture financiers. Unfortunately, Fanny herself was unable to locate a spare copy, instead suggesting that she could have a transcript made of it 'pronto' to send to the animators. However, ultimately it does not appear to have been optioned for animation.

The final phase of Fanny's foray into literary circles was book-ended (although she would release one more Frances Dale children's book in 1952) by two of her most bizarre publications, even by her own latter-day strange standards. Another new publisher, Andrew Dakers, who specialised in fantasy and philosophy; another new name, although at least the cover name of Phyllis Cradock was the one that she lived under this time. It is no secret, however, who this author is. The book jacket lets new readers know she has previously written successfully under the name Frances Dale; however, it outlined why these books were different:

> The Phyllis Cradock novels, she declares, are written through her and not by her, she being incapable of writing the superb prose or originating the lofty thoughts and philosophy they contain. Her Atlantean novels are both a literary curiosity and a portent for these days.

These Atlantean novels were *Gateway to Remembrance* and *The Eternal Echo*. Fanny claimed that both books were dictated to her by a priest who had died nine million years previously on the lost continent of Atlantis. The novels were published shortly after Aldous Huxley released his *Ape and Essence* book, and the publisher was the first to link the two. One book had the gift of seeing into the past, one the gift of seeing into the future. Both sounded 'a note of dreadful warning to a race either unaware or indifferent to the doom that threatens it. The truth of the one is substantiated by the truth of the other, and this justifies the publication of both, terrible as are the revelations which each makes.'

Fanny was creating quite a whirl of marketing and publicity. For *Gateway to Remembrance* she sent out a press release stating that she would be refusing all royalties earned for this work: after all, she was merely the typist and as such should only receive a typist's fee. The *Psychic News* gave a favourable review, saying that 'the story is well told. The vivid phrase, the gripping paragraph, the tense dramatic moment are all here, and the tale moves towards its climax with the logic of inevitability.' Other reviewers drew attention to the simple story of romance, the appealing and fascinating subject of Atlantis, its compelling originality and careful writing.

The similarly love-themed Atlantean follow-up, *The Eternal Echo*, was billed as the second of three tales. Whether or not Fanny ever received the dictated text for the third planned instalment, *The Immortal Voyage*, remains as lost as the city of Atlantis itself. It seems her psychic hotline to history was curtailed. It certainly never made its way into print nor publication.

Fanny had proved herself to be prolific and versatile in the types of publications that she could produce, and able to sell successfully. In the ten-year period between 1942 and 1952, she authored an impressive twenty-one adult fiction and children's books. This would only be the start of her writing, and other careers. Fanny had a range of other plans she was determined to bring to fruition yet.

JOBBING JOURNALIST

AFTER THREE YEARS LIVING the country life, Fanny and Johnnie began to feel restless. In 1945, wartime activity had ceased, and the pair felt safe and secure to return to their beloved London without fear of the hostilities placing them, and any home, in danger. Johnnie had a chance meeting with his father to discuss returning to the family business which prompted Fanny to 'give in' as they realised that they were 'sick to death of this flaming backwater' anyway.

With some glimmer of security under her belt from the initial flurry of fiction, they decided to look for a suitable place to call home in London. Despite having 'lived the life of two contented cabbages' for their three years in the country, they were far from financially stable. It was all a gamble. London had been devastated by the Blitz, which enabled them to afford a charming place at 29 South Terrace, Kensington, a stone's throw from the Victoria and Albert Museum. The property had been a victim of extensive bombing during the war and required a great deal of love and attention to bring it up to standard. Undeterred, they took up residence and set about making it home, within the confines of rationed materials, where they would remain for the next thirteen years. Now an extremely desirable area, the six-bedroom property was advertised for sale in 2017 at just short of eight million pounds.

Evangeline Evans, who thereafter became a lifelong friend, lived next door at Number 27. 'I met her first when I was about sixteen, I suppose. We lived in London before the war, then we sold and moved to Oxford, then moved back to South Terrace just opposite the Victoria and Albert in 1945. Fanny and Johnnie lived next door, so we must have got to know them then I think. My parents thought she was a quirky next-door neighbour.

'Her elder son, Peter, became my first boyfriend. I was about eighteen at that time, and he was twenty-one. He'd been born in wedlock, which was quite surprising for Fanny, but her husband had been killed. His parents adopted Peter on the understanding that Fanny would have nothing to do with him until his twenty-first birthday. So, he suddenly appeared. Fanny and Johnnie heaped every kind of luxury on him, which was enormous fun for me. We went out a lot and had fun. So that's how I got to know her particularly well.'

Peter stayed with Fanny and Johnnie for a while, but often found it all 'too much' and disappeared. 'He buzzed off and came back. Fanny was sure we would end up together; we did not,' Evangeline remembers. 'He was a sweet man. He ended up marrying Pamela, who worked as some kind of assistant to Fanny. Fanny did not approve of her. She did not like anyone who took anything away from her, in terms of affection. My father was an actor, so I was accepted: I was not a threat. Pamela was working with Fanny and was a great favourite, but then the favouritism shot out of the window.'

Jane Chapman remembers the time well. 'It was in her character. She did exactly the same with her eldest son, Peter. Pam was working with Fanny when they got together. Fanny disowned them. As long as she was in control, and people were doing what she wanted, she was fine. If they had a life of their own, she wasn't happy. Silly really, but that was just her.

'She had nothing to do with her sons while they were young. Christopher got in touch with her in his late twenties. Peter had been brought up by his father's family. Christopher was the same really, his father and aunt brought him up. Fanny never had anything to do with them when they were children, but got back together when they were older. She thought she could control their lives. When Fanny discovered they had lives of their own, she disowned them again. She obviously did not have very good motherly instincts.'

Always with an eye to outward appearances, Fanny and Johnnie made their first task entertaining. Of prime importance was re-establishing the contacts that may have forgotten them during their three-year stint in the country. Their diaries bustled with social occasions; they accepted every invite that came their way, whether they liked the sound of the event or not.

The war had taught them that life was short, and leisure should be spent with friends. And potential new contacts and networks too, obviously.

Food rationing and availability was a major issue across the country during this time. In London, in particular, the black market was rife; rationed foods were sold and exchanged for high prices in an attempt to satisfy the hungry, and wealthy city dwellers. Fanny and Johnnie had made a success of cooking and entertaining on the very little scraps of food that they found, and cultivated, in the country. London was an altogether different affair. Evangeline recalled the interior of South Terrace: 'The furniture was dreadful; everything was covered in sacking. She had incredibly bad taste, but made a huge thing of having impeccable taste. We never knew where she got the idea of saying it was all right.'

Somehow Fanny found herself drawn into the company of local housewives who made it their mission to campaign on the 'food problem'. The group of around sixty housewives lobbied hard, setting up a petition to present to the government outlining their demands and concerns against the current food policy. The petition caught the imagination of the Borough of Kensington, and other parts of London. The group was right-wing but non-party affiliated. The British Housewives' League was founded by Mrs Irene Lovelock (who became their first Chairman and later President) to act as the voice of the British housewife, providing advice and encouraging active participation in society. The League aimed to attract one hundred thousand signatures to present to their local Conservative MP, Richard Law.

The campaign soon attracted attention from the media, and crucially from the influential British Broadcasting Corporation (BBC). A reporter was dispatched to interview the housewives for a broadcast to the United States in order to shine a light on the situation being faced following the war. Fanny, by now a prominent published author and novelist, as well as being the daughter of Arthur Valentine (as he was known professionally), writer of the still popular play *Tons of Money*, quickly became the public face, the media spokeswoman, of the group for their food campaign.

The group held protest meetings across London, resplendent with banners proclaiming 'Women demand fair play' and slogans such as 'Food before Films'. Ultimately, the group demanded that the Minister of Food set up a national consumer council, on which housewives should be strongly represented, even suggesting that the Minister of Food himself should be replaced by a woman. The group became 'a thorn in the ministerial flesh'.

They called for the food situation to be regarded as an emergency in view of the extreme hardships that British housewives were currently facing.

During a meeting held in Chelsea Town Hall, a large grapefruit bought at the Covent Garden Market for two shillings was held aloft as evidence of the law-breaking black-market racket that housewives had been forced to enter into. Others brought along a dozen lemons bought for five shillings to show their vindication of a scathing 'food indictment' among the supporters. The British Housewives' League organised the food demonstrations through a sub-group initially called the United Women's Organisation, and eventually known simply as United Women.

At one meeting held at Livingstone Hall in Westminster, demands were put forward for: an increase in the meat ration; the return of dried eggs; the rescinding of all food cuts; a general increase in the standard of the nation's food; and for a fairer distribution as well as more food for British civilians than for prisoners of war. Fanny spoke passionately about the need for a petition. She was reported to say, in a brisk voice, 'We are profoundly disquieted at the level to which our food standard has been lowered. We are forced to surrender our meat ration to our husbands and children and are constantly underfed. We see no reason why we should be denied dried eggs for films.'

Fanny was appointed as the person responsible for the petition, with the reports in the *Evening News* listing her address and phone number should anyone have wished to add their signature to the already substantial ten thousand housewives. Several meetings approved of the petition. Groups of housewives voted motions of no confidence in the Minister of Food. Pathé newsreels relayed short films to cinemas across the country showing the growing disquiet among women about the food situation. A demonstration held in Trafalgar Square against bread rationing was captured on film, calling on an 'army of indignant housewives' to sign the petition in 'open revolt' to the rationing policy.

Quickly Fanny became not only the media spokeswoman, but the leader of United Women. Her mission was to lead on food objectives which were 'superior'. The group had drawn some criticism in demanding better rations regardless of shortages of food around the world. Often referred to as 'hot-headed hens', United Women aimed to put an end to maldistribution and wastage of food through exposing, constructively, chinks in the black market.

The notoriety of the food campaigning work, together with the endless entertaining they committed to at South Terrace, led the Cradocks to rub shoulders with some pretty lofty, and influential, characters. Fanny had an ambition to supplement her novel-writing income with regular newspaper columns, if only she could secure the correct commission. She knew she could write and write; any topic was possible as she sat at her typewriter 'woodpeckering' away. She sent some suggestions to the *Daily Express*, who showed a keen interest in some 'Frances Dale' food-related columns.

At the same time, Fanny had struck up a friendship, she recalled, with the French-born wine merchant, gourmet and prolific writer about wine, André Simon. He called her one day to say that the *Daily Telegraph* was interested in securing her writing services. He could easily facilitate an introduction should she be interested. She mustered all her composure to sound relaxed about the whole suggestion, but inwardly she was overjoyed. Two opportunities to feature in national newspapers at once; surely Fanny's fortunes were well and truly on their way.

Both titles wished to see Fanny to discuss plans on the same day, at the same time. Fanny somehow managed to negotiate a slight time difference, planning to scoot from one appointment to the next with ease. First up were the *Daily Express* who, according to Fanny, immediately offered her a series in eight parts under the title *My Kitchen*. Floating on cloud nine, she arrived to meet Evelyn Garratt, the women's editor from the *Daily Telegraph*, full of hope and expectation. Evelyn wanted to sign Fanny for exactly the same deal. Fanny explained she could not pass up the *Daily Express* offer, but greatly wished to write for the *Telegraph* too, if only they could find a way.

That way, at least initially, was to create yet another pseudonym for Fanny. Using her background and knowledge gained from her stint at the dressmaking business, Fanny was now signed up to be Elsa Frances, writing a series on clothes focused on the principle of 'make do and mend'. Her first article instructed readers how to make a smart long-quilled cap, in velvet or velveteen, satin or faille, fine wool or jersey fabric. Readers could, if inspired, write in to receive an exclusive pattern to make their own cap design. Fanny (or Elsa) gave additional ideas, if long quills were not quite your thing: feathers (to frame your face), contrasting lace (rose pink under black, or even turquoise under navy blue), fur trims (only if you were young), and sequins (for evening wear) would lift the basic design to 'exciting levels'.

Fanny, as Elsa, also encouraged readers to make a topless evening gown (not as risqué as it sounds) from an old dress, to emulate the style and grace of well-known radio star Joy Shelton. 'It is not difficult to do,' Fanny reassured; all that was required was last summer's flare-skirted silk dress, some inexpensive squares of netting, and of course sequins (to add a splash of glamour). Fanny suggested alternative additions to set the outfit off – how about two matching winged birds, which would be 'very new' and followed Paris fashion trends. For the less courageous, flowers could be stuck here and there. Ostrich feathers might be considered as a suitable trim, or even ruched taffeta ribbons. Only the very young could get away with leaving the dress quite plain, with only a wide contrasting ribbon sash to indicate 'extravagance' at any party.

There seemed to be no topic out of bounds for Fanny to write about, if someone was paying, and no name that would not be considered to attach to the growing list of publications. Her articles described how 'Quilted Bedheads Set New Decorative Trend', covered 'The Art of Pot-Pourri Making' and there were even features on 'Brighter Easter Cooking.' Fanny became Philip Essex to write a rugged newspaper serial entitled *Escape from Atlantis*, full of peril and intrigue. Articles on beauty were attributed to Mary Carden. Enquiries were made about acne, leaking scalps and other curious ailments on behalf of a series of mysterious 'friends' (and never the writer) to the *Daily Telegraph* beauty editor, Nan Sortain.

Fanny's typewriter had never been busier. Her schedule quickly filled up with a range of personal appearances at women's luncheon clubs up and down the country, in between hanging out at press parties in Schiaparelli's clothes, interviewing Norman Hartnell and other fashion icons of the day. She began to see less of Johnnie, who was still toiling away at his father's firm. Johnnie's health was deteriorating in much the same way as Fanny's diary was filling up – rapidly. His nervous system was weak, following several otherwise minor (at least usually) illnesses. He had his tonsils removed, and 'very nearly died' as a result. He had arthritis, chronic catarrh and was seldom without a cold. He had a spinal operation which resulted in his doctors insisting he take a few weekends in the country to recuperate.

Evelyn Garratt supposedly hit upon the perfect solution. She had an idea which would involve both Fanny and Johnnie, professionally, ensuring that they spent at least the next six weekends 'in the country' in search of worthwhile inns to visit. Their task was to stay at various hotels, eat at a range of restaurants and then submit their reviews for publication in the *Daily Telegraph*. Evelyn initially asked for a short series of six articles, paying eight guineas for each, plus expenses. Fanny and Johnnie seemed delighted to accept the gig.

For Evelyn, the only matter still up for consideration was which name to attach to the published articles. Fanny was already writing under a myriad of names and personas. Initially she was reluctant to add yet another one to the list. Evelyn assured her that it would be a very short-lived venture, so 'almost any name would do'. Fanny tells in her autobiography that she immediately thought of the name 'Bon Viveur' as it was 'sexless' and covered food, wine and travel, as well as keeping people guessing their true identity. In retrospect she suggested she was well aware of the glaring grammatical error that would follow the name around; however, she felt that (the more grammatically correct) 'Bon Vivant' simply suggested dealing with the table alone.

So, 'Bon Viveur' were born. An anonymous husband-and-wife team, scouring the country for the best food and fare that money could buy. They paid their bills, never accepted bribes and introduced themselves to the proprietors only at the end of their stay, letting them know that they would feature in an article in the *Telegraph* the following week. A simple concept, which today is commonplace but, at the time, in the early fifties, something new and ultimately popular.

However, all may not be as transparent as it first seems. In 1937, the London publisher Geoffrey Bles put together *Where to Dine in London*, a book for visitors to the capital as well as those who 'dine out often but seldom know where to go'. Geoffrey had a reputation for spotting 'new talent' and went on to publish the first five books of C. S. Lewis's *Narnia* series. The book intended to guide visitors to 'smart hotels and Bohemian haunts, chop-houses and taverns, places to dine at before the theatre and to drink at afterwards'. The book described nearly one hundred restaurants and included chapters on 'Food and its History', 'Restaurants of the Nations', 'How to Choose a Meal', 'The Marriage of Food and Wine' and places that can be enjoyed 'All Through The Night', with each area of London covered.

Not unusual in itself perhaps, unless the attributed author of this guide is considered. Like Fanny and Johnnie, he (if it was indeed a he) remained anonymous in order to conduct his research without interference. Like Fanny and Johnnie, his book was full of asides and opinions on culture and refinement, with strong opinions of the 'gastronomic greats' such as Escoffier and what they brought to London in transforming the cuisine choices from 'English' to 'Continental'. Like Fanny and Johnnie, it claimed to feature everyday places as well as those frequented by socialites, although it very much focused on the latter. Like subsequent Bon Viveur books by Fanny and Johnnie, it featured a flamboyant design resplendent with illustrated cartoon images of splendour and the splendid. Crucially, like Fanny and Johnnie, it is published under the name 'Bon Viveur'. Perhaps Fanny and Johnnie had stumbled across it?

Additionally, this was not Fanny's first foray into the world of food and travel writing. In 1950, under the name Frances Dale, she had published a volume entitled *Bon Voyage*. Equipping readers with the necessary information on 'How to Enjoy Your Holiday in Europe with a Car', the book was promoted as 'the actual experiences of the author' and is split into two sections: firstly, planning and preparation; and secondly, the trip itself, including the best route to take through France, Switzerland and Italy, covering hotel accommodation, food, wine, restaurants, as well as overcoming any language difficulties.

> *Bon Voyage* enables the Englishman who has never left his own shores to set out confidently in his small car with three passengers and the correct clothing and equipment, secure in the knowledge that the answers to all his problems are to be found in this instructive and friendly little book.

Bon Voyage recommended that readers take out a membership to either the Royal Automobile Club (RAC) or the Automobile Association (AA), who were both able to offer a range of facilities and services exclusively to members, such as insurance, breakdown cover and so on. Essential advice for planning a trip to the continent to be found in any guide book, but perhaps given more prominence in this volume than might be expected, suggesting that the publication itself was commissioned by those services.

Whichever way, *Bon Voyage* enabled Fanny to enter another realm of writing: travel writing. This had long been an ambition of hers. The book enabled her to show the connection between travel and food, and also between advice, review and recommendation which she would go on to explore and expand upon, with Bon Viveur and beyond.

Another anomaly came from Evelyn Garratt. When Fanny originally began writing a wide range of material for the *Daily Telegraph*, she pitched an idea for combining food and travel together in articles. Evelyn was not as keen and thought Fanny's travel writing required some work to make it more polished for publication. 'Muddled thinking, wordy, pointless' was the harsh feedback that Fanny needed to hear. As before, she acted skillfully upon the advice and thanked Evelyn for helping her to become a better writer.

Something changed along the way, and the changes continued to come as the Bon Viveur 'brand' developed. Weekends were dedicated to travel, hotels and reviews; weekdays for other work. The Bon Viveur column proved to be extremely popular with readers and restaurateurs alike. The 'high ups' at the newspaper were equally thrilled and asked for them to continue. The arrangement they had with Evelyn was fairly informal and, although Johnnie was included 'in brand', and it appeared to have been contrived to benefit his health, he had, at least initially, no official status within Bon Viveur. Contractually, Fanny was Bon Viveur; she received the payments despite Johnnie reportedly doing fifty per cent of the work.

Fanny pushed Evelyn for a more formal recognition for Johnnie, which presumably also entailed a payment equal to her already increasing fee for each article. Fanny knew that members of the public talked about Bon Viveur as a couple. The *Telegraph*, however, wished their articles to read as if the Bon Viveur signature concealed only one identity, namely Fanny, which would keep the articles more personal and appealing to read. In reality, the hidden persona of Bon Viveur was becoming more and more public as Fanny and Johnnie became more and more identified as a duo. They wanted to be recognised, for themselves and also for their work.

The Daily Telegraph columns came together under the banner of 'In Quest of Pleasure', and this also became the title of a series of four booklets in which the newspaper reprinted the columns for sale. The first, simply taking the name *In Quest of Pleasure*, chronicled the first series of columns. Written in the first person, Fanny as Bon Viveur opens with a foreword by way of introduction:

> In the autumn of 1950, the *Daily Telegraph* launched me upon a quest for honest, English fare, a warm welcome and a good service in the hotels, restaurants and the inns of England. My briefing was: 'Go out quite unprepared, go in unheralded, forget gastronomy and the standards of haute cuisine but, should you find them, report upon them faithfully.'
>
> Here are the first of my adventures on the roads of England. I chose at random necessarily, missing many establishments doubtless as good, or maybe better, than the ones I found and either praised or blamed.

> This booklet is now published in response to readers' request in a form convenient for the bookshelf or for the motorist's pocket; and if, in any small degree, I am assisting the quest for weekend pleasure in the countryside, I shall be richly rewarded for the snow, the rain and the sleet which were my portion at the times of writing – October, 1950 to March, 1951.
>
> Just one word of warning – summer tariffs tend to rise. Managements change. These things are inevitable; therefore, it is only reasonable to ask that you shall not be disappointed if you find tariff adjustments upon your journeyings throughout the summer months, if you find the names of new innkeepers in the place of those I quoted.
>
> Bon Viveur

Confusingly, the first four articles themselves refer clearly to a duo, with Fanny writing Bon Viveur as 'we' at every turn. They make their way from 'East Kent by way of Rochester' (where they discover the legend of Pickwick); visit Bath (in search of truffles and walnuts); trundle along the Pilgrims' Way to Winchester (where they see the spotless kitchen at their first hotel stop, with a pot of stock bubbling away nicely); and end up in Stratford-upon-Avon (the town with two lives).

All mention of 'we' is then replaced completely by 'I' and 'me' as the quest continues: racing through the Essex-Suffolk border country (complete with Constable scenes and coffee); Chichester (a town of plenty – of cake shops, but sadly no restaurants for gourmets); the 'turkey country' of Norfolk (where Fanny was overjoyed to find some different vegetables such as artichokes); rural England (or Hertfordshire in reality); the border villages of Kent and Sussex (with a choice of running buffet or dinner); a quick trip to Cambridge and the Fens (where the Bell Hotel in Ely was delightful); arriving rain-drenched in the Chilterns (but leaving when not offered a warm welcome); finally receiving a warm welcome in the Cotswolds (with a warning that tatty curtains and unswept yards would drive travellers away); sending a bouquet to Sussex (which would be perfect for honeymooners); and lastly ending up with a trip westward to Wiltshire and Somerset (where Fanny urged readers to complain if not satisfied).

Further 'quests for pleasure' came in the form of the subsequent booklets, collecting articles on 'Eating in England's Inns'; travelling 'In Search of a Holiday Hotel'; and finally, 'Eating Out in London', which took Bon Viveur well into 1952. Somewhere along the winding roads of Britain, the identity of Bon Viveur, once so secretly guarded, was unmasked. During this year they published – as Frances Dale and John Cradock, 'Bon Viveur' of the *Daily Telegraph* – *Around Britain with Bon Viveur*. The book was based upon their articles, greatly expanded and altered, in an attempt to 'stimulate holiday makers to closer appreciation of the good things to be found in Britain' in the same way that *Bon Voyage* had done in Europe.

Years of hard work and determination were beginning to pay dividends for Fanny. She was a successful fiction-writer, children's author, journalist, and had now added in-demand travel writer to her profile. Fanny named this time 'the harvest years' with both her and Johnnie entering a 'season of plenty'. Johnnie was able at last to take a step away from his father's company, leaving his job in 1952 to focus on being half of Bon Viveur instead. His role in the duo would remain under scrutiny for the rest of his life, but for now he focused on establishing his own area of expertise, deemed by Fanny to be suitably acceptable for the male in the partnership – as the wine connoisseur.

Bon Viveur would go on to publish a book on wine, *The ABC of Wine Drinking*, in 1954 with a further title, *Wine for Today*, written and published by Johnnie alone in 1975. For the second book, a lively foreword was written by Fanny, and her name included on the cover as a result; but the writing style adopted by Johnnie appears to be totally different, at times quite pedestrian in comparison with Fanny's.

While Johnnie developed his knowledge and passion for wine, the Bon Viveur writing portfolio continued to expand. The pair (or was it simply Fanny?) continued to work for the *Daily Telegraph* until 1955 when they asserted their freelance credentials to start a Bon Viveur column in the *Daily Mail*. At the *Daily Mail* the columns were clearly marked with both their names – Phyllis and John Cradock – in brackets after the Bon Viveur title, making it clear they were now, officially, a duo.

Taking their trips around Britain as a template, and possibly echoing the Frances Dale book *Bon Voyage*, they set about publishing a series of travel guides to popular, and not-yet-popular, places around Europe. The guides expanded on columns published in the *Daily Mail*, but the books themselves were not affiliated with them. The foreword reminds readers of their weekly articles and their modus operandi, suggesting that some level of legitimacy and approval came with that. They had spent years fending off criticism from other professionals for being 'amateurs' without any real knowledge or expertise in which to dish out advice. The readers mostly did not seem to care.

The book series was published by Frederick Muller Ltd, who had begun publishing a range of books in 1932. After several buyouts and mergers, in another coincidental twist of fate, they became part of the Hutchinson fold, Fanny's early publishers. The series was billed as the 'Continental Holiday Series with Bon Viveur' with each title labelled as *Holiday in the...* followed by the region to be explored. The first title followed Fanny and Johnnie as they trundled their way through the *Austrian Tyrol*, from the moment of planning to the 'last minute of return as the traveller fumbles for his key outside his own front door'.

The series was written with independent travellers in mind, not those on any kind of organised tour: new generations of 'Gay Adventurers' keen to seek individual experiences. 'The world is a book and he who stays at home reads only one page' became a favourite quotation of theirs, inspiring readers to set down their books – although presumably not their essential Bon Viveur guides – and strike free among the undiscovered lands of the continent that lay waiting for them.

It did not matter if readers were not experienced globetrotters, had no language skills to hand or indeed were fearful in any way; Bon Viveur were there to hold their hands as they helped and encouraged a sense of freedom. Fanny and Johnnie seemed to tap into a mood of at least a dream of 'a freedom to roam' among many, before regular holidays in Europe from Britain became commonplace. Whether or not happy bands of 'Gay Adventurers' set forth to explore, or remained at home and simply read about it, will never really be known.

As well as introductions to the area and chapters on the key places that Bon Viveur felt suitable to travel to, each book in the series had a number of standard chapters. These covered accommodation; food and wine 'at the table'; the clothes to wear; souvenirs and other shopping to purchase; key information for motorists; other travel information and a list of appropriate hotels; pensions and guest houses. A key section addressed what Fanny and Johnnie saw as 'the language problem' for travellers. 'No Spik Austrian', or Spanish, Dutch or the tongue of whichever area the guide was focused on, aimed to arm the weary traveller with a 'serviceable' list of phrases which could 'stab a frenzied finger until your first diffidence is overcome', allowing travellers to scream badly in the local language until whatever it is they were hoping to ask for was secured. So as well as planning a trip like Fanny, readers could also *be* like Fanny while away.

The guides ran to an eventual series of eight, covering Austria, Holland, Barcelona and the Balearics (originally planned to be South East Spain), Denmark, Belgium, Sweden, the Touraine and finally ending with the French Riveria in 1960. Each title claimed to be the result of personal experience and active participation, which meant a great deal of travel for Fanny and Johnnie over the seven or so years that the publications stretched. Fanny's passport, stamped with a multitude of visas around this time, provided a testament to her travels. Other titles, such as Southern Italy, were scheduled but never published.

In typically prolific style, Bon Viveur also, during these years, published further titles exploring food, accommodation and fun closer to home. In 1953 the *Daily Telegraph* published *Bon Viveur in London* which greatly expanded upon, and indeed replaced, the previously published *In Quest of Pleasure* guide, *Eating Out In London.* Fanny told of stepping into restaurants on behalf of the readers, not for private or personal enjoyment, but as a professional. The next year, with a different publisher and no mention of the *Daily Telegraph, Bon Viveur's London 1954* appeared, offering expert guidance on almost one hundred restaurants that had reportedly been personally tested by Fanny and Johnnie. The volume claimed that the duo, much like the maintenance and repainting of the Forth Bridge, were never finished in finding new restaurants to review. They were already partway through 'rechecking, adding, subtracting, sampling and rejecting' for the 1955 edition. This never appeared in print.

The Cradocks were by this time becoming experts in marketing, publicity and engaging enthralled audiences who waited with bated breath for more. Fanny encouraged readers who spotted their blue-and-white Ford Zephyr outside a restaurant or hotel to come in and tell them which other places they had so far left out of their guides. Alternatively, a postcard would suffice. The cloak of concealment had been shed. In the jacket for this publication they proudly announced that they were about to begin yet another veiled column, this time for the European edition of the famous American magazine, *Esquire.* Their first column, *Dining Out and About with Esky* (the magazine's cartoon mascot) was scheduled to appear in May.

1955 saw a return to the *Daily Telegraph* as well as to book form with *Bon Viveur's London and the British Isles* guiding readers 'where to dine, wine, visit, stay, relax and entertain' as well as shopping and exploring, of course. The book seemed to have been designed to appeal to visitors to Britain from abroad, citing the credentials of Johnnie as a 'Harrow-educated director of a successful family business, Travel Editor of *British Esquire*', as well as the pair as joint Food and Wine Editors at *Esquire*.

Wining and Dining in France with Bon Viveur was unleashed to eager readers in 1959, bringing attention to four hundred and fifty hotels and restaurants throughout France, where Fanny and Johnnie had supposedly themselves enjoyed eating. France, they reminded us, was the country Bon Viveur knew as the 'supreme' in fine eating and drinking. Presumably the establishments in which they did not enjoy eating, or which were less than supreme, were 'rejected' from this compilation. It is a wonder they had time to write anything, with the amount of eating, drinking and travelling they were seemingly doing.

While their final Bon Viveur travel book, a massive compilation, the extended *Guide to Holidays in Europe*, was published in 1964, they occasionally branched out from the usual, accepting special assignments which served to increase their booming sense of celebrity in the eyes of the public. As part of a series entitled *Dining with the Famous* for the *Sunday Express* in 1959, they spent two days in the company of the infamous Duke and Duchess of Windsor, at their home in Paris.

The Duchess charmed them with her ordinariness: 'I can assure you I am not at all a three-star Duchess' she told them as they discussed her favourite restaurants. The Duchess told Fanny and Johnnie she could cook: 'I must have cooked over one hundred thousand eggs and bacon rashers for the troops when we were in the Bahamas,' as well as sharing the secrets of her slimline figure. Six days out of every week she 'dieted' – no potatoes or bread, just lamb cutlets and spinach, grilled calves' liver with lemon juice, plenty of salads, fruit and grilled fish, plainly roasted game and poultry would be her limits. On the seventh day she ate with 'fastidious eagerness and an almost frightening discernment' to make up for it. She loved to entertain. She savoured wine with a quiet passion.

The Duke, Fanny and Johnnie recalled, was 'no gourmet'. He ate huge breakfasts, drank no wines, adored potted Morecambe Bay shrimps, and his favourite soufflé was haddock. He preferred fattening food, from Austria, Germany and, with some humour, America, although never put on any weight. Their different appetites and requirements kept their cooks and house-servants busy. So ordinary. Almost a template for the life Fanny and Johnnie not only aspired to but presented to the world at the same time.

Dining with the Famous continued with articles featuring their joyous times with the English playwright, novelist and short-story writer Somerset Maugham, and then Mrs Douglas Fairbanks Jr, or Mary Lee to less formal friends, as Fanny and Johnnie obviously were. The Cradocks were wining and dining with Hollywood celebrities, royalty and literary greats. The articles underlined how much they too were part of the jet-set, welcomed in as 'one of the club'.

Fanny and Johnnie were keen to expand into the world of gardening. They wrote articles detailing their own personal quest to transform their garden at home into a 'marvel' which would more than amply supply their gourmet kitchen. The articles clearly showed how readers could emulate their plans, obviously on a reduced scale if they were not so fortunate as to have several acres, outdoor swimming pools and walled garden spaces to cultivate. Readers at home perhaps would have the same troubles with planners from the local council should they wish to install smokehouses (for eels, mutton, beef, turkeys, trout, salmon, mussels and hams), a trout pond (to keep the smokehouse busy), an open-air rotisserie, orchards and space to make home-made wines.

The pace that Bon Viveur set was relentless. The subjects of their output were as varied as they were furious. It seemed that there were no topics that they would not consider writing about. In what was to become one of the most successful personas that Fanny would create, Bon Viveur columns and features continued weekly, and occasionally more frequently, across a range of newspapers and magazines until 1986, a few months before Johnnie died.

In later years, they wrote mostly about food and travel of course. Familiar articles were printed dealing with 'Turkeys at Christmas', 'Delicate Dumplings', 'Piping Hot Winter Warmers', 'Biscuits to Take the Family by Surprise', and even 'Gooseberries Galore'. They tried to inspire readers to reclaim British heritage foods such as tripe; they sang the praises of the best fish in the world (which came from Scottish waters); and continued to romp round the country in quest of pleasure, at as many hotels, restaurants and boarding houses as they could possibly squeeze in. Always with a typewriter, presumably, in their luggage.

Cooking the Books

Fanny had a burning desire to write a cookbook. It seemed like a fairly natural progression for her, already established as she was as someone who could 'write almost anything' and frequently did. Her work with the Housewives' League had shown her the importance of food in the lives of her 'ordinary' friends, and her experiences after the war living frugally in Warwickshire had equipped her with the skills necessary to make a very little go a long way. Besides, she was always looking for the next big thing, the next string to her bow, particularly if it was lucrative.

Fanny's agent did not initially agree that food writing would be the right course of action for such a successful children's and fiction writer. Competition in cookery books was fierce, with thousands on the market. Perhaps concerned about a potential drop in income for them both, his advice was to stick to the novels, keep building them up and all would be worthwhile.

Fanny recalled seeing a newspaper article that had been recently published discussing the fortunes of English novelists. She was dismayed to read that only a handful were 'rich'; a mere ten per cent earned enough to live on, and the rest flickered up and down over the starvation line. A return to a life of less than luxury did not appeal to Fanny, so she wrote her first cookery book regardless, promising to drop the whole idea if, and only if, it proved not to be of interest or a success. Failure was not something Fanny contemplated easily, but she conceded that if six rejection letters came flooding in, failure it would have to be.

There was no real need to be concerned. The very first publisher who was offered the book snapped it up. John Lehmann was already the publisher for the first two books by Elizabeth David, *A Book of Mediterranean Food* and *French Country Cooking*. Fanny admired Elizabeth greatly.

It is not clear how long Fanny took to write this first cookbook, published as *The Practical Cook* under the Frances Dale name. She described it, in dismissive style, as a 'makeshift affair geared to dried eggs and general shortages' despite its over three hundred pages of more than one thousand recipes, techniques and approaches to cooking. Fanny would later in her career very publicly mock Mrs Beeton and call her a 'fake' for collecting together other people's recipes and printing them in a book as if they were her own, which was a 'shameful thing to do'. It was also very successful, and enabled Mrs Beeton to publish a very popular cookbook.

It may have been that the entrepreneurial Fanny learnt a valuable lesson from the past, employing the same technique, then attempting to cover up her work through deflection.

Wendy Colvin, who worked with Fanny later in the fifties until the sixties, managing tours and acting as a general assistant, recalls that 'she collected recipe books. I had loads of old ones – she had them too; recipes you couldn't do today, but could adapt for today. She had more cookery books going back in history. She pinched all the Women's Institute ones; she adapted them so no one could say she had pinched them. If there was a Women's Institute place, a stall or whatever, she would get their books from fairs, she would send me to get them. I would pick up recipe leaflets. If anyone was selling a machine, she didn't want the thing, but she wanted the recipes. Other people would get things from other recipe books for her. She had a great collection, including special books like for Colman's Mustard or other commodities. If she was called upon for a recipe using a particular ingredient, like milk, apples, potatoes or whatever, she would recycle recipes and reuse them.'

The Practical Cook was published on the 2nd of June 1949 – the day after Fanny's mother died, she noted without any hint of emotion in her autobiography. In perhaps a strange twist of fate, the magazine of the Women's Institute, *Home and Country*, declared the book 'a major contribution to gastronomy … written by an obviously practical cook who clearly possesses an outstanding mastery of her craft' on publication. It may be that they did not recognise their own recipes after Fanny had recycled them, if indeed she had.

The book, in an early embellishment of the story Fanny always spun, describes Frances Dale as 'not only an exponent of good cooking and an expert cook herself, but also a novelist, a writer of children's books, a musician and a dress-designer. Her first interest in the art of cooking was awakened when, as a small child, she fled from the so-called "amusements" of her elders in Riviera hotels to find entertainment in the kitchens.' The book featured a cover illustration by Val Biro in a similar style to the *Gateway to Remembrance* novel of Phyllis Cradock. Inside, selected recipes, equipment and techniques were illustrated by Nigel Mould. In many ways the book is just another in what was becoming a long line of publications stamped with the emerging Fanny Cradock style.

The book was described by the publishers thus:

> In this up-to-the-minute Kitchen Encyclopedia, Frances Dale has supplied an exhaustive range of information for the home cook. The author is a cook-hostess, long inured to the present-day deficiencies in household staff, and she therefore writes with a full and sympathetic understanding of the difficulties her readers are likely to encounter. She fairly frankly admits to a great love for the arts and virtues of good cuisine. She invites experiments, encourages novelties and makes this work both an invaluable textbook and a stimulus to the individual imagination.
>
> In the vast range of recipes totalling more than a thousand, are simple dishes, needing the minimum of expenditure of labour and ingredients; hundreds of appropriately economical recipes and some exquisitely tantalising glimpses of what could be done in the past and may one day be done again. Notable are the chapters on garnish, with their annotated illustrations, so clearly set out that a beginner can follow them with ease; the menus for the cook-hostess, timed and scheduled to the last detail; and the time-saving chapter on batch cookery, so outstandingly helpful to busy women.
>
> Here is something for everyone, and a great deal for a great many by a woman who knows and understands her subject and writes of it with respect and enthusiasm.

These words could almost be written about any of Fanny's books in the future. This first book became a template not only for her cooking, but for her approach to food, particularly garnish. Recipes included in *The Practical Cook* appear time and time again throughout Fanny's career and become her trademark. Recipes for aspic and 'mock cream' sat alongside banana candles, doughnuts, blinis au caviar, tripe and soufflés. Unusual recipes are included too, for hedgehogs baked in clay, roasted cygnets, 'kababs' on skewers and recipes we now recognise as American classics, such as pumpkin pie. The *Bake-Off*-esque illustrations give a glimpse into a style of garnish and presentation which would, for Fanny, never change.

The book began with a few pages of common French cooking terms and their explanations in English, followed by a few pages of 'Do's and Don'ts' (supposedly derived from personal experience) before a whole chapter outlining Fanny's 'Approach to Cooking'. This mainly appeared to be lists and planning. Fanny said, 'Great chefs, like great artists in any field, are comparatively rare, but applied intelligence will make a good and often excellent cook out of any woman who sets out clear-headedly to reach her goal.'

The book was written to inspire housewives to achieve greatness in the home setting and could have been written with the women of the League in mind, and as a reflection of the changing household set-ups after the war. Fanny states that the 'clever hostess', which every reader should aspire to be, 'always plans her work so that she is ready for her guests one hour before their arrival. She then changes in comfort and makes a final tour of inspection before the guests arrive. She has no maids.'

The sheer variety of recipes included would have been enough to ensure soaring sales, but the sneaking in of bizarre ingredients, dishes and presentations seems to be what captured the imaginations of the readers. Reviews predicted Fanny would become 'one of the top flights of chef in the country' with her 'lively and practical style' and 'recipes to kindle the imagination'. The publisher knew this too, sending a copy to a friend with the following note:

'This is just published – it seemed to me just down your street. Except perhaps the "Baked Hedgehog"!!! All sorts of things out of the ordinary. If you don't want it, send it back!'

Fanny used the rave reviews and sales figures to persuade the *Daily Telegraph* to reverse their initial decision and print her eight-part *My Kitchen* series. Evelyn Garratt had told Fanny that they already had a cookery expert, Claire Butler, who helped them produce cookbooks 'with enormous sales'. Fanny must have had her eyes on that prize. The column described her as: 'Frances Dale, aged 40, married. Jobs: Novelist (nine novels), children's writer (six books) and writer on food and wine. Runs home, doing all cooking, personal laundry and interior decorating with husband and son.'

In turn, Fanny wrote another cookbook for the *Daily Express*. *Enjoyable Cookery* featured 'more than one hundred tested recipes by Frances Dale'. A companion to the pre-war book, *Economical Cookery*, this new volume gave many new ideas, such as a 'Chinese Cooking' section and even a chapter on 'Bachelor Cookery' as well as a look back at food fashions from the past in a section called 'Antique Food'. The book was illustrated with full-colour photographs as well as smaller black-and-white images of Fanny preparing items to show particular techniques. Many recipes are repeated from *The Practical Cook*, including the somewhat out-of-place pumpkin pie, as well as new ideas, not least an amusing nod to her future name: the Fanny Cake.

However, Fanny was already making plans for a sensational follow-up to *The Practical Cook*, such was its success. Fanny mentions in her autobiography that, despite her promise to the publisher, she already had *The Ambitious Cook* in 'fair copy' when its predecessor was published. *The Ambitious Cook* was written as a companion guide to *The Practical Cook*, helping the housewife to elevate the simple knowledge gained from the first volume to the 'elaborate and exceptional' this time round. Cook-housewives under Fanny's instruction needed to be energetic, enthusiastic and have a will to plan. Designed to help soothe the trials of the post-war years as well as demonstrate that cooking was an art, and 'like all arts can transform life', *The Ambitious Cook* was persuasive.

Fanny claimed her role, and greatest ambition, was to 'persuade the British housewife to stop regarding cooking as a chore and accept it as an integral part of life's pleasures and self-expression'. Fanny called on her readers to vary her recipes, disagree with her and include their own preferences as they branched out from her suggested dishes into creative flights of their own. Fanny urged readers to find a new way of reading the ambitious recipes and processes in the book. Readers should not expect to absorb them on first reading. They would require to be read at least three times, like mathematical problems, before any cooking could begin.

No hedgehogs or cygnets this time; however, plenty of recipes and presentations which again would become recognisable as classic Fanny Cradock over the coming decades. Gone too were the illustrations from Nigel Mould, replaced with similar designs by Evadne Rowan. Full-colour photographs were interspersed throughout too, in extremely vibrant and elaborate displays. Fanny seemed to decide that colour was required to transform the lives of post-war housewives, which she stuck to for the rest of her life.

Wendy Colvin recalls, 'She was a great one for outlandish cooking. She didn't hesitate, and those green mashed potatoes were typical. She had the idea, she wanted some colour, and still today they are one of the things people remember.' In *The Ambitious Cook*, Fanny claims that the green mashed potatoes were invented by her as a celebration for publication day of *The Practical Cook*. It was also the day after her mother died. Fanny took some ordinary mashed potatoes, added the green colour and piped the potatoes onto a large presentation board into the words 'Bon Appetit' to mark the day of publication in style.

The Ambitious Cook contains a chapter on wine; a whole section on eggs – and real eggs, not dried this time; recipes for oysters and stuffed aubergines; and a section on Christmas, which again became the blueprint for all subsequent discussion of the subject from Fanny. At the beginning of each chapter, Fanny includes inspirational quotations from notable cooks of the past. She says on the book jacket that, for this volume, 'Past and present have been plundered in this assembly of dishes for every occasion, all of which can be made in England today.' Particular reference is made to Brillat-Savarin, author of *Physiologie du Goût (The Physiology of Taste)* from 1825; Mrs Charlotte Mason and her *System of Cookery* from 1787; and Hannah Glasse's *The Art of Cookery Made Plain and Easy* from 1747, which Fanny would ultimately write an introduction for when it was reprinted in 1971.

Frances Dale would not appear on any other cookbook cover again, nor indeed on any published book after her final children's title, *Fish Knight and Sea Maiden*, was published shortly after *The Ambitious Cook* in 1952. Over the next few years Fanny wrote contributions, as Bon Viveur, to two *Daily Telegraph* books – a guide to garnishing in *New Dishes* in 1952 and ideas for children to cook in *Definitely Different* in 1954. The only other contribution credited to Frances Dale was in the 1956 publication *The Kenwood Recipe Book* alongside other experts including Elizabeth Craig, Philip Harben and Marguerite Patten.

Frances does receive a fleeting, and confusing, mention in the very first cookbook that Fanny and Johnnie produced together, as Bon Viveur. *Cooking with Bon Viveur* was published in 1955 by Museum Press, a short-lived publishing house operating after the war until the 1960s, which had also become home to Elizabeth David in the same year for her *Summer Cooking* volume. Johnnie wrote the closing chapter, 'Happy Marriages', which dealt not with his relationship advice but with wine. He told readers that 'Frances regards all sweet wines as being a nuisance,' even though Bon Viveur are introduced as concealing the pseudonym of John and Phyllis Cradock.

The book is an altogether snobby affair, matching the image they were projecting by the time the Bon Viveur brand was in full swing in the fifties. They told readers that the recipes in this book have been 'chosen essentially because they are in constant use, do not call for ingredients that are hard to obtain, and can be easily prepared before or even during a meal'. The exception, perhaps, is the inclusion of a recipe for 'Royal Roast Swan' which contains a footnote disclaimer that Bon Viveur cannot tell readers how to obtain a swan (legally). Should anyone have found one, legally or otherwise, they may have been unable to secure the gold leaf to gild it once spit-roasted or lacked the skill to paint their coat of arms on small banners to stake around it.

The book is littered with references to famous friends with whom Fanny and Johnnie had dined, who had shared the secrets of their larders with Bon Viveur, disclosing sacred family and professional trade-secret recipes which Fanny and Johnnie happily print for all to see. Many recipes are named after the couple themselves: 'Crêpes Bon Viveur', 'Scampi Bon Viveur', 'Salade Bon Viveur', 'Bon Viveur Family Trifle' and 'Gâteau Bon Viveur' among many others. Fanny writes in the introduction that 'No one, we maintain, has any right to lay down the law to you about cookery unless they can cook themselves.' She then continues to lay down *her* laws of cooking, including guidance such as 'never to ruin what might otherwise be a perfect dish by using bought mayonnaise'.

As further cookbooks were published, the message within them changed in subtle ways. Fanny and Johnnie were pictured completing various cooking tasks in their own kitchen at South Terrace for the *Daily Mail* publication, the heavily advert-laden *Bon Viveur Recipes*, which focused on preserving food. The theme of frugal cooking from store-cupboard ingredients was revisited in 1962 with the *Cooking with Can and Pack* book, attributed to Fanny and Johnnie Cradock, and again linking advertised or placed products in each recipe.

The next publication, *The Bon Viveur Request Cookbook*, promised 'dishes that are different, out of the ordinary and yet, most of them, far from extravagant'. Recipes made the most of available produce and reinforced the 'waste nothing' message of the time. Recipes were still introduced with their French titles, but readers were invited to replace ideas of roasted swans with gently sautéed cabbages and pickled eggs.

Fanny and Johnnie continued to put their names to collections of books for anyone (and, it could be suggested, everyone) who asked them to. As freelancers they exploited their freedom to roam, engaging with almost as many publishers and producers as publication would allow. Fanny entered into what would become a lifelong sponsorship deal with the Gas Board. She always recommended readers cooked with gas, never electricity, in all her books, remaining loyal to those that paid her way.

In 1959 Fanny wrote two books for the Gas Council, published under the House Wife banner, as Bon Viveur. The books, *Mr Therm's Encyclopedia of Vegetable Cookery*, attempted to reverse the 'British housewife's approach to vegetable cookery' which Fanny thought to be 'so extraordinarily casual and so fundamentally slapdash', resulting in the best parts of the vegetables being thrown away. Volume One – *Cabbages and Things* – educated readers on and celebrated seasonal British vegetables: how to shop for the best produce, how to spot the worst and avoid it, and what health properties were to be gained from each example. All cooked with gas, of course. Recipe ideas were colourful, appealing and accompanied by colour pictures designed to help the housewife enhance her own presentation. Volume Two – *Veg and Vim* – focused on the health benefits of vegetables, emphasising the vitamins as well as the beauty benefits to be gained from vegetable juice and cocktails. Colour and presentation were joined by diet tips for slimmers, where to get more protein if required, and ideas for how to still enjoy a party with vegetables.

The books were received well, with reviewers noting that in addition to vim and vigour, Fanny had introduced both wit and wisdom to the subject of vegetable cookery, in a 'genuine crusade for health'. The books were promoted as reference works for everyday use, using the usual Fanny trick of 'trimmings' and embellishments to transform the recipes into special occasional meals. Fanny was signalling to any would-be producers and companies that she could help to sell their products in surprising, innovative ways that were well received by the public and professionals alike.

Subsequent Bon Viveur cookbooks often repeated the pattern of being released in two companion volumes, encouraging readers to purchase both titles. Sales were high. The most successful of these were published by the

Daily Telegraph in 1964 and 1967 in original hardback volumes, and thereafter reprinted in various formats as paperback. *The Daily Telegraph Cook's Book* was published on the 16th of July 1964, and quickly topped the bestseller lists in August, securing sales equal to thirty-two per cent of the top five books in demand that month. The book remained in the top ten throughout September and October.

As was often the case, the descriptions of Bon Viveur given within the books list Johnnie first, ahead of Fanny, and underline their famous credentials as well as helping put the country 'back on its feet' after the war through supporting housewives to deal with food shortages, substitutes and rationing. The book also repeats the device of suggesting that the only reason Fanny and Johnnie have put together this particular book is due to the huge number of letters they received at the *Daily Telegraph* begging them to do so.

Winifred Carr, who followed Evelyn Garratt as the women's editor at the *Daily Telegraph*, wrote the foreword to the book and described it as 'a book to read in bed, at leisure, or while in the thick of it, in the kitchen'. The book was cheerfully illustrated in a newspaper cartoon style, with additional illustrations to show examples of equipment which may be essential as you progress through Fanny's instructions, such as a canelle knife or game secateurs. Details of a selection of carefully vetted places to purchase these items were then given at the end of the book. There are several full-page adverts contained within the original editions, mainly for gas cookers but also key kitchen ingredients, although these are not carried through to the paperbacks.

The book opened with a few chapters of explanation, again setting out the Bon Viveur way of approaching cooking:

> We have been cooking for a very long time, yet we have never discovered a good cook who was divorced, deserted or even kept waiting. The man who is urged to stay drinking one for the garden path, the garage doors, the road, and so on, will trot straight home if he knows that an otherwise superb meal will be ruined if he stays.

The books are written with a whimsical, conversational tone at the beginning of each chapter, followed by a huge selection of recipes shared by Fanny and Johnnie as their 'very favourites'. Otherwise the recipes reinforce the previously laid-down image of Fanny and Johnnie as creative socialites sharing their insider knowledge, particularly of French cuisine, with those less fortunate than they have been, in the hope that they will be able to dazzle guests, bosses and neighbours that were never really liked very much with their newly acquired culinary knowledge and expertise.

The 'sociable sequel', *The Daily Telegraph Sociable Cook's Book* of 1967, aimed to follow the great success of the original, turning housewives across the country from 'secretive cooks' who only feed their families, into 'sociable cooks' who share food freely and adore people who simply 'pop in' uninvited to their homes. Sociable cooks could come from wealthy or relatively poor backgrounds (Fanny and Johnnie knew both) but must be prepared to work beyond the basics, must be 'ambitious' about raising the standards of both everyday meals and the sociable spreads that they lay on for friends. Although this duo of books remained in print for many years, Fanny and Johnnie also published a similar title, *Fanny and Johnnie Cradock's Cook Hostess' Book*, in 1970, through Collins. It too headed up the bestseller lists.

Either on her own, or with Johnnie, Fanny amassed just short of fifty cookbook titles during her career. Many of these were linked to television series (which will be discussed in later chapters); many were linked to producers or promoting particular products of some kind. Fanny always attempted to make the books 'marketable', finding new hooks on which to hang the recycled recipes to secure a fresh purchase.

One popular area for the pair to focus upon was the festivities that surrounded Christmas, a sensational time for food, family and friends. Fanny knew that it could be a time of incredible stress and strain too, so to 'help' she produced a book which, at last, would let the ordinary housewife relax at Christmas – by preparing all year round. *Coping with Christmas*, published in paperback by Fontana in 1968, saw Fanny and Johnnie exhaustively share their plans for a perfect Christmas schedule, 'whether you're a well-equipped mother of four with six months in hand, or a hard-pressed career-plus-children housewife with two hours left on the 24th of December to start actually *thinking* about Christmas!'

The popular book covered 'it all' – how to make decorations, how to lay the table, what to drink and of course what to eat. The relentless Cradock-inspired Christmas kicked off in January, when Christmas puddings and Christmas cakes had to be made in advance, while this year's decorations were coming down. Fanny recommended they come down 'as soon as possible' and either be stored or burnt. This perhaps gave a clue to her true feelings on the topic of Christmas. Despite her eternal link to the festive season, she was not a fan.

And neither indeed would any reader be if they adhered to her suggested plan in every detail. Without doubt guests at Christmas would eat well, but it would be as a result of twelve hard months of preparation. Fanny acknowledged that this book was not intended to be followed to the letter, saying that 'the average wife and mum would end up dead or ravers if she attempted to act upon all the suggestions we put forward in this book!' Fanny was no average wife or mother, however, and had a lot of experience and knowledge to share.

Readers were supported to choose the items they wanted to focus on from the book to put together their perfect Christmas. Fanny merely was providing suggestions as a solution, backed up as always with references to all the gastronomic greats from the past, such as Escoffier and Mrs Agnes Marshall, in addition to more modern names like Constance Spry and Gretel Beer.

Fanny carefully plotted a history of each dish on the Christmas table, giving recipes en route for each variation, in case a reader's choice was more adventurous than the standard turkey and inspired hostesses wished to impress their guests with tales of medieval banquets of crane and spoonbill instead. Fanny conceded though that swan was no longer a viable option, which was just as well as every venturesome guest that had tried it had deemed it a 'total failure'. Fanny endorsed the view that the swan's sickly sweet, almost fishy flavour was repellent to most modern palates, her own included.

Ultimately the book remains a resource for the plucky at Christmas, and those with enough time on their hands to search through for the viable recipes which will be enjoyed time and time again. Other cookbooks that originated from the kitchen knowledge of Fanny, and perhaps Johnnie, were more practical in nature. There were titles focusing on the wonders of *Foil Cookery*; ideas which were both *Modest but Delicious*; books which included different *Soups* for every day of the year, and its sequel, *Puddings*; cooking for the freezer, or *Just for Fun*; books designed to get children cooking at home; introducing new ideas such as *Pasta*, or from new cuisines like French and Italian; or perhaps books which took readers through an alphabet of terms and recipes. Fanny would continue to write about food, cooking and entertaining if someone would publish it. Titles which bore one of the many names that Fanny wrote under were almost guaranteed to sell, and sell well. Publishers spun them out as quickly as Fanny could write them, which was one heck of a pace.

One book that Fanny had been keen to write all her life was a recipe collection and history celebrating her culinary hero, Mrs Agnes Marshall. Mrs Marshall was, at times, a forgotten culinary entrepreneur. A leading food writer in Victorian times, she had established a cookery school, sold hard-to-acquire cooking utensils and equipment for use in the kitchen, and published recipes for ice cream before anyone else, using liquid nitrogen and an ice-cream-making machine that she patented herself, which could freeze a pint of ice cream in five minutes. She gave public lectures on cooking and ran an agency for domestic staff. Mrs Marshall, like Fanny, was born in Essex, and was said to have studied cooking from a very early age, practising her art with celebrated chefs in Paris and Vienna. Almost as if Fanny had borrowed her story for her own.

Mrs Marshall died after failing to recover from a horse-riding accident in 1904. Fanny had her own theory on the demise of Mrs Marshall, which she claimed was more suspicious than the received version. Had Agnes survived beyond her fifty years, Fanny was convinced that she would be remembered very differently as a pioneer for women in food. She later did receive some acclaim in books and on television from British celebrity chef Heston Blumenthal, but not before Fanny made an attempt to place her name in the minds of readers in the seventies.

Fanny had to shelve plans to write her proposed book, *The Great Marshall Mystery*, as she could not track down the archive materials required to make it a success. She was furious, suggesting that Mrs Marshall's husband had destroyed them. However, she found a way to write about Agnes anyway, without being constrained by factual information. *The Sherlock Holmes Cookbook*, published in 1976 by WH Allen, may not immediately be the obvious home for her tribute, should anyone be searching for it; however, this is where it is to be found.

The Sherlock Holmes Cookbook is, even by Fanny's own standards, a strange cookbook. It was intended to be. Fanny returned to her earlier spiritual role to compile the book, supposedly, in a similar vein to her Atlantis novel. The given author for this book is Mrs Hudson, fictional housekeeper for Sherlock Holmes and Dr Watson. The inspiration for the recipes that Mrs Hudson shared, through Fanny, was gleaned from the works of Mrs Marshall. The premise was that Mrs Hudson had been fortunate enough to see Mrs Marshall during a brief visit to her cookery school in Great Mortimer Street, and had been inspired to write down her recipes, just as Mrs Marshall had done.

Fanny claimed that the idea for the book had originally come from the trustees of the Conan Doyle Estate, although she does not clarify if that idea included this complicated exchange of attribution or not. Many of Fanny's own recipes are included alongside Mrs Marshall's, as are Escoffier's. It seems Mrs Hudson was a fan of all the same people as Fanny. Each recipe included side notes and clarification from Fanny herself in an attempt to supposedly reduce confusion.

The book remains popular in Japan, where Fanny Cradock had not been a household name, meaning that Japanese readers were likely to be even more confused as to who had actually written the book. Fanny Cradock? Mrs Agnes Marshall? Mrs Hudson? Perhaps they did not care, preferring instead to simply enjoy the strange and surreal world of Sherlock Holmes and the food he may have eaten. The original hardback featured illustrations from long-time collaborator Val Biro, which were faithfully reproduced in the Japanese version, giving glimpses into 221b Baker Street.

The final cookbooks of Fanny and Johnnie were published in 1985, in three volumes of *A Lifetime in the Kitchen*. Volume One was *For Beginner Cooks*, Volume Two dealt with *Family Cooking* and finally Volume Three was for *The Ambitious Cook*. Why change a winning formula? Stretching to a staggering combined page count of almost one thousand three hundred, the collection gathers together almost every recipe from the culinary canon Fanny held, and many more. Modern dishes are included, with modern ingredients and modern techniques, in an attempt to make a marriage of experience and a demonstration that they still held some relevance in the world of cuisine.

Fanny stated they had received no additional remuneration for brand-naming the various products that they used with the greatest of success over the years. She did not clarify whether this included new sponsorship and placement deals to mention very eighties products like St Ivel Gold, a low-fat dairy spread, which Fanny now recommended for use as a potential substitute for butter, following nearly forty years of warning people of the dangers of margarine.

The introductions to each volume contain a potted history of their careers, or more accurately a revised version, as well as an outline of their motivation to discredit Mrs Beeton and reinstate Mrs Marshall to 'the limelight' that she deserved following a career based on merit and not publicity, as Mrs Beeton had achieved. Fanny said that both she and Johnnie were currently working on books adapting Agnes's recipes to contemporary requirements, which they hoped would go some way to seeing her recognised as she should have been. Fanny additionally claimed that she believed Mrs Marshall was deliberately murdered by arsenic poisoning to suppress her name and works.

Fanny's versions of Mrs Marshall's books never made it to print, which must have been a real disappointment to her. Fanny clearly had plans to continue writing and releasing additional cookbooks well after this set; however, the published legacy of her own cookbooks, stretching from 1949 until 1985, remains impressive. Sadly, after her own death, her estate (if indeed anyone has the ability to assume control of her written assets) have resisted the opportunity to reprint or re-evaluate her cookbook career, in some way mirroring the suppression Fanny suggested Mrs Marshall had succumbed to.

Beginning to Broadcast
1950s Kitchen Magic

Fanny was always quick to act positively on any opportunities that came her way. As many freelancers are, she was always on the lookout for the next big thing before whatever she was exhaustively working on at that time came to an end. It is barely conceivable that she had any time to consider her next move immersed as she was in novels, children's books, newspaper articles on any subject that came along, and her burgeoning career as a cookbook author. She did, however.

Following the publication of *The Practical Cook* in 1949, some interest in the volume was shown by BBC Radio's *Woman's Hour*. A magazine programme comprising a range of features, discussions and information aimed primarily at women, *Woman's Hour* had been broadcast on the British Broadcasting Corporation's Light Programme since 1946. At that time, the programme built heavily on the BBC's reputation for producing 'talks' for women, which grew significantly in number after the war. Programmes focused on subjects ranging from current affairs, women's employment and other areas of national interest to fashion, gardening, childcare and cookery.

When the review of *The Practical Cook* was broadcast, a friend of Fanny alerted her to the fact. Fanny herself, no doubt too busy at her typewriter, or perhaps abroad, had not heard the broadcast but was assured that it was positive about her book. Encouraged, she wrote to the then *Woman's Hour* editor, Evelyn Gibbs, with a letter that set a template for many hundreds of letters she would send throughout the next few decades.

Fanny, signing herself as Frances Dale, wrote expressing her appreciation for the mention but, in her own words, 'like Oliver, I would like to ask for more'. Fanny assured Evelyn that food and cooking really were the 'most favourite of my subjects' (just in case she had heard of her other exploits) and that if the BBC should consider Fanny for future broadcast roles, she would be most delighted. The letter[1] boldly asks Evelyn Gibbs to let Fanny know which 'branch of food and the home' would be most appealing to listeners, stating that she was just about to leave the country for four weeks. Fanny wanted to say thanks to *Woman's Hour* for the mention, in addition to a request to 'please' consider her for yet another new career, as a broadcaster.

The BBC initially did not bite. The editorial team at *Woman's Hour* underwent a few changes before Fanny was to try again. Janet Quigley had returned to the fold following a few years away from the BBC after she married in 1945. Prior to this, she was responsible for 'talks' for women broadcast on the radio from 1936. On her return to the BBC to take on the role of editor in 1950, she was keen to make changes to the format to include new subjects and styles of broadcast. She is often credited with transforming *Woman's Hour*, with the regular inclusion of many areas of discussion that were previously seen as 'taboo'.

The following year Fanny made contact with Janet Quigley, who agreed to look at some submissions. Fanny was quick to send them in for consideration, hopeful that the change in personnel would have a positive result for her personally. The recipe-based 'talks' that Fanny submitted were well received by some in the department who found them tempting. However, a recent change in policy favoured a focus on dishes that could be explained without the need for giving a 'recipe', which, it was felt, slowed up the programmes.

Fanny took the feedback with her usual vigour, and resubmitted various ideas for talks in which food was part of the story being told, but not central. Ideas such as the tale of an Essex village famous for an apple supposedly

---

[1] BBC Written Archives Centre RCONT1/Talks/Cradock 14th July 1949

planted by William of Normandy were pitched alongside stories of a two-hundred-year-old ham involving twin brother-and-sister survivors of a religious controversy, but none seemed to land with the *Woman's Hour* team.

One idea that did seem to connect, however, was a series of talks by Fanny in which she shared her memories of 'Eating Abroad' in various locations, encouraging listeners to expand their holiday considerations beyond the British Isles. No issues of featuring ingredients that were still on the ration, and light enough to be inspirational to those listening in.

Fanny was scheduled to have a voice test with the BBC on the 3rd of July 1952 by way of an audition so they could judge her suitability to be heard over the airwaves. The memo[2] that followed the test highlighted that she had a 'pleasant, mature, rather husky voice'. Fanny apparently read very badly at first but, true to form, she responded well to being produced and prompted. The reviewer, Grizel Paterson from the *Woman's Hour* team, found her to be 'extremely conceited' and 'very hard', although she was certain that she could work with her, and even shape her eventually into a good broadcaster.

She had passed the first hurdle, although her card had been marked in terms of her prickly personality. Grizel noted that Fanny was 'obviously wildly keen to get in with us' and had lots of interesting ideas in addition to her tour of Continental Europe. Ideas were something Fanny was not short of. The main concept she hoped to 'sell' to the BBC was a double act with Johnnie in which Fanny would teach her husband to cook. Fanny joked that Johnnie could barely boil an egg[3] by himself and suggested that, by following a set of instructions given by Fanny, perhaps other husbands could be motivated to join a 'noble army' who were beginning to cook. The idea was politely put on the back burner by the BBC until they could gauge reaction from listeners to Fanny's initial broadcasts.

There had been some discussion about the name under which Fanny would, and should, broadcast. She had, by this time, quite a choice. Her preference was to be known as Bon Viveur, for which she had gained permission from the *Daily Telegraph*, without any need to reference them, more than likely in an attempt to ensure that Johnnie was included from the very beginning. However, for the first series of broadcasts, it was agreed that the name Frances Dale should be attached.

---

[2] BBC WAC RCONT1 File 1 1949-1954 4th July 1952

[3] BBC WAC RCONT1/Talks/Cradock 4th July 1952

The first talks were scheduled to be broadcast at the end of August 1952. As Fanny kept insisting that she was just about to head off on a trip to somewhere or other, and would not be around on those dates, the *Woman's Hour* team suggested that Fanny pre-record a series of three talks, each concentrating on one country, and these she quickly produced. Due to the recent policy shift within the BBC to drop the use of dictation speed as a means of giving recipes, Fanny had suggested that she could ask listeners to write to her directly to receive copies instead. Although the BBC could see merit in this, they were concerned about the precedent being set for future broadcasters to do the same, so no such announcement was made.

The first talk was broadcast on Friday the 29th of August 1952. Frances Dale recalled 'Eating Abroad' in Italy and shared some of her tasty but inexpensive dishes. In the talk, Fanny relayed a tale of her recent trip to the coast of Viareggio with her family. Her reminiscences are romanticised and allow her to recall a journey of food that she encountered along the way. She saw a man carrying a wicker basket filled with 'the most delicious dough-nuts' which, when she makes them for her family at home, she is careful to fill with a cream substitute. Other foods she can't quite shake from her memory include spaghetti cooked with mussels, butter beans from a Florence restaurant and a delicious pizza which they had enjoyed at the end of the day with a beer. Fanny then went on to tell how this pizza can easily be recreated at home with puff pastry, slices of tomato, strips of anchovies, thin slices of cheese and small bits of olive 'if you have any to spare', making a splendid supper dish.

The next broadcast of 'Eating Abroad' came the following Friday and focused on the 'often basic fare' of sandwiches 'at all hours and in infinite variety' favoured by people in Denmark. These sandwiches, in contrast to ones that most housewives at home would be familiar with, were 'gay' in appearance and consisted of a piece of bread with 'many good things heaped on top'. Fanny suggested that these would make a splash at finger-food parties served along with pancakes dolloped with jam and a spoonful of cherry brandy, which happily could once more be purchased in Britain in miniature bottles for those not fortunate enough to travel to Denmark, as Fanny often did.

The final talk in the series followed the next Friday, with Fanny remembering some delectable meals she had eaten in Holland, including fruity bread a little prematurely intended for Easter. Fanny told how her trip inspired her to make her own version at home, as well as more frugal dishes such as soup with rice. Fanny was ultimately critical of the Dutch diet, in particular the preference to eat cheese for breakfast. She said that 'if anyone wants to put on weight, it is a wonderful idea'.

Fanny would not feature in any further broadcasts during that year, despite her attempts. Keen to try her hand at new challenges, she had submitted herself to do a test recording of live commentary for the Lord Mayor's Procession in London. The results were seemingly quite shocking. Fanny realised quickly that speaking without a script was not her forté and she vowed to forget all notions of live transmission.

However, she must have impressed someone within the BBC world, as she was invited to join the regular panel of the lively parlour game *The Name's the Same*, in which the experts had to attempt to discover the identity of their guest in the studio who bore the same name as someone famous. Alongside Fanny, the panel featured Frank Muir and Denis Norden, who would continue to have great success on television and radio in the years to follow. The fourth panellist was the American actress and singer Frances Day, who would later appear on the popular British version of *What's My Line*, a similar panel show where the experts had to guess the profession of the person in the studio. As it was felt that the names Frances Day and Frances Dale were too similar, and could easily confuse the listening audience, Fanny agreed to be listed as Phyllis Cradock. No doubt any listeners to both this popular series, in which Fanny would feature weekly from June until December in 1953, and *Woman's Hour* would recognise her unmistakable voice.

The Name's the Same transferred to television, without Fanny, despite her being recommended by the radio producers. The show had attracted a great deal of criticism from listeners who doubted that the panellists could guess the names so successfully without being given the answers beforehand. Despite doubts, the radio show went on to win a prestigious National Radio Award. The British television version aired for only a few months in 1954.

Fanny continued to bombard the BBC with proposals for shows and broadcasts. She knew she was making a nuisance of herself, but she was 'bursting with new ideas'[4] – some with Johnnie, as Bon Viveur, some on her own. Her campaign to be noticed and remembered was partially successful.

---

[4] BBC WAC RCONT1/Talks/Cradock 9th September 1953

She had several meetings with producers. One idea struck a chord with one of them who had an idea to produce a series of food and travel talks for *Woman's Hour* under the theme 'A Window Over the Kitchen Sink'. Fanny took the idea and ran with it, sending outlines of a staggering thirty talks for consideration; she even attempted to rename the feature 'A Window Over *My* Kitchen Sink', unsuccessfully. When the series ran, Fanny featured only once, in a piece relaying how she managed to forget about the household chores by thinking of Ibiza. The series would continue with a different guest speaker each week. This would be Fanny's final outing as Frances Dale on radio.

She felt that a food-based show that took dishes renowned for glamour and expense and recreated them for the ordinary housewife, simply and inexpensively, would be a winner. Of course, presented by both her and Johnnie, she felt it could not fail. Radio producers, however, felt that it was perhaps more suited to the medium of television, which seemed to surprise Fanny as an avenue that she had yet to consider. This resulted in more ideas to commit to paper and more letters to write.

Meanwhile, Fanny and Johnnie were invited to take part in a broadcast for *Woman's Hour*, in a segment entitled 'In Partnership' talking about their professional life. Fanny also began to make regular appearances on the early-morning magazine on the BBC World Service, *Hints for Housewives*, giving general advice on domestic questions, which also led to a small number of appearances on *Woman's Hour* and another BBC Radio programme, *Home for the Day*, focusing on advice for 'business girls'. BBC producers had agreed to experiment with a number of '"personality" speakers'[5] that they could test audience reaction with, of which Fanny was one.

Around the same time, at a dinner party hosted by Fanny and Johnnie, the BBC television producer of the popular cabaret show *Café Continental*, Henry Caldwell, was impressed not only by the food he was served, but also by the 'performance' that both Fanny and Johnnie put into the evening. He referred to them, according to Fanny's autobiography, as performing 'kitchen magic', suggesting that they should take to the stage. Initially reticent to agree, Fanny was won round by Henry who suggested that she appear in full evening gown just as she had that night for dinner, with the gimmick that she never got any marks on it while cooking. He would produce the show. Johnnie would need to learn to cook.

[5] BBC WAC RCONT1/Talks/Cradock 22nd January 1954

The pair swung into a period of creation, perfecting an 'act' which they could perform together at venues up and down the country, more often than not twice daily. For evening performances Johnnie would appear in top hat and tails, Fanny in full-length ballgown and tiara. Matinées were more relaxed, but only a little. The message was 'food is fun' and 'cooking can be, and indeed should be, glamorous'. Johnnie cracked open bottles of champagne; Fanny gave detailed instructions on how to cook perfect dishes at home. Audience members were invited on stage to sample the outcome, prompted (but not obliged) to say it was 'delicious'. They were also required to scrutinise Fanny's dress to confirm that nothing from the cooking process had made its way on to her attire. Fanny would tell the audience that 'Cooking is a cleanly art, not a grubby chore,' and, from time to time, 'Only a slut gets in a mess in the kitchen.'

On stage, Fanny and Johnnie would proclaim that cooking was 'child's play' allowing them to prepare the best food in the quickest time. 'There is nothing we do that a child couldn't do,' Fanny told audiences during the hour-long shows in which they produced seven dishes, including Swiss rolls, fruit soufflés, savoury omelettes and spaghetti. Always cooking without aprons, remaining cool and collected, Fanny and Johnnie invited the audiences to taste the dishes at the end of each performance, which also allowed for 'ordinary' people to have a fleeting meeting with them.

As they perfected their craft and honed their act to delight larger and larger audiences in department stores and halls across Britain, they were invited, as Bon Viveur, to be part of the *Daily Telegraph*'s 'Food and Cookery Brains Trust' event, which shared expert advice from an experienced panel including Constance Spry and Egon Ronay. Fanny wrote up the proceedings, with recipes, hints and tips, for the *Daily Telegraph* publication *Inside Information*, so making sure that Bon Viveur featured prominently. She gave advice on making a soufflé simply, basting meat (or rather not doing so), fish and chips fit for a queen, hosting a party, tips for sure-fire success with meringue, perfect pastry and a Swiss roll that never cracks. All would become staple segments of performances from Fanny in the years to come.

The Food and Cookery Brains Trust events were sponsored by the Gas Council, a relationship which Fanny and Johnnie would continue from 1955 until the day they switched off their final flame, with different geographical Gas Boards sponsoring local events. Fanny would maintain throughout her life that only gas would do, following this conversion in the mid-fifties, having had previous contracts and relationships with companies such as the Simplex Electric Company.

The Bon Viveur Kitchen Magic act was a success and popular with sponsors who saw it as a new way to introduce products to the growing audiences of mainly housewives around the country. The *Daily Telegraph*, too, seemed pleased with and supportive of the new venture which promoted them at the same time as putting Bon Viveur very much in the minds of households in addition to businesses.

The *Kitchen Magic* tours were hard work, but the investment brought dividends when television producers from the BBC began to show some interest in their demonstrations. Fanny sent script outlines to encourage them to see that their act could be developed easily on screen. She invited them to come and see them perform, and even offered to put on a special performance for their consideration. Persistence was beginning to pay off.

Cecil Madden, a pioneer producer for the BBC responsible for bringing new programmes to the screen, often championed the duo, although not all were convinced. In 1954 the BBC's current television cook, Philip Harben, 'dropped out'[6] of the organisation and Cecil suggested that the time was now right to give Fanny and Johnnie a chance. He was keen on the act including evening dress, which was opposite to Harben's presentations in butchers' aprons, and liked the notion of including an interactive element with an audience. Others thought Fanny to be 'an awful person' whose performances were 'abominable'. Fanny was working behind the scenes, however, to make improvements to both her performance and her appearance.

Fanny toyed with the idea of a full facelift to improve her chances of looking suitable for the small screen. However, the plastic surgeon she consulted disagreed, saying it would make no difference to her appearance as it was her nose that was 'wrong'. It apparently threw shadows all across her face, brought her eyes too close together and made her face look like a 'currant bun'. Charmed by the description, Fanny agreed, almost without consideration, to change her nose. She was delighted with the more 'telegenic' result. Instead of pretending that it had not happened and accepting the many compliments that followed from curious well-wishers who noticed 'something was different', Fanny wrote about the experience in her column in the *Sunday Graphic*, having photographs taken to show the

---

[6] BBC WAC TVART1/Phyllis Cradock/File 1/1953-1962 7th January 1954

before-and-after effect. Fanny sent the pictures to Doreen Stephens at the BBC to further remind her of her burning desire and absolute commitment to getting on screen.

Fanny later gushed about her operation: 'My whole career has changed since I got a new nose. They used to tell me I looked appalling on television – my craggy old nose threw shadows all over my face and made my eyes look close-set. I was so conscious of it that I developed a series of mannerisms as a cover-up... like talking with one hand draped over the bridge. Then I had the operation and discovered a whole new personality. I became much less aggressive and much more successful. My basic fee for a day's work has shot up to one hundred guineas – I used to be lucky if I made that in a fortnight. Now I have more dates to fulfil than I can accept!'

As the year trundled on, and Bon Viveur did more and more performances, each better and bigger than the last, BBC executives exchanged memos debating their merits. Somewhere along the line, Fanny was given a commitment to at least have an audition of this new glamorous 'joint cookery act'[7] with an audience. One of the Bon Viveur sponsors, the Simplex Electric Company, almost put an end to the venture before it had even begun by contacting the BBC to enquire when Bon Viveur would appear so they could add the information to their publicity materials. Fanny took decisive action to stave off any backlash, which was welcomed by the BBC. Doreen Stephens warned Fanny that any attempt to procure direct advertisement on the BBC would result in 'immediate cancellation' of any agreement that may be in place.[8]

The rehearsals and tours stood Fanny and Johnnie in good stead. Their audition was a success. They were offered their very first television programme, running to half an hour, which would be broadcast live on the 17th of February 1955 at the very late time of a quarter past ten at night, entitled *Kitchen Magic* after their show. Dressed glamorously, the duo were billed thus in the *Radio Times*: 'John and Phyllis Cradock, the Bon Viveur husband and wife cookery team, present an unusual style of cookery to a studio audience at the Television Theatre.' The invited audience of five hundred guests would watch as they prepared inexpensive party dishes, including their Swiss roll that never cracked, éclairs and a soufflé.

---

[7] BBC WAC TVART1/Phyllis Cradock/File 1/1953-1962 6th October 1954

[8] BBC WAC TVART1/Phyllis Cradock/File 1/1953-1962 14th October 1954

The day of transmission began with rehearsals at the Shepherd's Bush Empire at the unlikely time of four in the morning, which was the only time Fanny and Johnnie could snatch from a chaotic schedule that week. The rest of the day, and the broadcast itself, appears to have been a bit of a blur for Fanny. Johnnie was seized up with nerves. Fanny was upset at the end of the performance. It must have been an extremely nerve-wracking, and pressured, time. They had campaigned for this day for so long and, despite all their other career plans, this seemed to be the 'big' opportunity they had worked so hard to secure. Fanny burst into tears after the cameras stopped, assuming it was all a disaster, prompting Johnnie to say it was the only time he had seen her cry. However, neither of them really had to worry.

Fanny looked confident in her shiny evening gown, resplendent with a large buckle near to her chest and set off with a necklace of mixed-size pearls. Her hair was tightly curled and short, framing her face perfectly. Fox furs draped over her arms as she displayed the finished dishes. Johnnie looked comfortable at her side in a velvet and silk dinner suit, complete with bow tie and monocle, of course.

The BBC producers were happy with the broadcast. Cecil Madden even made a plea for their fee to be increased from forty guineas to fifty to compensate for their extra rehearsal time and the fact that they had supplied all their own equipment, including ovens and fridges, free of charge, leaving the BBC nothing to provide. Viewing figures were strong, despite the late time slot, and the newspaper reviews the next day could barely have been better. 'They proved themselves expert in holding the attention of probably their biggest audience and gave an unhurried, but crystal-clear explanation of their magic'; 'What a grand little show it was – good food, striking personalities and any amount of wit'; 'It was entertainingly instructive.'

Several newspapers mentioned their predecessor, Philip Harben, suggesting he would have to 'look to his laurels' after the Cradocks' half hour of cooking in party clothes. Only one review had a note of concern, spotting that, although the dishes made were indeed inexpensive, some of the items of equipment, such as electric mixers, they used to prepare them were not.

Fanny herself took the trouble of retyping and sending on to the BBC some of the hundreds of letters she said she had received, personally congratulating them on the programme and begging for more, for a series, for the recipes and for new ideas that may be inexpensive and easy for men to make. Doreen Stephens recognised that, despite Fanny's 'highly strung nervousness' and 'irritating mannerisms', everything had been worked out to 'a foolproof degree' and that they should be recommended for another spot.[9] This second spot would not materialise for several months, due to a combination of the busy Cradock schedule and tense negotiations with BBC bosses who were perhaps already becoming wise to Fanny's demands.

In the intervening months Fanny continued to send in various ideas and suggestions for programmes, including one based on material that Johnnie had filmed while the couple were in Naples. Producers who viewed the footage seemed keen on the possibilities it offered. The proposal was to film Fanny and Johnnie in the studio as an introduction, then to use the pre-recorded material throughout – cheap for the BBC and enabling the completed films to be repeated when necessary, should the Cradocks be in agreement. The films were never broadcast.

Not wishing to stand still, Fanny pushed on with the Bon Viveur tours, which were becoming technically ever more proficient. Bon Viveur were about to enter a new agreement to write for the *Daily Mail*; the paper's publishers also had interests in the newly formed independent television company, Associated-Rediffusion, who lured Fanny and Johnnie with the promise to make stars of the Cradocks. Nervous BBC producers watched them at work and were impressed by their innovative use of technology and cameras. They were also fearful of losing the Cradocks to Independent Television, and as such were keen to feature three more programmes before the year was out.

The resulting second BBC appearances were broadcast on the 4th of November. During the protracted negotiations Fanny pushed for another half-hour slot, which she almost achieved. Instead *The Cradocks Are Frying Tonight*, as it became known, was broadcast in two editions, each of fifteen minutes: the first in the afternoon, followed by an 'evening dress version' late at night. Fanny's script shows that they planned to demonstrate how to fry chips initially, and then different fillets and types of fish. If an extra thirty seconds was available, the completed dish would be garnished with sprigs of fried parsley, carefully placed on the finished plates with a pair of eyebrow pluckers, presumably Fanny's own.

The three other broadcasts Fanny had prepared were not filmed with the BBC. Instead, a new show called *Fanny's Kitchen* (presented by Phyllis

---

[9] BBC WAC TVART1/Phyllis Cradock/File 1/1953-1962 6th April 1955

Cradock) was prepared for Associated-Rediffusion and broadcast on the rival, independent network in October, November and December of 1955. The new television alternative to the BBC had launched just a fortnight previously, in September 1955, with a gala opening night heralding in a schedule of variety, celebrity, drama, news and sport. Fanny added a touch of glamour to TV cookery with a mid-morning slot in 'her own kitchen' as she prepared a Madeira cake, choux pastry and then pancakes over the weeks. *Fanny's Kitchen* continued until 1957, but her time on Britain's second channel was only just beginning.

Regardless of her foray into Independent Television, Fanny was evidently still wildly keen to secure more slots with the main broadcaster in Britain, the BBC. However, despite the will of most of the BBC team, Doreen Stephens was having 'considerable difficulty'[10] with Fanny who did not seem able to appreciate the BBC's point of view. The Corporation had already committed, however, to broadcasting a major undertaking of a performance with Fanny in early 1956.

Fanny had suggested the idea behind *Challenge in the Kitchen* to Alan Sleath, a pioneering producer at the BBC in the forties and fifties, early on in 1955. A famous French chef, Raymond Oliver, had reportedly said that women could not cook as well as men, and he would be willing to test this out against an Englishwoman. Naturally Fanny, sensing the opportunity for publicity and prestige, was keen to accept the challenge. She also spotted an opportunity to involve her new sponsors, the Gas Board, in a television extravaganza which could be broadcast across Europe. Monsieur Oliver was represented by the French equivalent of the Gas Board, Gaz de France, as well as being connected to RTF, the French broadcaster. The BBC had recently become a partner in Eurovision, and collaborative broadcasts of this type between British and continental television companies held considerable appeal.

The resulting show was a grand affair – as much off-screen as on it. The date was set as the 9th of January. The venue was the prestigious Café Royal on Regent Street, London. This was not a BBC production, but they had agreed to televise a reduced version of the event the following evening, which entailed restaging parts of it on the 10th of January for transmission. Elaborate plans for staging were drawn up, which had to be approved by

[10] BBC WAC TVART1/Phyllis Cradock/File 1/1953-1962 14th November 1955

Monsieur Oliver, Fanny and both television companies. Both Fanny and Raymond were eager to have the best camera angles, the best access to the judges, the best of equipment to prepare their meals on, and the best in one-upmanship as they went along.

As sponsors of the event, the Gas Council were providing the cookers to be featured on stage, and other essential equipment. They were keen that Monsieur Oliver cooked on a different type of cooker to Fanny, who was by now firmly associated with the Parkinson Cowan eye-level grill cooker. Monsieur Oliver requested a 'backless oven' to be on stage, facing the audience, in order to have the capacity to increase his showmanship. This caused some consternation with the Gas Council who felt such a 'prostituted model' would confuse the audience and misrepresent the finished product. The BBC were not concerned with selling a product, only in broadcasting an entertaining show; however, they showed interest in using a backless oven for future programmes[11] should the Gas Council be able to supply them. They responded favourably, saying: 'As a matter of fact there is nothing new about this since Harben, Patten et al, have from time to time used a backless job; and, on one memorable occasion, an ovenless one as well!'

Correspondence between the organisers of the event and the BBC indicates that Fanny was beginning to display diva-like personality traits and demands, which required some management. They appeared, however, to match the temperamental outbursts from her opponent, Monsieur Oliver, like for like, which must have made for a difficult production. Both stars were nervous of the 'Challenge', realising the pressure that came with the opportunity of such a grand, live, outside broadcast across several countries. Monsieur Oliver hoped the outcome would place him firmly in the bosom of the BBC as a television cookery presenter; Fanny was keen on any and all the publicity she could muster to further her career.

Challenge in the Kitchen, billed as a 'culinary duel between the sexes', had three esteemed judges, including Constance Spry who had been part of the Food and Cookery Brains Trust tour with Fanny, and knew her well. This did not give Fanny any advantage, however, as Constance let Fanny know beforehand that she would judge her more harshly as a result. Fanny arrived ready for battle in a 1911 Renault with 'glittering brass fittings', in a dress she had designed herself in apricot satin embossed with ostrich feathers,

---

[11] BBC WAC T32/486/1/Challenge in the Kitchen 2nd January 1956

with a three-foot train. Raymond wore a white cotton dinner jacket with wine-coloured facings. The duellers went to their separate 'kitchens' on stage to commence battle.

The judges, after much deliberation, pronounced the battle a draw. For the reduced show for television the next evening, Monsieur Oliver, according to Fanny, initially refused to participate unless it was announced that he was the winner. However, the restaged show went ahead as it had the previous evening, and the draw was broadcast as planned. Fanny, however, came out as the winner in the eyes of the press and the public. The flurry of newspaper stories covering the event reinforced the persona with which Fanny would remain identified for the rest of her life. She was described as cooking in ballgowns with 'silver foxes' and diamonds, while at the same time picturing Monsieur Oliver in traditional chef's outfits. All of the press coverage focused on the battle of the sexes, questioning whether Englishwomen could indeed cook as well as Frenchmen? The *Challenge in the Kitchen* proved that that was very much the case.

Fanny's father wrote to her the next day to let her know 'how proud, how tremendously proud, am I to know that I am the father of such a daughter'. BBC producers let Fanny know how delighted they were with the broadcast, disguising their frustrations at the time. Fanny must have thought that the stage had been set for a whirlwind of offers for television. They never really materialised during the remainder of that year, although monthly editions of *Fanny's Kitchen* were still broadcast on Independent Television, along with a new, short-lived, show with Johnnie called *Chez Bon Viveur* where they discovered 'new things' to eat while abroad and recreated them in the studio for housewives at home. Fanny also appeared on a couple of magazine shows, again on Independent Television, discussing 'easy and delicious picnic meals' on *Summer Magazine* and as a guest on *Talking About Wine.* As the year end approached, Fanny and Johnnie also filmed two *Bon Viveur Christmas* specials for Associated-Rediffusion.

However, as was becoming the norm, behind the scenes Fanny was planning the biggest, most extravagant performance which would eclipse all that had come before it, including *Challenge in the Kitchen*: a stage-cooking performance at the Royal Albert Hall in London. Never before had anyone attempted such an event. Fanny was convinced that it would be the perfect vehicle for her and Johnnie in terms of publicity and the possibility of television coverage.

Rival food demonstrator Marguerite Patten, who had already featured on the flickering television screens of the BBC, had recently been engaged in a tour of Britain showing housewives how to cook particular dishes. As part of the tour, called *Melody Fare*, Marguerite had been booked to appear at the London Palladium. She gave a perfectly ordinary food demonstration, in between performances from variety acts. She would later take part in a similar show, again at the Palladium, but this time was asked to combine food and fashion, wearing a special evening dress at each entrance.

Fanny was keen to outdo all those whom she saw as rivals in the food world. In later years, Marguerite would turn her back on the linkages between glamour and cooking, stating: 'We had to make cooking very worthy because we were dealing with rationing.' She did not approve of Fanny's approach entirely, even if perhaps she had inadvertently inspired it, saying, 'She brought a sense of a gracious entertaining thing, though I disapproved of her evening dress and spangles.' Marguerite maintained mixed views about Fanny throughout her life. 'I did not like her as a person because she was a bully – we were judges together at the Festival of Britain and she massacred me in the meeting – but I would defend her ability to the end of my days.'

Fanny was also known to inspire a few rivals too. Graham Kerr, known as the Galloping Gourmet, attributes his famous leap on screen to Fanny. 'I was told,' Graham said, 'that Fanny went to paratrooper training school to learn how to fall and roll in one fluid movement, which she then employed when making an entrance down a sweeping staircase at her parties! It might just have been this piece of gossip that got us thinking about jumping chairs as an entrance!'

Never one to acknowledge other contemporaries, Fanny had long maintained that she had been inspired by the great chef, Escoffier, and that it had been her mission to reintroduce his teachings to the housewives of Britain. She had the idea to dedicate the grand evening to Escoffier to demonstrate her love for him, or perhaps resulting from the news that the Escoffier company had agreed to sponsor the performance. Around the same time, in the story she tells, a mysterious friend called her to say she had discovered a book of Escoffier's unpublished recipes in the vaults of the Bank of England, and wondered if Fanny might be interested to make good use of them? The coincidence seemed perfect, especially as the Escoffier company granted Fanny permission to use and publish the recipes in the *Daily Mail*.

Fans were offered the opportunity to secure a ticket for the performance through giveaways in newspapers. All tickets would be numbered, and holders of the lucky numbers would win a range of prizes from cookers to rolls of linoleum, gift packs of food and wine, and even a model hat. Readers were enticed with the prospect of seeing other stars in the audience, who would be sitting in the inner-row seats around the 'boxing arena' and tasting some of the food prepared by Fanny and Johnnie. Ordinary ticket holders just may have the opportunity of a tasty sample too.

In June of 1956, Fanny's public relations team sent an offer to Doreen Stephens at the BBC to have exclusive rights to broadcast the Bon Viveur show, in collaboration with the North Thames Gas Board, planned for the 11th of December that year. The proposal outlined a two-part performance, completely scripted, running for approximately two hours.

'For the first part, Fanny and John (wearing ball dress, tiara and white mink; velvet dinner jacket) will present "Christmas Dinner with the world's greatest chef, with recipes never used before." There will, of course, be a considerable publicity build-up before the event concerning the recently found manuscript of Escoffier in which among other things he bequeaths a menu of Christmas dishes; and these will be cooked and served with all due ceremony – soup, fish, meat, game, goose, turkey, sucking pig, an unusual Christmas pudding and the real Pêche Melba as served to the Diva inside the curved wings of a swan sculpted in ice and carried in the dark to the stage on an illuminated base, giving the effect of an actual floating swan.'

Part Two would, somewhat incongruently, feature Fanny and Johnnie as patrons in a bistro in France, playing roles in a comedy feature called 'Chez Bon Viveur'. The elaborate proposal received a short response from the BBC stating that they may be interested in broadcasting a quarter of an hour or perhaps thirty minutes of the show, should the material be strong enough. It did not appear to be, as the final agreement placed a fifteen-minute segment of the entire two-hour show, to be transmitted live from the Royal Albert Hall at eight-thirty on the evening of 11th of December 1956. This was scheduled to be followed by forty-five minutes of *Vera Lynn Sings*.

On the evening, stress levels were high, with Fanny later referring to it all as a 'madhouse'. In addition to the entire evening being filmed before the live Royal Albert Hall audience, which included many invited celebrities including television cooking rival Philip Harben, timings had to be absolutely perfect so that Fanny could link seamlessly to the BBC television cameras at precisely eight-thirty-two-and-a-half for her fifteen minutes of fame. When the signal came, Fanny's hand was on the door of her gas cooker ready as she without hesitation greeted the TV audience with, 'Hello, viewers – here we are in the thick of it at the Albert Hall…'

Television viewers missed out on the opening shots showing the famous concert hall bristling full of excited guests, all dressed smartly for an evening out on the town in London, waiting patiently until Fanny's voice came booming over the loudspeakers introducing Georges Auguste Escoffier to them. The first to appear, wandering out of the darkness, was Johnnie, dressed in dark dinner jacket with silk detailing, a dark bow-tie and crisp white shirt with matching handkerchief in his top pocket. From the opposite direction came Fanny, dressed all in white. She wore a long satin ball dress, partly concealed initially by a fur stole, sparkling with jewels. Triumphant trumpets serenaded the couple as they took their places on stage, behind tables laden with food and wine. Fanny grasped hold of Johnnie's hand, tightly, before beginning the spectacle of their lives.

The broadcaster Leslie Mitchell, who not only lent his voice to the first broadcast of the BBC on the 2nd of November 1936, but also to the first announcement of Associated-Rediffusion, the ITV company, on the 22nd of September 1955, was plucked from the invited ring of celebrity tables to try one of the completed dishes. Fanny looked apprehensive, but his review was simply, 'Delicious!'

Fanny and Johnnie went on to present a large mincemeat pie, decorated with a pastry image of Mr Therm. Their able assistant, Susie Tyfield, who Fanny introduced as 'our youngest pupil' and 'Escoffier's youngest disciple', brought on a huge ice-sculpture swan to the stage as Fanny told the story of Dame Nellie Melba and the now famous Pêche Melba. Escoffier had presented his version in a similar ice swan, surrounded by roses and ferns and flavoured with real vanilla pods ('not that terrible essence') to finish off the Master's classic dish.

After the interval, the stage set was transformed into a French bistro, with the 'miracle of Kitchen Magic' and the Bon Viveur team raring to show how to make a soufflé in a gas cooker. Both Fanny and Johnnie adopted different outfits – and personalities – for this change of pace. Fanny assumed a rather dodgy French accent, and was now wearing a white short-sleeved dress featuring an elaborate fern-like design, bound tightly with a belted waist, with a high-necked collar and a modern, Dior-like pleated skirt. Johnnie was dressed in a stereotypically French striped top complete with beret and round glasses. The pair hammed things up, with Fanny discussing her approach to cooking ('Zen it ees shild's play!') before asking those watching to 'Think about that woman next door that you have never really liked, but you are too nice to tell her, so you take it out on the sauce.' Johnnie affected an equally dodgy, but inexplicable, cockney accent: 'Cor blimey, I forgot to light me bloomin' cooker!'

After thirteen-and-a-half minutes the soufflé that emerged from the (at first forgotten) gas cooker was wonderfully risen. Fanny held it up to the audience to ensure they had a good look as she delivered the punchline to the whole event: 'You see, ladies and gentlemen, you can't possibly go wrong with gas!' Fanny then dropped all pretence at any accent other than her own to thank the audience and to take a bow.

The evening – and, more importantly for Fanny, the experimental broadcast – was a success. Again, newspaper reports the following day all mentioned the elaborate evening dress, the scale of the spectacle and the inclusion of Escoffier's lost recipes. These recipes were printed in the accompanying programme for the evening, along with adverts for gas cookers and acknowledgements for all other items used on stage. One illuminating credit betrays the secret of Fanny's never-spoiled ballgowns, which she so fiercely maintained had remained clean throughout, as cooking was not a grubby chore. Perhaps through links established during her days as a dressmaker, or from her time as fashion editor with the *Daily Telegraph*, she no doubt came into contact with new and innovative materials, not commonly known by the public. Most people at the time would skirt over the description of her ballgown, made by Madame Cordeau in a 'silicone stain-resisting satin', whereas today we would surely recognise this to mean that the dress was wipeable, so as to appear clean at the brush of a cloth, or a swift swipe of the hand, maintaining the stage secret ahead of anyone scrutinising it.

During the year that followed, Fanny continued to submit a range of ideas for new television programmes to the BBC, with limited excitement as a response. Her outlines varied from programmes that answered viewers' common problems in the kitchen to spots featuring celebrities enjoying the food that they cooked. Fanny was keen to secure a spot in the early evenings, between six and seven, when she knew that housewives would be most likely to sit down and watch. The BBC had mixed views about both Fanny and the timeslot. She had garnered a reputation relatively quickly for being hard to handle; and the BBC were reticent to launch into any new venture with her on screen, especially if the vehicle was not quite right.

Fanny continued to feature in a range of BBC shows on radio, passing on her endless tips for holidays to the continent and as a regular contributor to the panel on the topical discussion show *These Foolish Things*, often alongside Gilbert Harding. Fanny and Gilbert, who was often described as 'rude' following his appearances on television, would become firm friends. Gilbert had attached his name to some early promotion for Fanny and Johnnie before their first television appearance, telling his fans that the announcement of their television debut was 'the best news for some time'. Following his death in 1960, Fanny and Johnnie pitched an idea to the publisher André Simon to collate a collection of essays about Gilbert to be written by his friends, in lieu of a memoir. In the published volume, *Gilbert Harding by his Friends*, Fanny lamented that 'The planet is without doubt more drab since his passing.'

Regular appearances at the Ideal Home Exhibition featured in Fanny's hectic schedule, creating eggs served as swans, snails which 'looked appetising' stuffed with mushrooms, or skinned trout with aspic jelly 'tinted with lavender' and garnished with lemons cut to resemble water lilies for Queen Elizabeth at Olympia. Crowds gathered to catch a glimpse of Fanny, with Johnnie by her side, at work. Newspaper articles carried headlines such as 'Cooking in Full Evening Dress' and 'Janet Learns About Magic in the Kitchen – How to Cook in Evening Dress' with tittle-tattle stories of minor accidents such as Fanny falling at home while her hair was in curlers, resulting in one of the curlers cutting into her precious new nose and ultimately leaving Fanny with no option but to spend a day in bed. The headlines appeared more regularly than Fanny and Johnnie did on screen, however, with only a couple of episodes of *Fanny's Kitchen* left to run.

It was at the Ideal Home Exhibition that Fanny would meet Wendy Colvin, who went on to work alongside Fanny as her faithful assistant for at least a decade. 'I had been working freelance with the *Daily Mail*,' Wendy recalled. 'I was responsible for the VIP stands. Somehow we just clicked, we got along like a house on fire. She made me laugh. That seemed to appeal to her as most people were afraid of her, even then.'

Wendy worked with Fanny behind the scenes, at home, on the road and in the television studio. 'She was exciting to be with, but also terrifying. Some days people would be terrified to talk to her. There were certain things you would never do around her; you had to know your place and not step over the line. You would never go into her bedroom, ever. I never went into her territory if she was out. I wouldn't have dared to use her bathroom or loo; I was careful.'

Wendy realised quickly that Fanny had a complicated personality. 'Fanny was fun, even when she was the devil. She could have been bipolar. When she was good, she was very good; when she was bad, she was horrid. Fanny was a damaged person. She so wanted to be liked and loved, but as a result she wanted to own people. Johnnie was the only person she ever trusted. I loved Fanny. I think people who knew her could not help but love her. I was well aware of her faults, but there was something about her, I couldn't help it. If you were an open-minded person, and open, she was fun. She was very friendly if she liked you. She was friendly until she hated you.'

Wendy did not appear on screen with Fanny. 'She went for boys,' Wendy recalled. 'She could not have lovely young girls on screen with her, it would have shown up her age. It was always boys. I was in the background whisking up the egg whites, always out of camera.' Wendy got to know how Fanny liked to be supported. 'I did her *mise en place* and placed every knife, every bowl exactly where she needed it to be. She used to tell me that, when presenting on television, she could not look down: she had to pick things up and chop without looking at them. If it was not right it blew her. It was a real responsibility. She was a very professional artist on television – she loved the camera on her and saw it as a great opportunity for her. She loved the feeling of oozing charm and personality to people, pulling the audience in with little bits of speech like "don't tell your husband" and so on. She was very good with her audience and they loved her wherever she went. She really did have a tremendous following.'

It was not until September that a new venture on Independent Television came to fruition, in a programme which would never have made it on screen at that time on the BBC. *It's The Tops* was a series of six planned programmes (which would be extended to seven), hoping to break the mould of magazine programmes in the UK. Heavily linked to advertising, they would emulate the more 'human' approach taken by such product-heavy shows in America. Fanny wrote the scripts and selected the advertisers she wanted to feature, although it is hard to imagine that she would have refused any requests she gathered. She did, however, tell the press conference to launch the programme that she would draw the line at bottled sauces, butter substitutes, pressure cookers and malt vinegar, which she felt was only suitable for cleaning refrigerators and polishing furniture.

Fanny shared her vision which lay at the heart of the idea: that viewers looked upon adverts as part of the entertainment when watching television. She waged a war against the Chancellor of the Exchequer to reduce the 'iniquitous purchase tax' that kept refrigerators and deep-freezes beyond the reach of millions of housewives in Britain. She happened at the time to be 'trying out' what she claimed to be 'Britain's largest domestic fridge', on loan to her by the manufacturer, in her own kitchen at South Terrace. It appeared to be quite at home nestled among the eleven cookers she also had installed. At the same time this allowed for a whole new range of products to fill the appliance, such as Fropax frozen foods, 'the finest frozen foods in the world', who employed Fanny and Johnnie to promote their products across newspapers, books, live shows and broadcasts. Viewers were encouraged to write in to the show for further details on any of the products they liked the look of.

It's The Tops echoed their stage performances of *Kitchen Magic* which were still on a seemingly endless tour of the country, reaching areas of Britain where their Associated-Rediffusion shows were not broadcast. At that time, the independent television network opted in and out of many programmes locally, with franchises such as Scottish Television only appearing late in 1957. Fanny was well aware of this patchwork of possibility across the country, with many potential viewers left without the option to tune into shows such as *It's The Tops*, even if they wished to. During one trip to Edinburgh, to appear at the Usher Hall, the press reported that mounted police were required to control the crowds, such was her popularity. However, while *Kitchen Magic* kept Fanny in the public eye in those areas, she knew that the main opportunity for her to reach the majority of housewives and families was to return to the national broadcaster, the BBC.

The BBC, with strict guidelines on advertising, especially subtle forms of it, were cautious to say the least. Memos and other correspondence bounced around between BBC producers and executives debating Fanny and Johnnie's future on screen. The majority of memos note that, although producers often found Fanny to be unlikeable to them, to the audience she was very attractive, always giving an extremely professional performance. Debates and disagreements centred upon the commercial enterprises Fanny found herself involved with, on and off screen, while broadcasting on Independent Television. Would this count her out from any future BBC opportunity, or could it simply be disregarded as an additional unrelated activity that she did for another company? Fanny was becoming so entwined in sponsorship and promotion, it was increasingly difficult to separate the two. The flip side was that she was able to produce an entirely packaged act for television, and not merely a presenter's contribution, making it a cost-effective proposition for the BBC.

Wendy Colvin remembers Fanny's approach to getting companies to work with her. 'She was very good at using the Fanny Cradock name for things, and being aware of it. She was also an intensely mean woman, inasmuch as if she could get anything for nothing, she would. She was paid, paid, paid. Whether it was Anchor Butter or the Gas Council, different people used her. In return she would drop into her performances things like, "I always use butter, never that other stuff," things like that.

'When I worked with her, I made her something one day using ready-made puff pastry. She used to say that I was the only person she would ever have cook for her, especially in her own house. She thought the pastry was delicious, assuming I had made it. I had to confess it was bought. Fanny being Fanny, she immediately saw the opportunity, so contacted the company who had produced it and did a deal with them. From then on, she would always say, "It is so time consuming to make puff pastry, I always use this one!" She was just like that.'

As the deliberations stalled any return to the BBC screens, Fanny busied herself by plotting a dramatic return to the stage, in a play featuring cooking along the same lines as the second act of the infamous Royal Albert Hall performance, feeling that what theatregoers lacked at that time and therefore deserved was some light entertainment mixed with expert food knowledge. Who better to stage such an extravaganza than Fanny, with Johnnie by her side?

The result, a three-act play modestly entitled *A Cooking Story*, emerged during 1957 for a short run at the Arts Theatre in Great Newport Street, in London's West End. The Arts Theatre had built a reputation as a members-only club for the performance of unlicensed plays since it opened in 1927, and was the theatre where Ronnie Barker, later of *The Two Ronnies* fame, made his debut in 1955. The Arts Theatre became home to try-outs before they transferred to larger West End venues or indeed before they ventured out around the country. This was the plan hatched by Fanny; she wrote to her contacts list at the BBC to share her ambitious idea.

The programme for *A Cooking Story* reveals the three acts, produced by John Valentine (which may have been an amalgamated name to allude to Fanny's father but disguising the true identity of her brother, Charles) with only two other actors billed to appear alongside Fanny and Johnnie: Tony Church and Gwen Nelson. The play would begin with 'Breakfast with the Cradocks', in their flat on a summer Saturday morning. Fanny and Johnnie would play themselves, naturally, with Tony taking the role of Willy Wickham and Gwen as his wife, Joan. In the second act, Willy and Gwen travel to France the next day where they eat lunch at Chez Françoise, a restaurant in the Pas de Calais area. Fanny and Johnnie play the French restaurateurs. The final act sees Willy and Joan returning to dine with Bon Viveur in their flat again the next evening. All three acts allowed for an array of food to be prepared, served and enjoyed on stage. The recipes were listed in the programme should anyone wish to recreate them at home. Each and every item of equipment, clothing and service included in the performance was outlined in the programme, including Madame Cordeau's hidden-in-plain-sight silicone stain-resisting satin ballgown worn by Fanny.

This first outing for the play was not the overnight success that Fanny longed for. As with their display of acting abilities at the Royal Albert Hall, audiences were not convinced. Undaunted, and believing in the project utterly, Fanny set to work to reinvigorate the play. Perhaps driven by the knowledge that *Tons of Money* had resulted in exactly that for her father, she was sure that this play could run and run, with the royalties running over. The reworked show became *Something's Burning* and returned to the Arts Theatre in the summer of 1958.

In the intervening months, Fanny and Johnnie sold their house on South Terrace and moved to 134 Shooters Hill, in Blackheath near to Greenwich in South London. In *Something's Burning*, they had similarly upgraded. Still in three acts, the action now initially took place in the kitchen of the Cradocks' London home, on a Friday summer morning, before moving to a restaurant in France, and then back again to the London home for a Monday evening dinner. Only one additional character had been written into the play: Mrs Plum, played by Mollie Hare. Otherwise Fanny and Johnnie played themselves, and the same characters under different names, Françoise and John Huggins. Although Fanny and Johnnie had moved from South Terrace, they were joined on stage by their neighbours, and friends, and emerging actors, Tenniel and Evangeline Evans.

Something's Burning ran for a fortnight at the Arts Theatre, and did not exactly set the West End alight, despite planned appearances in the audience of celebrity friends Alfred Marks and Hughie Green. The reviews were, at best, tepid. Some reviewers even reported the name of the play incorrectly: anything from *Something to Burn* to *Something's Cooking*. The *Evening News* called it 'pretentious nonsense'; Fanny and Johnnie were berated for their lack of acting ability and the play for a lack of plot.

Evangeline recalls, 'We did a perfectly ghastly play with her, *Something's Burning*, in London. Tenniel and I did it with her. Tenniel was out of work, so it was a chance; we were all going to make our fortunes. We rehearsed in her kitchen; she cooked the food. Awful food. We sat at a table on stage – Fanny cooked on stage, which was a frightfully good idea at the time, after the war, with the country not back to full luxury... One thing we ate, was pancake with corn inside it. Tenniel and I were sitting on the edge of the stage and he said to me quietly, "Don't eat it." It was absolutely poisonous. We all had food poisoning. We mimed eating it. Poor Eric Croall, who directed the show, and was used to working with them at Associated-Rediffusion, was terribly ill. He was a Christian Scientist and not strictly speaking allowed to be ill, so while Tenniel and I rolled around being terribly sick, he couldn't.'

Evangeline remembers it as a really nightmarish time, rather than the fantastic opportunity she and Tenniel had hoped it would be. 'It was ghastly. Someone wrote a review: "What a tragedy, when the Moscow Arts are here doing a marvellous play, that they are producing *Something's Burning* which is a complete disaster." The whole thing only ran for two weeks, but we couldn't get the smell out of the curtains for months. It really was dire. There was never anything like that again. As I say, it was an inspired idea at the time, to have a cooker on stage and for Fanny to cook a meal during the performance with people having the recipes printed in the programme to take home. It should have been a marvellous idea. Fanny really had a business brain, but all I remember was that she was so grubby. Fanny and Johnnie did not eat any of the food they prepared for *Something's Burning*. She was feckless about what was kept and reheated. We were all lucky to be alive at the end of it...'

However, Tenniel, Evangeline, Fanny and Johnnie remained friends. 'We did not worry about little things like being poisoned. She was an extraordinary "thing" in our lives. She gave huge presents at Christmas. One year it was a cardboard box of wine glasses, full of glasses that had all been used – they had not even been washed. They had obviously been used for a party and Fanny had not given them back, so gave them to us. It was just Fanny, you put up with it. She was completely unlike anyone or anything. I have to say, as much as I miss her, I am rather relieved never to have met anyone like her again.'

Unsurprisingly, *Something's Burning* did little to enhance Fanny's chances of a return to the screens of the BBC. However, her 'celebrity' did continue to rise. She featured in a four-page spread in *Vogue* magazine giving readers a glimpse of the 'down to earth' natural 'born showman' who was undoubtedly a 'hard-headed businesswoman' and at the same time remained 'essentially feminine'. Readers could recreate Fanny's fabulous gowns at home using patterns sold by *Vogue*.

Around this time, Fanny's son Christopher was living with her in London, as part of a late-flourishing reconciliation. Fanny would mention her 'children' in interviews and publicity, reinforcing her image as a domestic mother figure. As was becoming the norm for Fanny and Johnnie, she was also welcoming other young people into their home, supporting them to succeed in life. One such young person was Jane Cornelius, later to be Jane Chapman, Christopher's wife.

'My family got to know Fanny when I was about six,' remembers Jane. 'My parents worked for the BBC. My father, George Cornelius, read the news on the Light Programme. Fanny and Johnnie were coming down to Cornwall and stayed at the Bristol Hotel, Newquay – we used to go there for Christmas. Fanny and Johnnie stayed there as Bon Viveur; they were doing write-ups for the newspaper. We went over and saw them; my parents struck up a friendship with them which lasted for years. They would often come down to Bristol to see us, and we went up to London. I remember we stayed for the Coronation. I often used to see Fanny when I was a child, she was always lovely towards me. Her and Johnnie both.'

Fanny, in particular, seemed to take a shine to Jane. 'Mum and I would go up and watch Fanny at the Ideal Home Exhibition. One year, when I was fourteen, I was about to leave school. Fanny was asking what I was going to do. I hadn't the faintest idea. Fanny had the idea of me moving up to be with her. She had an idea of getting into the debutante scene, she wanted to get into that crowd, and I was her ticket into that. I went up to Vicky Clayton's to do the finishing course. I rather liked it, so I went on to do their models' course. All this time I lived with Fanny. I did various things with her, went along to television recordings, helped her out at dinner parties. She was ever so sweet to me, she treated me like a daughter.'

When Christopher's marriage to his first wife, Nikki, broke up, he came to live with Fanny for a short while, towards the end of the year. Jane was there at this time and became involved with their collective plans. 'We were going back to Cornwall for Christmas, all of us, Fanny, Johnnie and Christopher. On Christmas Eve my father sang at the Cathedral and we all went out for dinner afterwards. Suddenly Christopher and I were kissing each other under the mistletoe. Fanny looked up and asked, "What's going on here?" From then on it was downhill. Once Fanny realised that I was together with Christopher, she disowned us. Christopher and Fanny were too alike to do anything much together. They wouldn't have got on even if I hadn't got in the way.'

At the same time, Fanny was pitching an altogether more homely proposition to the BBC, this time nothing at all to do with cookery.

The new home on Shooters Hill was in need of some transformation, to the house and the garden, which Fanny and Johnnie felt that they could do themselves without any professional help. Fanny pitched to BBC producers an outline of an outside broadcast series following their progress from the 'highly vulgar and full of beaverboard'[12] house as it stood at the time to a much more desirable home, suitable for the burgeoning stars. In addition to the television series, Fanny envisaged several accompanying articles in newspapers, and eventually a book, to encourage other homeowners to transform their modest homes too.

The BBC were not sure that such a series would hold the interest of more than a limited number of viewers, nor that it could justify the 'considerable amount of film effort and money'[13] that would be needed. It was suggested that Fanny take her idea to ITV, who may be more amenable, particularly as the plan involved exploiting the television exposure 'to the full' for her own gain. The BBC did eventually use Fanny and her gardening expertise for the television programme *Living Today* in 1963, in a semi-regular slot called 'In a Town Garden'. Fanny let the news slip to the press at the time, claiming that she was to become the only woman on British television to have her own gardening programme. 'I had to fight a major battle with my own

---

[12] BBC WAC TVART1/Phyllis Cradock/File 1/1953-1962 16th September 1958

[13] BBC WAC TVART1/Phyllis Cradock/File 1/1953-1962 3rd October 1958

garden when I moved into my home in South London,' she was reported to say. 'I collected a lot of blisters – and some know-how too.'

The new home in Shooters Hill, Langton House, would eventually feature an impressive kitchen stretching to thirty-three feet by fifteen. The Cradocks installed five cookers in the kitchen, with a further six elsewhere in the house. They also had a trout tank (everyone needs access to fresh fish), a still room and a smoke room. In the garden they planted sixteen orange trees alongside their very own grapevine. Fanny prepared meals on a three-hundred-year-old wooden chopping block, cooking dishes in her Picasso-designed saucepans. She was not short of recipes to choose from, boasting that their cookbook library alone had 1,127 titles, with a further 280 dedicated to wine.

The Cradocks were interviewed at their home in 1959 as part of the Independent Television series *Success Story*, produced by Associated-Rediffusion, who were employing Fanny and Johnnie at that time. No doubt Fanny and Johnnie assumed that the programme would be in celebration of their success, rather than in any way critical. However, the interview dug deep into their motivation, and provided a candid glimpse of their career to date, much to their surprise.

The interview was conducted by Dan Farson, a British writer and broadcaster whose sharp, investigative style contrasted with the BBC's more deferential culture. He was famous for taking risks that were possible on ITV, and for doing so where other interviewers would not. Dan was credited with ushering in a 'new generation' of television investigations. In his series *Success Story* he met popular figures of the time, and grilled them.

The voiceover set the scene, stating that since starting out in business together, the Cradocks had been successful in making their love of food into a paying concern. Reminding the audience that they had been first famous in journalism, the establishing shots show Fanny and Johnnie at home with Fanny at work in the kitchen, wearing a large, patterned fifties-style skirt and blouse. The table is set grandly. Johnnie is shown pouring champagne for their guest.

Fanny had prepared a seafood platter for the occasion. However, Dan soon noticed something odd. 'Er, you realise they are moving?' he asked his hosts, peering doubtfully at a winkle in its shell. Fanny looked incredulous and simply stated 'No!' Both Fanny and Johnnie looked ruffled; Johnnie started to offer an explanation that it 'must be the quality of the champagne' that had affected Dan's powers of visual perception, while Fanny interjected:

'They've been boiled, dear!' before beginning to examine the winkles herself. She was forced to admit that he was perfectly right, they were moving, but attempted to dismiss it as a rogue uncooked one that must have fallen onto the plate. Fanny sipped nervously at her champagne, looked around the opulent and elegant dining room and asked Dan, 'Which ones are you going to eat – the live ones?'

Dan conducted the interview with a series of controversial questions, implying that Fanny and Johnnie were not 'real' cooks and indeed may themselves not be all that they seemed. 'Would you deny that your performance is rather like a circus act?' Fanny tried to lighten the tone: 'I don't have any clowns or elephants, except Cradock,' as she looked at Johnnie. 'Do I deny that I have made a gimmick out of cooking in evening dress with tiaras and all that – certainly not. I have cooked in evening dress since I was a small girl; it is all in our memoirs which are not published yet.' Fanny nervously tackled her seafood again; Johnnie looked pained and puzzled.

Turning to the idea of cooking in a ballgown, Dan asked, 'Surely you must get dirty?' Fanny answered with the line that they offered a five-pound note to anyone who could find a mark on them after they finished cooking, money which they had yet to pay out. Dan went straight for the jugular with his next question: 'What I am getting at is that you aim above all for publicity, which must inevitably influence your cooking?' Fanny looked uneasy as she answered, stating that their aim was for recipes that worked and cost what they said they would. Johnnie offered some help: 'We believe normal cooking lessons are dull, with people in white coats, rather like a school lesson. If you dress it up with humour, they will imbibe more knowledge that way, subconsciously. They will go back to try these new things. It is not a chore. People can eat better.'

Dan would not let things drop. 'With you it is also big business, though, isn't it?' which clearly riled Fanny. 'Oh, I wouldn't call it big business, dear,' she replied, shaking her head. 'There's not much left when those gentlemen have got their teeth into it.' Dan suggested that their new home and kitchen were well stocked with free equipment and food as perks of the job. Fanny came close to losing it with him, before remembering perhaps that the cameras were there. 'Has it ever dawned on you that you never really get anything for free? That if you get something which doesn't cost you anything, you probably have to spend more than you can afford in "getting it free"? It is a vicious circle, you know,' Fanny grimaced.

Bringing the interview to a close, Dan asked how Fanny and Johnnie would explain their terrific success? Fanny fluttered her eyelids and looked modest, still unable to shake his previous comments, stating that she would only be able to say 'Thank you.' Johnnie chipped in that their success had been built upon recipes that worked, that they did not set out to fool anyone, they did not 'put across a line'. This allowed Dan to repeat, 'To a certain extent you do; in your demonstrations you go after the circus aspects as I said earlier…' but Johnnie was quick to add, '… just to arouse interest.'

The interview must have made Fanny and Johnnie wonder about their place on Independent Television. If their 'own channel' could treat them in this way on screen, were they in reality welcome and respected?

However, Fanny and Johnnie returned to the screens of ITV as part of a new magazine show for young people, *Lucky Dip*, billed as 'The Junior Newspaper'. *Lucky Dip* began in February 1959 and was broadcast at five o'clock on a Tuesday each week until March the following year. Fanny and Johnnie were the resident cooks, inspiring young people to become 'happy cooking children' each week with a variety of demonstrations, ideas and suggestions suitable for young people to make to surprise and impress their parents as well as each other. Fanny had previously tried, unsuccessfully, to interest the BBC in this concept. The segments were extremely successful, allowing Fanny and Johnnie to publish a series of four spin-off books, the scarily-in-retrospect titled *Happy Cooking Children*, covering the basics of cookery, outdoor cookery, preparing young people for a professional career as chefs and also catering for their own parties.

The segments, and the books, proved to be popular with young people and their parents too. Fanny and Johnnie received record-breaking correspondence figures following their performances and used the thousands of written fan-mail letters as a collective evaluation of their work, pointing the way forward based on feedback and what these young viewers appreciated the most. Fanny collected together the evaluation in a document to send back to the BBC in an attempt to secure their much-sought-after return to national broadcasting.

Fanny begged to be welcomed back to the BBC which she insisted was 'our first love'.[14] Johnnie wrote to BBC officials with the feedback, making a plea to the place which launched them, the place which had given them their

---

[14] BBC WAC RCONT1/Phyllis Cradock/File 2a/1955-1959 22nd December 1959

first break, to embrace them once again. He was very clear that they did not want to languish in the afternoon schedules in a 'how-to-cook-it' cookery programme; instead, they knew what viewers wanted to see in order to inspire them to cook, or not: a performance-based entertainment show.

As the decade drew to a close, Fanny produced a short series of Christmas cookery programmes for ITV and also prepared to publish her autobiography, which borrowed its title from their stage play, *Something's Burning*. Although subtitled 'The Autobiography of Two Cooks' as it included Johnnie's story too, the book was entirely written by Fanny. Letters she wrote to the BBC claimed that it would tell the story of how the institution had given them their start. However, in reality it disparaged their involvement, glossed over their support and highlighted some reticence on behalf of the BBC to welcome them 'home'.

Taking Over Television
1960s Colourful Cookery

As the sixties swung into action, with society beginning another period of change across Britain, so did Fanny Cradock. Her autobiography, *Something's Burning*, was published and seemed a fitting tribute to her past, or the past she wanted to be believed. Fanny's original preferred title for the memoir was *Never a Dull Moment*. She wrote to friends that an autobiography should only be written once in life, so she was at pains to make sure it was as accurate, or at least as accurately incorrect, as she could muster. She plumbed the depths of her family's minds in order to plot out her past, filling in where gaps in knowledge appeared – or where perhaps there remained a truth or two that simply would not do – creating a history that she would more or less stick to for the rest of her life. Certainly, it became her blueprint for the sixties, a springboard that she would use to catapult herself into a new sphere of celebrity.

Reviews noted that both Fanny and Johnnie were well respected in the 'gastronomic world' (despite in reality having only 'discovered cooking' a few years previously) as 'experts with pan and pot who rose rapidly to fame in the last decade'. The autobiography promised to be a tale of inspiration, sophistication and determination to succeed. Readers were promised that they would absorb a little of their culinary magic too, allowing them to approach the summer season of social events armed with the knowledge that

Fanny Cradock would share with them. The main thrust of the book is that Fanny had worked hard to become a 'success story'.

Headlines of the day began to refer to Fanny as the 'Dizzy Dame', playing up her eccentric persona, which was compounded by stories in the autobiography. Seeing the words 'one of the goofiest, zaniest, fizziest, nicest characters I've ever come across' would no doubt have impressed Fanny greatly. The reviewer commented that her voice was 'like a blunt file struggling through armour-plate', but Fanny just laughed it all off, declaring, 'It has been rather boring to go through life saying down the telephone, "Don't call me sir, I'm madam!"' in response.

Wendy Colvin who worked alongside Fanny at that time recalls: 'Fanny was very, very real but she was also such a phoney. You could not believe her past. She invented herself. She claimed that her mother was born abroad and that her Gran was a lady, or something. She also wrote Johnnie's story as well as her own story. I really do not know what the truth is at all.'

Close friend and neighbour Evangeline Evans has a similar view: 'She was an incredibly colourful and amazing woman. She was remarkable. I married in 1953; I had two sisters older than I. We all had talents, but none of us had careers. Women in the middle classes simply did not work. Here suddenly was this extraordinary woman who was working. Maybe she was a feminist; certainly she was fiery, firm and alarming and fought her way to the top. Maybe Fanny would not have been noticed now, it is all much more commonplace.'

Evangeline continued, 'It was her character; her father wrote plays. One never knew quite how much she made up about her childhood, her grandeur… She was not married to Johnnie for ages, although we did not know she was not married to him. They did not tell us about it. One or two of her husbands were still alive at the time. It feels so difficult to unravel the truth. She spun different stories. She made things up as she went along and forgot what she had said. Life was never dull; there was always a drama next door.'

Wendy continues, 'I met her brother; he was always coming in for money. She was determined to keep him out of the way. He was supposed to be her manager, but I thought he was an alcoholic. He always smelled of booze. She was sort of very private about her real life. Whatever the "real" is. She lived this cartoon, storybook life. I don't think Johnnie was a major in the army, but I do not know for sure. She created it, and his monocle. She lied about it in so many books she began to believe her own lies.

'She loved being Fanny Cradock: the adulation, the publicity. She talked about her and Johnnie as the royal "we" – she would have loved to have been in with the real royal family. She said her Gran was a duchess, that they came from "the big house". There was something in that, about Fanny, that was very common. She claimed to be half-French. She was born as Phyllis, not Fanny. She put these things in, like insisting her surname had been "De Peche". Johnnie had some children; she would not let him see them or talk to them. Johnnie's wife did not want anything to do with him. Fanny did not encourage him…'

'She had amazing parties,' Jane Chapman remembers, 'like her memoirs party. Seeing all the famous people in a relaxed atmosphere was nice. Christmas was always fabulous. It was all celebrities, but it was nice seeing them just as people. She was in charge; it was her party, she was the star of the show.'

The party to celebrate the launch of their collective memoirs, *Something's Burning*, had a *My Fair Lady* theme. Guests were greeted by a floral-covered Fanny as Eliza Doolittle atop a large carriage, while Johnnie was dressed as a supposedly typical Cockney. The star-studded party was filmed by Pathé to be shown as part of their news bulletins at the time, in cinemas across Britain.

At the beginning of April 1960, Fanny was invited on to the Associated-Rediffusion programme *Late Extra* to discuss the autobiography, in a fairly standard approach to 'chat show' publicity for a new book. However, as with everything where Fanny was concerned, this was far from standard. *Late Extra* had started on ITV in July of 1958, broadcast as the name suggested late at night, around eleven o'clock. The programme was billed as 'a new slant on the happenings around town' and gave viewers the chance to meet the people who were hitting the headlines in sport, music and the world of entertainment, direct from 'the heart of London'. The show underwent some tweaks in the first few years, changing presenters, formats and segments, but continued to introduce the 'personalities who give late-night London its glamour, vitality and spirit' to viewers in London, and also Wales. Other ITV network locations did take the show, albeit irregularly.

Fanny's appearance marked yet another tweak. In the final show of its then-current format, Fanny appeared as a guest with compere Kenneth MacLeod, interviewer Neville Barker and comedian Barry Took, in a casual bar setting. This was the last show of the series to feature 'pretty girls' who would 'decoratively fill in the background'. Fanny was there to chat about her book, certainly, but also to be introduced to the viewers as the new host of the show. She would take up the reins the following week, replacing the entire presentation personnel in a bid to say 'farewell' to the glittery night-club atmosphere and the glamour girls that the programme had become known for.

Fanny's presence would signal a new direction for *Late Extra*, and for her too. Headlines claimed, 'She's in charge.' She would *not* be giving any cooking tips at all. The promotional materials claimed that 'She is a fantastic ebullient personality in her own right, and the programme will now revolve around her.' Fanny would, of course, be joined on the revamped show by Johnnie; however, she would be doing all the interviews herself. The newly formatted show would also feature songs by Lorie Mann, a popular jazz singer of the time.

It must have been a tough show to feature on as a guest, with the outgoing team facing their final curtain, but Fanny would disguise her fear well with her usual façade, throwing herself into a new role which relied on her to take control and carry the show.

Heavily scripted, *Late Extra* continued to feature a range of guests such as the theatre critic Kenneth Tynan and the formidable, award-winning actress Dame Edith Evans. Fanny had her work cut out each week. The critics were not convinced that the change of format, and crucially of presenter, was a winner. After just three broadcasts, reviewers were calling for Kenneth MacLeod to be reinstated alongside headlines such as 'Commercial network shows are slipping' which would not please Fanny or executives at ITV who relied on advertising revenue. Fanny was singled out as the reason for the programme's loss of bite and sophistication, with her style too plain, too polite and too good-mannered for viewers.

Late Extra came to an abrupt end on the 22nd of June 1960, after Fanny had presented a mere eleven weeks of chat, glamour and London life. The show would not return, and Fanny similarly left behind her brief career as a chat-show host. She joined a regular, revolving cast of experts on an after-noon show aimed at women, *Change of Scene*, which was only shown in the London area once a week. She continued to feature with Johnnie on the afternoon magazine programme for younger viewers, *Lucky Dip*; and carved out some new cooking shows, such as specific programmes helping viewers to prepare new ideas for picnics and a new semi-regular show, which capital-ised on their never-ending tours around the country, called *Kitchen Magic*.

Fanny even had a role in the ITV Christmas extravaganza, *Alice Through the Looking Box*, a star-studded ninety-minute parody loosely based on the Lewis Carroll story, which was shown across the ITV network at teatime on Christmas Day 1960. The *TV Times* heralded the festive pantomime with a fanfare of publicity. '*The Looking Box* is of course the goggle box and the contemporary heroine is a television baby-sitter.' Alice was played by Jeannie Carson, from the American sitcom about a young Scottish woman living in New York City, *Hey Jeannie*. Fanny played a role befitting of her, The Duchess. Other notable cast members included Spike Milligan (The White Rabbit), Harry Secombe (Humpty Dumpty), Ron Moody (The Mad Hatter), Bob Monkhouse (The Cheshire Cat), Joan Sims (The Chambermaid) and Ronnie Corbett (The Dormouse).

Something about the Independent Television network just was not clicking with Fanny, however, and she continued to hanker for a return to the BBC screens. She kept her voice known with the national broadcaster by featuring on several radio shows, mainly cooking and offering household advice but also as a special guest on game shows such as *Does The Team Think?* It was the prized coverage of television that Fanny really longed for, however. She was constantly submitting suggestions for new shows, including a series based on helping mother in the kitchen and another attempt at the outside broadcast programmes from continental Europe, while giving ever more elaborate pledges of loyalty to the BBC.

One idea did offer a glimmer of hope, leading to a brief return to the BBC studios at Lime Grove. Fanny pitched an idea for a children's television cookery programme aimed at 'children without hearing', enabling children to learn 'colourful no-cooking cookery' in order to express their unique sense of decoration and design. Fanny and Johnnie were booked in November of 1961 to demonstrate swans made from boiled eggs and an exciting presentation of a chequerboard sandwich in a single episode of *For Deaf Children*, which had been a staple part of the BBC's children's programmes since 1952. Fanny seemed disappointed that the programme was a one-off, submitting (retyped on her own headed paper, apparently for ease) apparently unsolicited feedback, sent directly to her from viewers, to BBC producers in a campaign to broadcast more in this series. No more slots in the *For Deaf Children* series were given to Fanny.

Fanny and Johnnie consoled themselves with a new series on ITV in which they celebrated British food, with dishes made from ingredients produced in all parts of Britain. On *The Cradocks* they tackled a different dish each Monday in just seven minutes of broadcast time. The recipes for each show were printed in the *TV Times* listings magazine, with one 'mystery' ingredient missing, which would be revealed on air by the Cradocks themselves, thus enabling viewers to cook the dish successfully at home. Fanny and Johnnie demonstrated (supposedly) quintessentially British dishes such as Hunter's Pot, Russian Roll and Oven Omelettes all in a bid to confusingly celebrate 'the finest foodstuffs in the world', encouraging British women to 'broaden their culinary horizons'. Fanny was quoted in the *TV Times* explaining the idea behind the programme, a change in direction from the previously fiercely French-orientated instructions: 'We know you don't want the same old dreary dishes over and over again. We have learnt a lot from the women of Britain.'

Around the same time, Fanny and Johnnie made a short commercial film for the Gas Council with the title *Kitchen Magic*. The film was fairly futuristic, resembling the popular American comedy-drama of the time, *Bewitched*, with Fanny appearing in a puff of smoke to help a struggling housewife realise that 'cooking could be fun'. With Fanny and Johnnie's help, 'nothing could be simpler' than cooking elegant meals, presented wonderfully, just in time for the husband returning from work. Fanny herself looked confident and elegant in several changes of costume – from pink shift dress to pristine white suit, to patterned blouses. Smiling, perhaps a little too enthusiastically, as she worked, Fanny assured the newly-wed wife that her cooking could yield 'really exciting' results, if she followed Fanny's ways.

Independent Television brought many opportunities for Fanny to be seen on screen in roles other than cooking: as herself; as a celebrity; as an authority. In 1962, she featured as one of the featured 'leading women of the day' giving her views on what she thought was *The Trouble With Men*. Alongside other women, such as Barbara Cartland, Barbara Castle, Marjorie Proops and Margaret Thatcher, Fanny gave a monologue to camera with her views.

The show was labelled 'unsuitable for male children over the age of twenty-one' which set the scene for a powerful dialogue of 'war, between men and women'. Fanny sat on her television kitchen stage set, attired in a sparkly dress with white fur trim, long satin gloves and an imposing necklace, to talk directly to the camera. Essentially, she felt men were only happy when they were 'kicking little balls around in a muddy field'. When it came to business, Fanny maintained that men were unable to even discuss things 'unless you fill their tums first'.

The controversial nature of some programmes, and hosts, at ITV must have been a constant source of frustration for Fanny. In the late fifties, she appeared on a supposedly 'all women' edition of a show put together by popular host Hughie Green. The show was live and featured a studio audience, who were also all female. Fanny was the first guest. Hughie, in a way that would become normal for Fanny throughout her career, tried to deliberately antagonise her with his first question. 'Tell me Fanny, don't you think women today have far too much to say for themselves in everyday life?' Fanny was fuming, as Hughie had planned, replying, 'I am amazed. How dare you say that. I thought you were a more intelligent man.'

It had all been a set-up, and the ruse had worked. Hughie introduced his next guest, who turned out to be singer and entertainer Danny La Rue, famous for his cross-dressing performances. He arrived on set in full female costume to perform a musical number before joining Fanny and Hughie, who were still arguing. Hughie goaded Fanny with more remarks. Fanny became more and more heated, before turning to Danny for support, referring to him as a 'very beautiful young lady', asking 'Tell me, my dear, what do you want to do as you grow older? Do you want to be at the disposal of any man?' Danny answered in his deepest, brashest, most laddish voice: 'When I get older, all I want to do is sit back in my easy chair and smoke my pipe.'

Fanny appeared to be the last to realise that Danny was in fact 'all male' and, according to Danny himself, 'she nearly had a heart attack' when the penny did eventually drop, much to Hughie's amusement. Less so for Fanny. Danny would later incorporate Fanny into some of his routines, dressing as her, cooking in an evening gown.

Not all ITV ventures were at Fanny's expense, however. The network additionally gave her the opportunity to experiment with different formats, including some that were new to British viewers. As an advertising platform, ITV was already well linked to producers in traditional advertising slots, and through product promotion on its many magazine-style shows. 1963 would bring a major innovation in the form of a seven-minute advert, or 'info-mercial', popular in America but never seen on British television screens before. Seven minutes was at that time the entire permitted advertising time for each hour of broadcast. The first experiment was intended to promote olive oil, with Fanny and Johnnie demonstrating a wide range of culinary uses, both in the preparation of food and direct table use.

The advert was funded by the International Olive Oil Council, and as such did not promote a particular brand of oil. Olive oil at that time was still recognised mainly for medicinal uses such as clearing earwax, and was more commonly available at chemists' shops than in food stores. In order to gauge the popularity of the experiment, Fanny produced a companion recipe book featuring dishes that made good use of the 'natural and pure' olive oil. These included sauces and mayonnaise, 'gaspacho', Chicken Hawaii, various hors d'oeuvres and even a chocolate gingerbread cake, all using pure and natural olive oil, of course. Demand for the book exceeded all expectations, with over two thousand housewives writing in for a copy. Advertisers and television executives hailed the experiment a success, particularly noting that television was an effective way to 'sell women anything' in an entertaining and instructive way.

Fanny must have been endlessly frustrated at the short but sweet segments in other programmes that she was being offered on ITV, continuing with yet another slot in the popular magazine series for young people, *Tuesday Rendezvous*. Fanny and Johnnie appeared together, in a mocked-up kitchen supposedly resembling their London home, preparing simple dishes at a solitary table surrounded by kitchen cupboards. Fanny wore her hair swept back to show her vivid make-up. Her wardrobe featured a range of smart, casual suits with blouses and silk scarves, all set off with ornate brooches. Johnnie stood by her side, usually in a suit and tie, but occasionally in a short-sleeved shirt with a cravat.

'I used to go with her to a children's programme on one of the channels, Associated-Rediffusion,' Jane Chapman remembered. 'She had a section in it. It was fun I suppose; I did not do anything. I would trail along and watch what was going on. Johnnie was always around, and little Johnny, their "helper boy". He was older than me, but he was a sort of apprentice or something to help them out. He was with her professionally wise, slightly different to me, so he did what she told him. He eventually disappeared too: all of a sudden, he was gone. Perhaps he had a life of his own which she didn't like?'

Jane also remembers Johnnie during this time. 'Johnnie was lovely; he appeared very long-suffering, but he took all that he gave. It came over that he was always on the wine, but he was not. He just took everything that came, especially on camera; he would not answer back. At home, she would not do anything without him, she loved him. He kept her under control. He was very much the downtrodden figure in public, but it was all an act; in real life they were lovely together. He just took it because it kept her happy.'

Fanny submitted a pitch to the BBC for a series that would teach the housewife 'the basics' of cookery; but due to some changes in personnel, particularly of those who supported Fanny the most, the programme would not, at least initially, be commissioned, despite widespread agreement that it would make an excellent series. Fanny instead appeared on the afternoon magazine show, *Home at One-Thirty*, which was later rebranded as *Living Today*, preparing a range of 'three-course meals in fifteen minutes', which had become her stock-in-trade during the *Kitchen Magic* tours of Britain. Fanny had demonstrated some of these meals on radio previously, with listeners writing in to call Fanny a phoney and a show-off who was clearly telling a 'pack of fibs' about the time involved. On television there would be no disguising the truth. The idea for the 'basics' series meanwhile made its way on to the BBC World Service radio, broadcasting to people from Britain now living around the world.

Fanny hoped to turn it into a series, with housewives 'challenged' to appear on screen with her. BBC producers at the time were less keen. Fanny had the idea to visit housewives in their own kitchens to help with the issues they faced on a daily basis. Common concerns included: why meringues weep; why fruit cakes crack; why fruit sinks in a cake; why omelettes stick to the pan; how to cook rice; or how to cook a perfect roast bird. She had pitched the idea to audiences during the runs of *Kitchen Magic*, collecting their enthusiastic responses by way of evaluation for television bosses to ponder. Fanny suggested two possibilities for the series: traditional outside broadcasts if the viewers' kitchens were deemed suitable, or a series of kitchen pictures back-projected in a studio to make a reasonable reconstruction of a home kitchen, avoiding the need, and expense, of outside broadcast.

The BBC found the idea 'impracticable on many counts'.[15] They appeared to be frustrated at Fanny's attempts to repackage the same idea over and over again in different guises to get viewer participation on the screen. As for the idea of back-projection, this was dismissed as something that the BBC had already done, not a new innovation. Indeed, it had featured in some segments of Fanny's fifteen-minute meal challenges in the afternoon programmes.

[15] BBC WAC TVART1/Phyllis Cradock/File 1/1953-1962 13th November 1962

Undeterred, Fanny found a way to include other people in her television kitchen set-up: celebrities. Late in 1963, the BBC screened the first of a short series of programmes, *Kitchen Party*, filmed in the studio but as a recreation of Fanny's own kitchen in Blackheath, in the style in which she entertained her celebrity friends at home. In what seemed like a return to the days of *Late Extra* on ITV, the fifteen-minute programme would be transmitted late at night on the BBC. Celebrities such as Barbara Cartland were promised to appear while the pilot episode was in pre-production; this, if successful, would be the first to be transmitted of a planned series of six. Fanny would carefully write out the recipes featured on each programme to be sent to viewers who wrote in to request them. Around two thousand did at each transmission.

The *Daily Mirror* ran a feature about *Kitchen Party*, with the headline 'Fanny is back!' They told readers that the BBC had built a replica of a corner of the Cradocks' wonder kitchen in their home in Blackheath, London ('one of the finest anywhere'). Fanny would prepare dishes surrounded by familiar paintings and plants, wearing the kind of glamorous, lacy dresses she would at home. The Cradocks would also stage a replica of the kind of meals they gave to friends. 'We all eat in the kitchen,' Fanny assured the reporter. 'We cook and chat and spend the entire evening there.'

The first programme was aired on the 14th of October 1963, with Scottish actor Ian Bannen, farmer turned radio and television personality Ted Moult, and glamorous stage and screen star Fenella Fielding the first batch of celebrities to be featured. The chatty, informative style of the show introduced a cooking and eating 'party' atmosphere, with Fanny demonstrating a range of omelettes and pancakes, from the simplest to the highly elaborate, for her guests. Fenella Fielding then attempted to cook, with guidance from Fanny, an omelette on her own.

One review, of the episode featuring David Jacobs and Polly Evans, in the *Journal Weekend* magazine found the 'contrived intimateness' of *Kitchen Party* 'most sickening', with the idea of celebrities being thrown into a very basic cooking programme simply to attract viewers being 'the worst' and an unnecessary intrusion in the learning of culinary art. Fanny was noted to be 'doubtless very gifted', but talked too quickly for viewers to be able to jot the recipes down. Johnnie was criticised for being 'a little slower' when chatting about the wine, suffering from 'long winded affectation'. The celebrities were accused of 'going through the motions of interest and curiosity', asking the obvious questions and setting Fanny up to provide her prepared answers.

'The atmosphere was thick with jolliness and false comradeship,' the review concluded.

All six episodes of *Kitchen Party* were eventually filmed, featuring stars such as Alfred Marks, Annie Ross, Nicholas Parsons and Betty Marsden; however, hiccups in scheduling meant that their broadcasts were sporadic. BBC bosses thought the fifteen-minute films were excellent to have on standby to fill vacant slots in schedules, while producers felt them to be fresh and different, noting that they would be better placed to be shown as a series, to build an audience. Fanny and Johnnie were kept in the dark about transmission dates, with some episodes not seeing the light of day until late into 1965, causing some embarrassment to Fanny and awkwardness among her 'friends' who had appeared.

Fanny submitted more ideas to the BBC, including a parlour game, which she claimed to have invented, based on guessing historical characters from very limited clues. She felt that *More Light Please* could easily be adapted for children's television if it was not considered suitable for an adult audience. BBC producers thought it to be too complicated to have legs, so passed on it. Memos shared between BBC departments at the time indicate a level of frustration with Fanny and the 'complications of coping with her'[16] although also that she was 'surprisingly amenable and open to criticism nowadays'.[17]

This reputation was beginning to spill over into the general press too, with stories of brushes with police officers when Fanny was fined for careless driving in her seven-thousand-pound Rolls Royce. Parked illegally near to Olympia in London, Fanny was asked by police to move. She admitted in court to becoming abusive, upset and rude, resulting in her reversing her car into another parked vehicle. However, Fanny claimed she was not guilty, as she was merely following the police officer's instructions to reverse.

On another occasion, Fanny was fined twenty pounds and disqualified from driving for three months by Oxford magistrates for driving at a dangerous speed, around fifty-five miles per hour, between The Slade and London Road in Headington. Fanny pleaded not guilty. At the time of the incident she had leant out of her car window when stopped, saying to the

---

[16] BBC WAC TVART3/Johnny and Fanny (Phyllis) Cradock/File 2/1963-1970 16th October 1963

[17] BBC WAC TVART3/Johnny and Fanny (Phyllis) Cradock/File 2/1963-1970 24th September 1963

police officer: 'Going too fast, officer? Guilty. I am in a hurry. I am going to open a festival.'

Stories about her terrible driving would follow Fanny around forever. She was acutely aware of the perception it gave to her public, and crucially potential employers; not that she attempted to cover up any possible stories in the press, merely to tone them down for fear of losing work. She once wrote to a journalist to ask: 'Will you please realise that your jocular references to "hurled through East London" will register instantly with someone whom we have not yet met as our being lunatic drivers of a dilapidated vehicle! When in fact we are extremely experienced motorists who have driven hundreds of thousands of miles professionally.'

The BBC were naturally hesitant to consider Fanny for a major new cookery programme planned for transmission in 1965. However, they found it near impossible to discount her at the same time, particularly as the planned show could loosely be considered to be the one that she had been pitching to them for years. The Adult Education department had the go-ahead to produce a ten-part cookery programme aimed at young people who wanted to learn how to cook, as well as older people who wanted to bring their cooking knowledge up to date. *Basic Cookery by Modern Methods* would demonstrate the underlying principles of cooking and introduce the latest labour-saving methods and equipment.

Each edition of the series would focus on a different element of cooking, from meat and vegetables to sauces, soups, pastry and puddings. A leaflet providing detailed recipes from the series had also been approved, but not yet written. The only thing that had not been secured was the presenter. Initial ideas included featuring different demonstrators for each specialism, with one overall presenter linking the series.

A very long shortlist was drawn up of possibilities, both people with television broadcast experience and those without. Notable names included Ruth Morgan from *Woman* magazine and well-known wartime cookbook author, Ambrose Heath. Ambrose was thought to be too old, however. Those with television experience who were considered included Molly Weir (it was felt her Scottish accent could become annoying), Marguerite Patten (who was ruled out for being too like a 'lady demonstrator' and, ironically, for doing advertising spots on ITV), Philip Harben (also on ITV, and considered to have poor and often incorrect content), Zena Skinner (who did not have enough personality) and Robert Carrier (who was thought to be too sponsored).

From the list of twenty-seven possibilities, twenty were interviewed for this new, high-profile position. The BBC were ploughing a great deal of resource into this show, and rightly wanted it to be a success. Eventually five people were selected to do a ten-minute demonstration by way of an audition, Fanny among them. The other four, all women, came from a variety of domestic science, home economist and newspaper backgrounds. They all pitched their auditions against Fanny.

Despite including Fanny in the final five, it was clear that the BBC, in some quarters at least, hoped that she would be discounted following the audition. Quite the opposite happened. The other four were considered to be competent, but ultimately so dull, so unoriginal and so uninteresting compared to Fanny. She was noted to be fresh, riveting, commanding the attention of her audience. Fanny had new and up-to-date ideas as well as a strong background, they thought, in traditional methods. She was able to offer simple scientific explanations for what she was doing, and why. BBC producers were concerned about employing someone without television experience for what would be essentially a series of demanding thirty-minute solo performances. The other four needed considerable rehearsal and training even ahead of their auditions. Fanny impressed the team with her enthusiasm for the subject and her sense of fun, leading them to think that she would be a reliable pair of hands who would also encourage and interest viewers.

Not everyone was convinced. Doreen Stephens, who had previously worked with Fanny, suggested five additional names, combining personality with demonstrating experience, to be considered carefully before any final decision should be made. No one was able to outdo Fanny; and so she was, reluctantly by some and enthusiastically by others, hired to present what had now been renamed *Home Cooking*, due for transmission in 1965.

Negotiations ensued; dates for rehearsal in London and filming in Bristol were set. Fanny was not initially pleased to discover that the programme would be transmitted early in the morning, preferring a more family-friendly prime-time slot. She set to work creating the accompanying booklet, which the BBC were extremely pleased with, noting that it would 'sell like hot cakes'[18] in something of a change of policy and perspective for the BBC. Fanny was, as ever, keen to include Johnnie in the series. However, it was decided that in Adult Education programmes, there was no place for a

---

[18] BBC WAC T57/103/1/Home Cooking/General/18th December 1964

double act, which would make the whole thing more like light entertainment. Fanny instead suggested that Johnnie could take action pictures for the booklet, which despite her persistence did not happen. Executives did recognise that Fanny required some help and support on screen, however, in order to make her 'a much more relaxed, less aggressive and pleasanter person',[19] so agreed to pay one of her assistants who worked with her at home, David Auty (also known as Frank), a small fee provided that he did not talk, even if he appeared occasionally on screen and was seen to help.

Filming of the ten-part series went well. The first edition of *Home Cooking* was screened on Sunday the 25th of April 1965 at ten o'clock in the morning. The show received a great deal of pre-publicity in the *Radio Times*, the listings magazine for the BBC, and was subtitled 'a personal approach by Fanny Cradock'. The *Radio Times* encouraged viewers to sit down in their dressing gowns with a tea or coffee and watch *Home Cooking* as a family. Surely each family member would be interested in the chance to become a cook? The *Radio Times* also let it be known that the booklet to accompany the series was available, providing a record of all the basic information and the recipes, so viewers could simply sit back and enjoy the entertaining lesson while Fanny guided them through the preparation of various sauces and salads to revitalise family meals.

Throughout the series, Fanny turned her attention to the things that most people found so difficult in the kitchen: soups; pastry; casseroles and roasts; grills and poultry; pasta and rice; egg dishes; fish; cakes; and finishing the series with puddings and pies. Filmed on a monochrome set, Fanny matched wonderfully in a black and white outfit, somewhat resembling a Christmas pudding. Her dark, short-sleeved dress with a belted waist had a white, jaggy trim round the neck. Fanny never stopped on screen. She talked constantly. She wiped surfaces. She cleared equipment. She showed completed dishes. The set was simple: a work surface with a gas cooker behind. Fanny was assisted in the studio by David, seen (but not heard) dressed in chef's whites, complete with a chef's hat. The only sound he was allowed to make was of pleasure at Fanny's completed meals.

Fanny introduced dish after dish, saying 'This gives me a strange sense of satisfaction' as she did so. She passed on tip after tip with lightning speed, insisting that her views were 'only an opinion, not a fact, however it is, so...'

---

[19] BBC WAC T57/103/1/Home Cooking/General/10th February 1965

Wendy Colvin recalls how Fanny used to prepare. 'She spent hours and hours on things, perfecting techniques. If there was something she could not do well, she would not do it. She never faked anything, unless it was boring to watch, like mashed potatoes. She was honest about it all: she would say, "I made these earlier." It was all done with the audience in mind, she knew what would work well. She knew you could not really whisk egg whites on camera. She loved to break eggs with one hand, perfectly. She used a fork so that there was no noise when she whisked it up. She piped with one hand; it was a technique she worked hard to perfect. She never liked to credit anyone, but I taught her an awful lot. Like how to skin a tomato on the gas stove. She would then recommend it as "her way" to do it.'

Fanny repeated her mantra about never wearing an apron, as 'Cooking is a cleanly and creative art and not a grubby chore.' She explained that all her students, however, did work in aprons, until they were suitably qualified to go without. For this they required a target, set by Fanny. If able to complete a full week's work (standard hours of nine until six, Monday to Friday and a half day Saturday) in unmarked aprons, they received a bonus payment of five pounds and were then free to discard their aprons forevermore, should they wish. Students learnt, and viewers should also, that master chefs always wear white in professional kitchens. They never have time to change should they be asked to speak to diners in their restaurants, so must remain unmarked throughout service. Fanny made this more glamorous in her own kitchen, on stage and now on television, by wearing gorgeous outfits.

'In real life, Fanny was a very dirty woman,' Wendy Colvin thinks back. 'She never washed her hands. She would blow her nose on a teacloth and then wipe surfaces with it. And the state of some of her dresses! She would wear trousers at home to cook in.'

However, on screen, viewers were dazzled, in the way that both Fanny and the BBC had hoped. They were riveted as predicted, and the booklet did sell even faster than hot cakes. As *Home Cooking* had been recorded instead of the usual live broadcasts, the BBC were able to consider repeats of the series; however, they were not immediately scheduled. The booklet sold in excess of one hundred and fifty thousand copies, thanks mainly to Fanny herself slipping into her demonstrations that there really was no need to look away from the screen to write anything down, it was all available in the booklet. This would become her catchphrase as her television career progressed, and booklet sales escalated.

Fanny's father, playwright Arthur Valentine
(ANL/Shutterstock)

Fanny as Frances Dale, in her first publicity photograph as an author
(Photo courtesy of Chris Duffy, The Auchtermuchty Food Museum)

Johnnie Cradock, Fanny's most memorable husband
(ANL/Shutterstock)

Fanny as Frances Dale, reading her novel *Gateway to Remembrance* (1949)
(Len Cassingham/ANL/Shutterstock)

Frances Dale bashing out another novel at her typewriter
(Photo courtesy of Chris Duffy, The Auchtermuchty Food Museum)

Frances Dale, novelist, in a publicity shot for her Atlantean novel *Gateway to Remembrance*, dictated to her by a priest who died nine million years earlier

Fanny Cradock as she appeared in the 1950s

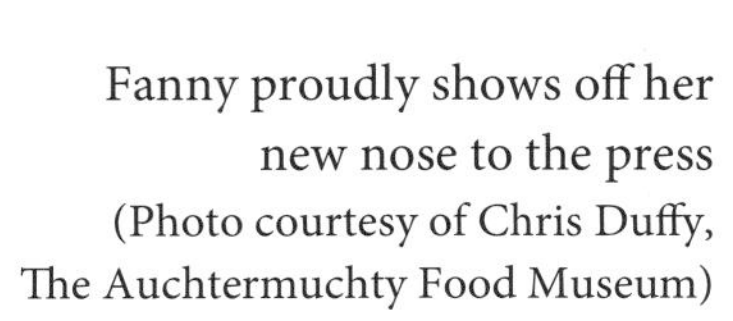

Fanny proudly shows off her new nose to the press
(Photo courtesy of Chris Duffy, The Auchtermuchty Food Museum)

Fanny beginning to broadcast, 1955
(*Daily Mail*/Shutterstock)

Fanny and Johnnie in *Chez Bon Viveur*, as they would appear on television
(Reg Warhurst/ANL/Shutterstock)

Fanny and Johnnie as Bon Viveur
in their kitchen at home
(Photo courtesy of Chris Duffy,
The Auchtermuchty Food Museum)

Fanny wears an outfit she made from
the Bon Viveur newspaper columns
(Wallace/ANL/Shutterstock)

Bon Viveur on stage, giving a demonstration at the Ideal Home Exhibition 1957
(George Elam/*Daily Mail*/Shutterstock)

Fanny and Johnnie sample the food at the Mirabelle Restaurant, London, 1956
(Henry Bush/ANL/Shutterstock)

Fanny and Johnnie in a publicity shot taken in their kitchen at home, 1955
(*Daily Mail*/Shutterstock)

Fanny and Johnnie demonstrating, 1957
(Photo courtesy of Chris Duffy, The Auchtermuchty Food Museum)

Putting the finishing touches to a grand 'swan' display
(Photo courtesy of Chris Duffy, The Auchtermuchty Food Museum)

Fanny and Johnnie in a posed publicity shot, 1960s

Arriving at the Café Royal, 1956 (Wallace/*Daily Mail*/ Shutterstock)

Fanny and Johnnie arrive at the *Daily Mail* Ideal Home Exhibition in style, 1955 (ANL/Shutterstock)

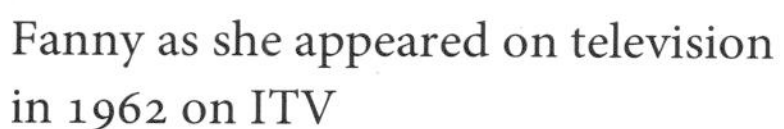

Fanny as she appeared on television in 1962 on ITV

Fanny being interviewed about her television series

Fanny on the BBC in 1970 in *Fanny Cradock Invites*, cooking Belgian cheese rissoles for a cheese and wine party

Fanny and Johnnie in their garden at the Dower House, 1970

Fanny and Johnnie in a publicity shot for their television series, *Fanny Cradock Invites...*

Fanny and Johnnie attending an event in 1972

Fanny and Johnnie sampling a pub meal costing 35p at the Hare Arms, Norfolk, judging a 'Bar Meals Competition' in 1974

Fanny and Johnnie as they appeared on *Celebrity Squares*, 1975
(ITV/Shutterstock)

Fanny and Johnnie celebrate the publication of their book *Time To Remember*, 1981

Book signing for *Time To Remember*

Fanny, an author again, as she appeared on the covers of her
Lormes of Castle Rising saga novels

Within the BBC, Fanny remained a divisive character. She prompted a great deal of enthusiastic and positive response from viewers, but executives continued to make remarks such as 'For people who like her she did a very efficient job'[20] when discussing her achievements. When it came time to review the library of her recordings, suggestions were made to 'junk'[21] nine of the episodes and save only one of the ten to make much-needed space in the archive department, which was moving to Villiers House in Ealing. The episode selected was 'Casseroles and Roasts', for reasons unknown.

Fanny provided all the equipment and resources for filming, part of her way of ensuring that only the products that she was connected to appeared on screen, at the same time convincing the BBC that she was value for money as they did not have to. They supplied the studio set, cameras, rehearsal space and a basic crew. Following filming of *Home Cooking*, however, Fanny began what would become a regular occurrence. She wrote to the producers to let them know that certain items that she had sent to the studio had not been returned safely to her afterwards. The BBC investigated fully to try and locate the missing equipment, without success. The matter was passed to the insurance manager. The items that had been lost somewhere along the way included several antique copper jelly-moulds from the eighteenth century, which were extremely rare, and a couple of copper frying-pans. Fanny was asked to attempt to purchase replacements and send the receipts back to the BBC in order to be compensated.

Despite reservations internally, the BBC realised that *Home Cooking* was a winner with audiences, and they were keen for Fanny to replicate the format. She proposed a series that would build upon the knowledge gained in *Home Cooking*, intended as a follow-on from its predecessor. Initially called *Advanced Cookery* but later changed to *Adventurous Cooking*, it was once again a 'personal approach', but 'went beyond everyday cooking in the normal household, to dishes which add vitality to family meals and a professional touch when entertaining friends'.

As before, a series of ten episodes was filmed, covering vegetables, fish, cheese, meat, poultry, economy dishes, cakes, puddings, fruits and climaxing in the 'art of easy garnish', essential for any entertaining purposes. Fanny chose her wardrobe carefully so as not to overshadow the food too much.

---

[20] BBC WAC T57/103/1/Home Cooking/General/24th September 1965

[21] BBC WAC T57/103/1/Home Cooking/General/2nd May 1967

She would wear pinafore dresses over elaborate paisley-patterned blouses as she stood at the gas cookers to explain her techniques. A young assistant, Simon, would be briefly introduced, to show the more menial of tasks, leaving Fanny to dazzle the audience with close-up shots of fennel fronds spread out against her hand 'so you can see it' should anyone be able to find such an exotic herb for themselves.

Fanny and Johnnie promoted the series by appearing on the BBC2 programme *Late Night Line-Up*, a chat-show format with an intellectual edge, focused on open and candid discussions with guests. The pair seemed relaxed and comfortable, Johnnie wearing a formal suit and Fanny in a flouncy, see-through-effect lace dress, with her hair swept up to one side. Fanny flirted with the host as he quizzed the pair about food and their past careers in journalism. 'Writing was my first love,' Fanny claimed, before telling him that she was currently writing novels again, collaboratively with Johnnie. He would research the facts and figures, while she did the 'deathly prose'.

In an attempt to demonstrate that she was just as 'adventurous' as the title of the new show suggested, Fanny declared that she would attempt to reheat a cheese fondue for them all to enjoy, in a risky experiment with no certainty of success. Happily, it worked. Fanny encouraged the other guests to dunk cubes of stale bread into the perfectly smooth fondue and 'get as much as you can in one dollop' before shovelling it 'right in'. She followed her large mouthful with a quick shot of kirsch, demanding that everyone else followed her lead.

Adventurous Cooking was transmitted again weekly on Sunday mornings at ten o'clock from the 17th of April 1966 onwards, but this time had an additional repeat late on Monday evenings. Fanny was well aware of her star quality and pulling power where audiences were concerned and had already negotiated a hefty increase in her fee for this new series, to two hundred and ten pounds per programme. However, she became concerned that she was not being fairly remunerated for the repeats and scrutinised her contracts before taking advice. Fanny felt that she should be paid a repeat fee in line with dramatic actors, who at that time included in their initial contracts the payment of a 'special additional fee' which was paid if a programme was expected to be repeated, regardless of whether it subsequently was or not.

BBC officials thought very differently. They classed the 'performances' given during talks and demonstrations under an Educational Contract as distinct from 'acting' and the fees for repeats were, in their thoughts, justifiably lower. Fanny would receive seventy-eight pounds for each programme that was repeated, which the BBC thought she should be very happy to receive.

The BBC followed their run of *Adventurous Cooking* with a repeat showing of the *Home Cooking* series on BBC1's sister channel, BBC2, each Tuesday at around seven-thirty in the evening, ensuring that Fanny was seen on British screens almost weekly during this time. Her work at ITV had ended. She was now fully fixed and committed to the BBC, which was her ambition, and they seemed just as committed to her. There was never any consideration of having her under permanent contract, however, perhaps due to her hard-to-handle nature or perhaps simply for business reasons. Each show warranted a new contract, and a new negotiation on the suitable fee as her celebrity increased.

Between cooking programmes, Fanny appeared on other shows as a 'celebrity' in her own right, often alongside Johnnie, such as with Chan Canasta, the famous television magician from the fifties, taking part in a series of experiments in the art of psychological perception, or as an unlikely panellist on *Juke Box Jury*, judging whether the latest musical releases were a hit or miss. She featured too with Frank Muir in *Call My Bluff*, the panel game featuring two teams of celebrities in a 'duel of words and wit', and as a panellist on the food-related quiz show *Know Your Onions* with Nicholas Parsons. There was even a brief return to dramatic roles, with Fanny appearing as Lady Macbeth in the bawdy cabaret series with Alan Randall, *Whatever Next?*

Next was firmly still food, however, with the prospect of more cooking on television being what interested Fanny the most. She filmed a series of three Christmas shows which were broadcast at the end of 1966, featuring her classic dishes of Escoffier's Christmas pudding with brandy butter, Christmas cake, large mince pies and stuffing for geese and turkey, all of which she had done on television before, and would do again as future Christmas recordings would arise. Her ideas for new cookery shows continued to flow in at the BBC, including opportunities to show her 'trainees' in action, or to feature the recipes of 'the greats' Escoffier and Alexis Soyer. Fanny really wanted to secure the prime-time slots that she so coveted on screen – and on BBC1, the main channel – so her outline ideas often stipulated that they be aimed at 'early evening' and not 'general hours' as was the preference of BBC executives. Recent experiments with early-evening cooking slots featuring Zena Skinner had not been as successful, or popular, as the channel had hoped, however, and they were reluctant to schedule Fanny into a time when families were expecting to see 'entertainment'. Letters appeared in newspapers across the country from viewers appreciative of Fanny, even from people who did not agree with her methods in cooking but felt that her entertainment skills were 'second to none'. Fanny knew that people were tuning in to watch regardless of whether they wanted to cook or not.

Fanny would stick mostly to the formula she had established for *Home Cooking* and *Adventurous Cooking* for her series for the remainder of the decade. They worked well, were enjoyed greatly by audiences and resulted in the sale of ever-increasing numbers of the booklets produced as companions. *Adventurous Cooking* was followed by *Problem Cooking* in 1967 and then *Ten Classic Dishes* in 1968, both of which were shown at various times across both BBC1 and BBC2, with regular repeats. *Problem Cooking*, which did feature one of her trainees from home, Peter, was shown at teatime, when Fanny knew that housewives were busy in the kitchen themselves and unlikely to be watching. Press releases promised that 'wearing a striped hairband and diamond rings' Fanny would make *Problem Cooking* look as easy as pie. Newspaper reviews focused on how glamorous Fanny was looking and how able she was to hold the attention of viewers 'who have no intention of setting to work in the kitchen'.

Fanny wrote flirty letters to the then controller of BBC2, David Attenborough, who would go on to be a television sensation in his own right, saying that she was 'sizzling with a new idea'[22] that she simply had to meet with him to discuss. Fanny clearly felt the meeting went well, writing back saying she wasn't sure if David had been twinkling at her or with her. David took the trouble to reply, 'I do assure you that all twinkles were totally with – none whatsoever at.'[23] Now Sir David Attenborough, and unable to recall the detail of the events decades later, he merely commented that 'I have no recollection of it, I did not take up any of her ideas, if she said I did I must put it down to the onset of senile amnesia…'

Despite the put-down, Fanny was successful in securing what seemed like the perfect vehicle for her style of cookery, and presentation, late in 1968. Shown on BBC2, *Colourful Cookery* did exactly what it promised, allowing

[22] BBC WAC TV ART 3/Cradock/File 2/18th March 1968
[23] BBC WAC TV ART 3/Cradock/File 2/9th May 1968

Fanny to show an array of extremely colourful ideas to the nation. Each episode was only fifteen minutes in length, but was Fanny's first glimmer of colour on screen, and at peak viewing time. Fanny described the series as 'about cooking for everyone – from the little girl in the bedsitter to the harassed housewife with little time to spare'. The accent would be on dishes that cost little, and which were not too difficult to prepare. 'Even the most economical dishes can be made to look appetising and attractive.'

Colour televisions were still relatively rare at the time, and the idea of cooking in colour drew some criticism, suggesting that those who may benefit from it most would not be in a position to afford a colour set. 'May I ask how many of these hard-up housewives can afford three hundred pounds for a colour television set?' one angry letter to the *Radio Times* asked. Some viewers moaned about the decision to put the show on BBC2, where 'all the good things are', meaning that difficult choices had to be made in households wedded, in the days before remote controls, to watching the 'main' channel, BBC1.

Reviews, however, were strong, suggesting that Fanny had with this show saved television cooking from the Dark Ages and placed it firmly among television's 'civilised entertainments'. Others called it 'one of the most entertaining around' with 'most of the colour coming from Fanny herself', which could just as easily be enjoyed in monochrome. Newspaper reports described Fanny's apple-green dresses with navy trimmings for those viewers unfortunate not to be able to marvel at the colours.

Shirley Conran, writing as women's editor for the *Observer* prior to her days as a bestselling novelist, published a discussion piece about the cost of colour television sets, which were out of reach for the 'common man'. She noted that: 'Although TV long ago replaced the sitting-room fire as the family focal point, most of the British still seem happy with their monochrome sets and see no point in paying extra to watch Fanny Cradock in glorious colour.' Opinion was divided. One viewer wrote to a newspaper claiming that Fanny was far too fussy when it came to her 'presentation', saying 'the various dishes look great until she starts adding decorations – leaves, flowers, ferns, you name it, she displays it! I saw the programme on a friend's colour set last week, and I thought that what seems merely fussy in black and white looked almost vulgar in colour.' Others felt strongly that 'her flamboyance is no doubt the secret to her success – some of the other cookery experts who have appeared on TV seem unutterably dreary in contrast.'

Fanny provided a follow-up to *Colourful Cookery* with the equally colourful *Giving a Dinner Party* series, which also featured Johnnie providing valuable information on the choice of wines at special social functions in the home. Fanny took viewers through all the stages of party-giving, with alternative menus as well as help with table settings and decoration. Johnnie, at various points in the series, would appear to show appropriate wines for each course, passing on his top tips on how to serve them. By this time, Fanny and Johnnie had established good relations with wine companies such as Avery Wines in Bristol who supplied them with the majority of the wine that they featured on screen – in accordance with BBC guidelines on product promotion at the time, of course. Or so they thought.

The series hit the screens around the same time as Prince Charles was invested as the Prince of Wales, in the summer of 1969. Royal occasions were linked to parties in the minds of viewers and broadcasters alike, and the BBC capitalised upon this. Shown in the evening following the Wimbledon finals, *Giving a Dinner Party* (occasionally referred to by the BBC as *How to Give a Dinner Party*) was a fifteen-minute programme shown just before nine o'clock on BBC2, pitched against the national news and weather on BBC1. The idea for the series came from Fanny and Johnnie's 'earliest memories' of the parties supposedly thrown by their grandparents, reimagined for the more modern cook-hostess. Fanny told viewers, 'We do not tell you what to do but merely share with you a cross-section of what we do ourselves.' The accompanying booklet was heavily promoted, including recipes and essential tips on etiquette – although Fanny claimed to abhor that word, preferring the more straightforward 'how to do' certain things, such as laying the table correctly. 'Lavish expenditure can never guarantee a successful party,' Fanny reminded those tuning in. 'The only thing which really matters is that your guests know you have taken pains within your limitations of time and money.'

Fanny had continued to campaign for a fairer contract for both her and Johnnie, with an impressive array of successful shows, often repeated, and their associated recipe booklets. The production of the booklets had, up until this time, been included in the individual contracts for each series, as a one-off production fee. The non-returnable fee for the text for *Giving a Dinner Party* increased greatly to one hundred and eighty-nine pounds, giving the BBC exclusive rights to the content. However, a new clause was added setting out additional royalties which were to be paid to Fanny should the booklet sell in excess of fifteen thousand, which her booklets regularly now did. She would receive ten per cent of the published price of each copy sold in the United Kingdom and fifty per cent of sales in the United States or any other country.

As the sixties drew to a close, Fanny's sense of colour and flamboyance was only beginning to show itself. Her sense of business seemed to be escalating towards a brighter, more prosperous decade to come.

Ever the Entrepreneur
1970s Fanny Cradock Invites...

By the time the swinging sixties had shuddered into the shade of the seventies, Fanny and Johnnie were riding high. Fanny's life and career were both seemingly successful. Fanny was rarely off screen, with one hit series after another, each being repeated across BBC1 and BBC2 to fill in the gaps while eager viewers waited for a new instalment. Books, newspaper columns and public appearances flowed as regularly as Johnnie's wine recommendations. Public perception of Fanny and Johnnie was of a wealthy, well-to-do couple who worked hard but made it all seem effortless. Maintaining this image was the real hard graft.

Fanny and Johnnie had outgrown their home in Shooters Hill and had moved to more suitable premises in Watford. 134 Shooters Hill went on the market for seventeen thousand pounds, a modest equivalent of around three hundred thousand pounds today, and they sank all the money they had into their new home in the country. So much so that, when the BBC requested the return of an accidental overpayment of six hundred and eighty-two pounds in lieu of repeat fees, an arrangement had to be made for Fanny to repay the sum in instalments of fifty pounds, as she claimed to be unable to settle in full immediately. The BBC eventually wrote off the debt. At the time, it was reported that the Cradocks had been involved in, ironically, a gas explosion on their yacht while in Cannes, which caused them to have to turn down a great deal of work, as well as the expense of chartering a private flight home. Fanny made sure that the BBC were fully aware of the newspaper stories relating to the incident.

The Dower House, on Grove Mill Lane, was about a mile and a half outside of Watford itself, set in three acres of land and surrounded by open country, farmland and woodlands, so quite a change from the hustle and bustle of London. Described as a 'fine gentleman's residence', the house itself dated from the seventeenth century, with further extensions and improvements made in the eighteenth century. Flanked on one side by the river Gade and on the other by the millstream of the nearby Grove Mill, the Dower House was a formidable home for the formidable pair.

Fanny and Johnnie spent a couple of years remodelling the Dower House to their own requirements, which by this time were quite substantial. Grand hallways were fitted with wrought-iron staircases and decorated with bespoke murals by the renowned West End theatre renovator, Miss Joan Jefferson Farjeon, who was also responsible for the gilt ceiling work in the dining room. This, after all, was a party house, and a show-off home. Fanny had the kitchen reconstructed to suit her individual needs, concealing Parkinson Cowan cookers under work surfaces, installing refrigerators, rotisseries and other essential equipment wherever she could. Electric swing doors allowed easy access to the kitchen area, and wide stable-style doors allowed Fanny to keep an eye on goings-on outside while she was at work inside.

The master suite was entirely self-contained, with a bathroom and a dressing room almost equal in size to the bedroom itself. The guest wing had three bedrooms for overnight partygoers to stay. Only to be expected, the wine cellar was particularly extensive, formed within an old corridor bridge originally part of a neighbouring property and crossing the river Gade. Fanny installed a separate freezer room to store the mountains of food that were produced, tested and never wasted at the Dower House.

The grounds of the house were magnificent, featuring high white gates leading to circular courtyards with pleasant elevated flower beds and a well dating from the fourteenth century. The formal gardens were supplemented by split-level terraces and were landscaped within an inch of their lives. A walkway led to a partially walled solar-heated swimming pool, impressive at over twelve metres long. The pride and joy of the Dower House exterior were the vegetable gardens and orchards, where Fanny and Johnnie cultivated all, or nearly all, of the produce they required. The Cradocks had three enormous greenhouses, one almost twenty metres in length, and two slightly smaller ones, a mere fourteen and ten metres respectively, all within handy strolling distance from the large garden room, a quiet retreat from the main house.

However, it was not simply Fanny and Johnnie who lived at the Dower House. The Cradocks required a crack team behind them, to ensure it all looked smooth on the surface. Fanny had the more modest wing extension converted into staff quarters with a separate living area, basic kitchen, a bedroom and small bathroom; suitable for several 'young ones' to live and be on hand to work, learn and prepare.

Fanny had surrounded herself with young people, professionally, for some time. Part image, part necessity, part making up for her own offspring's missing (for her at least) childhood and perhaps partly to provide a start in life that she had not had herself. As with most things Fanny, it is difficult to establish the real motivation. Fanny often talked about the youngsters as having apprentice-type roles, where she and Johnnie would train them in all things food, wine and hospitality, enabling them to go on to have careers in the industry. The image of Fanny and Johnnie as 'parents' and 'grandparents' was a major part of their brand, and their appeal, as well as their work on children's television and publishing children's books. All this despite the truth of their own children, hidden at that time.

Of course, it also meant that she had a willing army of helpers who could test, retest and test again every recipe that was suggested, or every preparation that was required for television, stage or photography for books, magazines and newspapers. The first of these 'little helpers' was a young fan called Johnny Harper, who, at the age of twelve, lived near to the Cradocks in Shooters Hill in the 1950s. He would spend all his days working in their kitchen in return for an education, courtesy of the Cradocks. 'Little Johnny' as he became known did everything from serving at the Cradocks' parties, appearing on stage during *Kitchen Magic* and also from time to time on television as part of the *Lucky Dip* programme.

Little Johnny Harper attracted a great deal of press coverage, with headlines claiming, at age fifteen in 1962, that he was 'Britain's youngest butler' and styling him as a 'juvenile Jeeves' at the Cradocks' side. Johnny received a wage of five pounds a week, as well as access to the 'high life' with Fanny and Johnnie of course. According to the reports, he travelled in their Rolls Royce and accompanied them to France. Under contract until his twenty-first birthday, Johnny was primed to tell everyone his plan was to take over from Fanny and Johnnie eventually. 'I want to cook for thousands on TV, on stage. And by myself,' he told reporters.

Young people came and went. A steady stream of enthusiastic applicants would write to Fanny, initially perhaps for advice on how to break into the industry, and would then be invited for an 'interview' to see how their skills (and personalities) matched up to Fanny's exacting, and intimidating, standards. As already mentioned, David (also known as Frank) Auty appeared on screen with Fanny during the 1960s, helping to clear away items in the kitchen and pass ingredients ready to be cooked. Viewers became used to seeing young faces on screen, helping out but never speaking. That would require a whole different contract. Other young helpers included Franz Stadler, from Switzerland, who tended to the garden and acted as a general 'houseboy' when required, a role also held by René who was also, coincidentally, Swiss.

The move to the Dower House allowed for a more immersive experience, with the young staff being on hand 24/7. Fanny had long had hopes and plans to open a cookery school, or at least talked of it openly to create the impression that she would do so. In 1966, a young hopeful attendee of the prospective school, Peter Botterill, wrote to Fanny asking to apply. Instead, he was summoned, aged seventeen, to attend an interview and an 'audition' in Fanny's kitchen in Shooters Hill, which he passed. He was invited to 'join the family' and stayed with them for over four years, including the move to the Dower House.

The new house (and the considerable financial investment from the Cradocks) had some purpose, or more accurately several purposes, over and above simply being the home that they felt befitted their status. Fanny and Johnnie invited popular weekly magazine *Woman* to come and view their hard work for an 'At Home with...' feature, complete with elaborate photographs of the interiors, in February 1970. They described it as their 'dream home' and garden. Fanny shared her tips for interior design, including choosing a peacock-blue bedroom as she found the colour extremely restful, warm and luxurious. The style matched the history of the 'stately home'; however, modern touches were included. Their television was hidden from sight until required under a fitted, green wild-silk cover. Fanny's 'dream kitchen' was shown off in all its glory, with time- and labour-saving devices to inspire readers to apply a similar common-sense approach to planning their own kitchens.

Fanny never let go of the notion of filming a television series in her own kitchen, consistently reminding the BBC of her idea. In the early months of 1970, the powers that be at the Corporation finally relented. The new Fanny Cradock series *Fanny Cradock Invites...* would be filmed entirely on location at the Dower House in the bespoke kitchen, with the cast of eager young helpers, well, helping.

Following the by now familiar pattern, Fanny scripted up a series of thirteen episodes, each focusing on a different type of occasion or celebration, informal parties that Fanny would 'invite' viewers to share with her and recreate at home. Johnnie would feature occasionally, as required really, to recommend and discuss suitable wines depending on the occasion. The premise was that Fanny would share her knowledge of doing everything she did at home when entertaining, single-handedly, with only the benefit in recent years of assistance from the young helpers; it should then be easy for viewers to do so at home, without any such help. Times were changing in British society, and Fanny was keen to reflect this on screen. Her assumption was that both husband and wife would now be out at work, and any entertaining duties would need to be slotted in to this new routine.

Fanny devised six types of informal party to feature based upon viewer letters and requests, with each party idea featuring across two, or on one occasion three, of the twenty-minute episodes of the series, again shown in colour on BBC2 at ten o'clock at night. The week the series began, BBC1 was showing highlights of the Commonwealth Games from Edinburgh at the same time. The series would begin with a cheese and wine party, followed by a cold Sunday brunch, a teenagers' party, a simple Saturday dinner, a television meal and climaxing with a hot buffet party.

The *Radio Times* featured a two-page interview spread to herald the new series, with the Cradocks interviewed at home in their new kitchen, of course. The article began by stating that 'Fanny Cradock is a very powerful lady, and also very sexy...' to demonstrate how she was viewed at the time. The interview took place on the terrace as the students, hand-picked from over one and a half thousand applicants, lolled around the pool. Fanny's heritage was established, with the usual mentions of cooking at the Royal Albert Hall ('I once played for six and a half thousand people,' she cheerfully announced) before mentioning her newspaper and writing careers. The interviewer watched as an episode of *Fanny Cradock Invites...* was recorded. Before the cameras rolled, Fanny criticised Frank for not doing something or other correctly but praised 'star pupil' Peter who she was sure would go on to have his own restaurant eventually.

Fanny's professional credentials were really drawn out in the article. She apparently worked without a script, in a relaxed manner with everything you see on the screen happening in real life too – no cutting, splicing or refilming required. This was key to Fanny's success, after all. She was, the interviewer noted, a great cook. Fanny's television producer, Betty White, remarked that Fanny had a certain quality that drew in viewers and inspired them to have a go in the kitchen.

When asked why she continued to work so hard, Fanny answered honestly. To maintain her lifestyle, a certain level of income was required: 'So that Johnnie and me can have a ball. There's a Rolls in the garage plus an MG; there's this divine house and garden, which you rightly said is the one place that can conjure up another world. I started off with riches, through rags and now I'm back to riches again; but without Johnnie they just wouldn't be worth a damn.' The interviewer clearly met with Fanny's approval as her final words to him were, 'You can call me Fanny and you must come again.'

The television series began with Fanny admiring the views from her own kitchen window, looking out at the millstream at the Dower House. Fanny welcomed viewers into her own kitchen 'at last, instead of the studio', with her hair swept up with a large bow at the back of her head as she showed the audience round every nook and cranny of her beloved work area. She introduced Peter 'who you will all know', and Sally, 'a newcomer, but a very good one', as her assistants helping to produce buffet parties that would make all the neighbours even more envious.

Fanny Cradock Invites... ran from July 1970 until October, and was greeted with successful reviews as had become the custom. The idea of informal parties hit the imagination of the British household at that time, with exotic cheese and wine becoming ever more available, to some at least. Others improvised with what they could get hold of, all displayed and prepared in the Cradock way whatever was on the plate. One reviewer was left feeling quite giddy by Fanny's yellow trousers and Johnnie's twinkling monocle. Another, however, was appalled at the way Fanny behaved towards those on screen with her. 'The way she treats her helpers would make a worm shrink back into its hole. Whether it is her husband or just someone placed conveniently to collect the washing up, they are her minions.' One viewer wrote in to their local newspaper to say, 'I was so fascinated by the designs on Fanny Cradock's frock, I missed half of her recipe for beetroot soup.' Regardless, Fanny was happy to have all the column inches she could achieve; and, as she reminded those watching anyway, the recipes were 'all in the booklet'. The repeats of *Fanny Cradock Invites...* continued to roll for the next two years regularly.

Fanny took a break from producing a full television series following *Fanny Cradock Invites...*, preferring instead to feature on various BBC game shows making the most of her celebrity status. With Johnnie by her side, she challenged family couples to a 'Great Omelette Race' on *Bruce Forsyth's Generation Game*; she rejoined the panel of *Call My Bluff* for another 'duel of words and wit'; she sat alongside Nicholas Parsons on the 'game for punsters and crossworders', *Password*; and popped up on the recently-poached-from-ITV BBC version of Jimmy Tarbuck's variety show, *Tarbuck's Luck*.

Meanwhile, the BBC had a new proposition for Fanny. Not a series of her own this time, but a regular segment in their flagship early-evening news and current affairs programme, *Nationwide*. *Nationwide* aimed to reflect the news and opinions from around Britain in a relaxed, 'light entertainment' style similar to the later *That's Life*, and the BBC's current early-evening magazine programme, *The One Show*. The nation was in the midst of European fever, with the prospect of an upcoming referendum to decide if Britain should join the 'common market' of European Communities, which would eventually be held in 1975. So, Fanny was alternately dispatched to various European destinations to report on their food and economy and to highlight any key differences to Britain, and also to recreate some popular European dishes in the studio for viewers to enjoy. She shopped in Belgium, Germany and Venice, and prepared European dishes with produce bought closer to home.

In Venice, a colourful Fanny was seen in a pink and white blouse, with a denim-coloured jacket and jaunty, almost cowboy-style hat, arriving at the local market by gondola. She barked a few instructions in her version of the Italian language before sampling winkles, the correct way. In the studio, the colour continued. Often seen in white blouses with red polka dots, or green and white patterns, with large white silk scarves and dark-coloured trousers, Fanny worked at a simple surface, with a gas cooker behind her. While making omelette royale, she would hold a bowl of stiffly whipped egg whites over the head of her assistant, Sally, to demonstrate how stiff they should be. In some segments, she focused on common household 'bugbears', such as tins of sardines that could only be part-opened with the attached key. Her solutions involved ordinary garden pliers from the toolbox, or kebab skewers. She would mutter to herself, 'That's right, Fanny,' as she shared her tricks, ending with a reassuring, 'You need not have any problem with that little one again, need you?' as she smiled and wrinkled her nose to camera.

The segments were an opportunity for Fanny to realise her long-held desire to connect food and travel on our screens, as well as producing some cookbooks as companions to the films, published by the BBC. *Fanny Cradock's Nationwide Cook Book* collected together the recipes she discovered while on the continent, while the short series of two *Common Market Cookery* books focused on a wide range of dishes from France (which Fanny approved of) and Italy (which she despised). Fanny planned additional books in the series looking at other Common Market countries, but these never made their way onto the bookshelves of Britain.

Nationwide devoted one entire episode of their series to covering the grand final of the annual Cook of the Realm contest, held in April 1972. Fanny was well used to participating in cooking contests by this stage in her career, but her role here was to be entirely different. Twelve amateur cooks from around the United Kingdom, each winning a local heat, were invited to the stage of the BBC's Television Theatre and given three hours to prepare a menu of original recipes for a panel of judges, including Fanny Cradock, Jimmy Young, Una Stubbs and a young Esther Rantzen, who was beginning her transition from well-respected BBC researcher to becoming a presenter and reporter with the channel. Fanny was additionally called upon to provide expert comments on each of the menus. The winning amateur cook was awarded a prize of a hefty one thousand pounds, and a fabulous new kitchen fitted at home.

The contestant representing the southwest area of England would return to the screen alongside Fanny a few years later, their names becoming forever entwined. However, making her first nervous and nerve-wracking appearance on television, having her menu critiqued by Fanny Cradock and her recipes judged for the viewers' delight on Wednesday the 26th of April 1972 was none other than Devon housewife, Gwen Troake.

As part of Fanny's ongoing career diversification plans, she was popping up doing personal appearances at all sorts of events and public openings. If they paid her (and Johnnie of course) to attend, she would be there, providing the full-on Fanny Cradock experience in return. Whether it was helping to judge 'Britain's Supersausage' at the Sausage of the Year contest in Westminster, or cutting the ribbon at a local jeweller's, Fanny would turn her expert hands to it all – especially if there was some publicity attached, which was nearly always the case. Wherever Fanny appeared, the cameras were on hand to capture her movements.

Occasionally things backfired a little – sometimes a lot – and the press attention was less than favourable. Fanny and Johnnie had been booked to appear at a charity ball to raise funds for the community centre at Botley Park Mental Hospital (as it was known then in less politically correct times) in Chertsey, Surrey. The lavish event was compered by the British actor and television presenter Shaw Taylor, best known for fronting the real-life crime programme on ITV, *Police 5*. The event was billed as one at which stars and guests would mingle; there would be no 'top table', giving guests the opportunity to meet their television favourites.

Nothing seemed right for Fanny that night. Expecting the red-carpet treatment, she was left disappointed and embarrassed when no one was allocated to meet her in the car park on arrival. Although not there to judge the food, Fanny was less than impressed with the cold buffet being offered to paying guests. 'God, I could do with a bowl of hot soup,' she told fellow guests. Fanny was offered a white bread roll to eat with her selection from the buffet, and proclaimed loudly, for all to hear, that she only ate brown. However, things boiled over considerably when Shaw Taylor spoke to her at the table and made the mistake of calling her Fanny. 'How dare you call me Fanny before we've been formally introduced?' she shouted at him, and then added to Johnnie, 'We will go. This is no place for me.' Fanny and Johnnie reportedly 'stormed out'.

The next day, Fanny claimed to not even know who Shaw Taylor was. She told the press, 'Everyone could hear what was going on and we did not want to put up with it any more. It was bad form.' Shaw himself felt that 'she got all stirred up over nothing'.

In the late 1960s, Gyles Brandreth was president of the Oxford University Debating Society. Part of his role involved inviting lots of politicians, celebrities and other well-known figures to come and debate. 'One of the biggest personalities of the day was Fanny Cradock,' he recalls. 'So, I wrote to her. I got a lovely long letter back, saying she would be delighted to come to the Union. It was all very exciting. I advertised she was coming. I did an interview saying she was coming. She saw it and wrote to me asking, "Are you making a monkey of me? Are you making jokes about me? Are you belittling me, young man?" Her letter was three pages, typed. I wrote back saying no, assuring her that in my quest for publicity I had learnt a lesson from all this, and reiterating that I didn't want to lose her. She wrote back saying, "You are clearly wonderful; I wish you were my son... If I wasn't married to Johnnie, I would marry you!"'

On the day of the debate, Fanny and Johnnie arrived at Oxford University in their Rolls Royce; a day Gyles remembers fondly. 'She was a triumph. She spoke brilliantly, she was easily as good as Robert Morley who was one of the great raconteurs of the time.' The debate had been at the beginning of December, so with her thank-you letter to Gyles, Fanny included an invite to her Christmas party at the Dower House. 'I brought my girlfriend, Michèle, who is now my wife. Anyone of the era who was famous was there. As we arrived, Fanny and Johnnie were on the doorstep with Lionel Blair. The big film that year was *Butch Cassidy and the Sundance Kid*, and as I saw Fanny and Lionel together, I said, "Oh look, it's Butch Casserole and the One Dance Kid!" which I thought was pretty good.' Fanny must have laughed too, as Gyles was welcomed into the party.

Gyles remembers the occasion. 'It was full of famous people, including Nicholas Parsons. The party was very generous; fabulous wines, incredible buffet food laid out in the kitchen, it was wonderful. We were by far the youngest people there, and the only unknown people there. Everyone else was famous. It was a very successful evening and, as a result, we became friends. We returned to their home on many occasions. We were sometimes described as her oldest, dearest friends, even though we had only really just met.'

Fanny had a failed business venture with a frozen foods manufacturer, Bird's Eye, who had hoped to sell a range of 'gourmet' Fanny Cradock ready meals. Fanny had maintained a connection with the company after attending the launch party for their fish fingers in 1955. In the intervening years, Fanny and Johnnie had both been strong supporters of the 'freezer revolution', promoting deep freezes in articles in the *Daily Telegraph* which showed how to easily create a glamorous 'party menu' from your chest freezer. The new collaboration fell flat on its face eventually, due in part to an economic downturn, leaving Fanny and Johnnie without the promised projected annual revenue of fifty thousand pounds.

Fanny had sunk a considerable amount of time, effort and resource into the development, and was left less than happy at the outcome. She turned the experience into a positive with the publication of the *Fanny and Johnnie Cradock Freezer Book*, which mentions the whole sorry incident in its foreword. Fanny herself would then take swipes at the company, without ever mentioning them, whenever she was able. At the opening of the Alpine Everest National Food and Freezer Distribution Centre in Perivale, Middlesex, she told reporters: 'I know a lot about deep freezing, and I can say that the freezers and the food supplied by Alpine Everest are of the very finest. It is a pleasure to wish a company well when that company is founded on honesty and its business conducted with integrity.'

Fanny and Johnnie were asked to judge the East Anglia Young Gas Cook of the Year in 1974, filmed in Norwich, Norfolk for inclusion in the local news bulletin by a young, fresh-faced, slightly intimidated and naturally timid Judy Finnegan, who would go on to present the popular *This Morning* magazine programme for ITV in the late eighties and nineties. Judy had recently joined Anglia Television with a flourish from Manchester rival Granada, becoming the first female reporter for the *About Anglia* news team. Fanny swept into the proceedings in a striking cream trouser suit, wearing her jacket off the shoulder and set off with a wide-brimmed matching hat, jangling with excessive jewellery. The young hopefuls were all installed behind Fanny's favourite Parkinson Cowan gas cookers, tending to their cupcakes and slicing tomatoes.

Fanny wafted around examining the work at hand while Johnnie peered over his heavily polished monocle. Judy could barely get a word in, so instead interviewed some of the children. They had all seemingly been primed to talk of the merits of French menus. She asked one thirteen-year-old boy: 'Is there anything sissyish about boys learning to cook?' Fanny was outraged by the standard of cooking in schools, claiming that schoolchildren were simply 'handicapped with their ingredients', being forced to cook with the most outrageous and inappropriate things, such as frozen peas in July. Fanny was sure that this (and other popular produce sold by Bird's Eye no doubt) was the cause of poor food standards in Britain.

Television cooking programmes in Britain were undergoing a bit of a metamorphosis in the early seventies, and somehow the style and grandeur of Fanny Cradock, which had been so popular up until that point, was not matching the mood of the country. The BBC had begun to use a young Delia Smith on *Woman's Hour* in 1972 to discuss cooking issues; and, although Fanny still appeared from time to time, Delia was becoming a more prominent voice. Seasonal food, inexpensive food and simple food were the trends, with Delia promoting soups, sauces, spices, oils and simple ways with eggs, leaving Fanny's fanciful creations looking a little bizarre. Fanny had covered all these topics in her early ventures on television, and by the seventies did not feel that viewers needed her to repeat them. Her audience, so she suspected, wanted to see elevation, being transported to the high points of society through food, not scrambling about in the kitchen making do.

Delia began her first television series the following year. *Family Fare* took a swipe at Fanny and her overblown ways. Delia produced simple and attractive dishes that could be served every day or jazzed up for special occasions or dinner parties. Delia ran through fish pies, stews, pork braised in cider, homemade scones, shortbread and ratatouille, followed by ideas for using up leftovers. Fanny continued her trips around Europe cooking up zuppe Inglese, stuffed pimentoes, oeuf en Brie and other delicacies from her trips to Denmark, Venice or Belgium. Delia's *Family Fare* programmes ran and ran in an afternoon timeslot, with housewives experimenting with the hearty and nourishing ideas she shared for simple suppers at home.

The run of successful series that Fanny had been accustomed to did not return: partly her design, and partly due to this shift in focus for food on television. The main television extravaganza for Fanny happened in 1975, when she was commissioned to present a series of five fifteen-minute programmes that together would enable viewers to prepare the perfect Christmas celebration. *Fanny Cradock Cooks for Christmas* was originally shown mid-afternoon on BBC1 in mid-December to very little fanfare.

Fanny did not seem to be excited about the prospect of sharing her ideas for a perfect Christmas day, again. She had been doing the same recipes on television, on radio and in print for the previous twenty years. On screen she sounded a little exasperated, annoyed with the viewers for requesting the same things over and again from her. She delivered though, never one to disappoint; after all they were so very popular when she did them the first time around. Then the second, and every time thereafter too. For the previous few Decembers Fanny had demonstrated the wonders of her round Christmas puddings, mulled wines, roast ducks, iced Christmas cakes and even ideas for Christmas decorations on her weekly semi-regular slots on the *Nationwide* programme. The simple studio set-ups required very little preparation or imagination from Fanny. The recipes were included in her *Nationwide* cookbook.

Fanny had been working at the BBC for two decades and was used to being paid job by job; she never had a permanent contract. Each show and series had been contracted separately, each fee being negotiated against the previous one. She earned a flat fee of around fifty pounds for each filmed recipe, which was slightly more than the forty pounds she might receive for a game-show appearance, but less than the one hundred pounds offered for chat shows such as *Parkinson*. Trips abroad for filmed segments, such as to Venice, were paid at a higher rate of one hundred and fifty pounds at Fanny's demand, to cover the 'fees' of both her and Johnnie appearing on screen, not including expenses such as flights and accommodation, much to the BBC's dismay. The per-show fees increased slightly year on year, reaching the dizzy heights of seventy pounds by 1975, still a far cry from the heyday of her career in the sixties.

For the *Cradock Cooks for Christmas* series, Fanny negotiated a rate more in line with her expertise and experience. If it were to be a prominent series bearing her name in the title, with her as the star, featuring her recipes that the audience was demanding, her fee would need to match. Fanny was paid two hundred and twenty-five pounds for each fifteen-minute episode, with an additional hundred pounds included in the contract to cover 'consultation' on the format and content – the intellectual property transaction of the day. She would write the accompanying booklet as before, including all the recipes featured on screen.

The studio set-up for the five programmes remained similar to those featured on *Nationwide*, with Fanny supplying all the equipment shown, including the by now synonymous Parkinson Cowan gas cookers. Each pot, Tupperware bowl and serving plate was brought into the studio by Fanny and her team of assistants, as were the ingredients and ready-prepared final dishes for presentation. Even the Christmas tree and decorations came from Fanny's own supplies.

Fanny was joined in the studio by Sara, the latest in a long line of assistants who worked with her on a variety of projects. She fetched and carried without muttering a word (for fear of attracting a higher fee), only occasionally whipping the required spatula off before it had actually been required. The programmes were devised, rehearsed and filmed all in one take, as before. Fanny was the professional, after all, and did not require retake after retake, edit after edit to make engaging shows. As such, she was still reasonably priced. Bringing in her own products to be used allowed additional behind-the-scenes opportunities for product placements and lifelong sponsorship deals to be honoured. Viewers with eagle eyes were able to spot an apparently rogue wrapper from a packet of Lurpak butter as Fanny unmoulded her perfectly round Christmas pudding, blaming someone else for leaving it there, but letting it linger on camera long enough to be recognised. Fanny knew the tricks of the trade: she had invented them, and wasn't afraid to use them.

Fanny went into overdrive publicising the booklet, which was available to buy to accompany the series, at almost every breath. 'It's all in the booklet,' had long become her catchphrase on screen, but for this Christmas series Fanny seemed keener than ever that viewers would rush out to purchase their own copies. Delia Smith and others were by now producing similar booklets for their programmes, so competition was fierce. BBC bosses were watching and wondering if Fanny was still relevant to television cooking programmes in Britain in the seventies.

The series began with ideas for that perfect, and unusual, Christmas bird involving manoeuvring mushrooms under the bird's flesh, baking it in a bath of murky stock from a nearby kettle, stabbing the poor bird with forks while you thought of that neighbour that you never really liked, before shredding it into manageable pieces with a perfectly safe, sterilised pair of ordinary garden secateurs, hopefully avoiding any damage to your hands during the process.

Fanny moved on to demonstrate Escoffier's wonderfully round Christmas pudding made in misshapen kitchen sieves, steamed for hours on end and served with bright green brandy butter. No Christmas would be complete without a cake, or two. Fanny showed both a traditional cake and a new one: her very own White Christmas cake, complete with advice on making edible almond paste (not from facial cream) and icing that would not crack your teeth on first bite. Fanny's imagination went stratospheric when it came to mincemeat creations, from pies big enough that men would like them, to puff-pastry perfections, pancakes, Swiss rolls and even the stomach-churning mincemeat omelette, served in the French style: baveuse, or still slightly wet in the middle. Fanny completed the series with ideas for petits fours all made from her very favourite choux pastry.

The entire five episodes really served as a 'greatest hits' of her cooking career, with a Christmas sparkle. Tucked away in the afternoon schedule, they would not reappear for many, many years. Other programmes would be repeated sporadically, but *Cradock Cooks for Christmas* was reserved for amusing clip montage shows in the 1990s, not being revived again for television viewers at least until Nigella Lawson resurrected Fanny's vodka-flamed Christmas pudding as part of her *Christmas Kitchen* series in 2006. This prompted the BBC to show the originals from over thirty years previously, starting an annual tradition of repeats of *Cradock Cooks for Christmas* on cable and satellite channels in the United Kingdom, and more recently a return home to the BBC with on-demand access on iPlayer. Demand for copies of the booklet soared, with copies dug out of old cupboards and flung onto eBay attracting record prices of two hundred pounds each, far outstripping the original fifty pence price tag.

Fanny would have no idea that this series in particular would be the one to be preserved entirely in aspic, elevated to cult status and freezing an image of her, now iconic, as slightly dotty, slightly barmy, ferocious to her assistants yet crinkling her nose sweetly to camera, dressed in pink chiffon with a poodle bow in her hair. She certainly did not expect it to be her very final series of cookery programmes, although she knew it would be the last for a while. As Fanny packed up her Tupperware bowls for a final time once the five programmes were done, it was time to put her plans for yet another career change into motion.

A Change of Gear

The seventies were a real period of change for Fanny and Johnnie: change that they had worked hard to plan for, almost as hard as they had planned their entire career. Reaching the 'age of retirement' (Fanny was sixty-one in 1970 and Johnnie sixty-six, both usual retirement ages in Britain at that time) was something that neither of them took to easily, Fanny especially as she continued to work almost every hour of every day. Nonetheless, some form of retirement was a goal to which they both aspired. The move to the Dower House was the linchpin in their plan: a 'forever' home that absorbed all their available funds, but which allowed them to multiply their earnings, or so they thought.

In the lead-up to the move they had considered many options for the future. Not only did they realise that they themselves could not continue forever; they were also acutely aware that television audiences may, just may, eventually tire of seeing them on screen. Besides, the couple had become accustomed to a certain lifestyle (at least, that was what the public-facing image suggested) and, even with the skilfully negotiated contracts for each programme and appearance, television alone would not pay the bills, or even go anywhere near doing so. Philip Harben had said that during his time at the BBC he was paid on average four hundred pounds a year; but he was able to earn an additional fourteen thousand from cookbook and sponsorship deals, which were often generated on the back of his small-screen appearances. Fanny was the same. She still had the newspaper columns, the personal appearances and the lifelong ties to certain producers and products; but would any of these continue if she were to disappear from view?

Despite constant press stories suggesting that they were intense rivals, Fanny had remained in contact with Philip Harben throughout the fifties and sixties, meeting from time to time, presumably to discuss 'business'. A perfect opportunity for Fanny, perhaps, to crow about how successful she was on television and in print. In 1969, the year before Philip died, he invited Fanny to a lavish lunch at his gloriously open-planned home in Hyde Park Gardens Mews.

Philip Harben's nephew, Charles Kenyon, was also invited. 'Uncle Phil served chicken, which he had cooked on an electric rotisserie that was installed in the kitchen wall.' (Fanny would later install a similar contraption in her kitchen at the Dower House, proudly showing it to the television audience of *Fanny Cradock Invites...*) 'He did his famous flaming ice cream as pudding; I remember him bringing it to the table. After lunch, Fanny asked me to drive her to Woolworths on the Finchley Road, before taking her home. I was driving my grandfather's bottle-green 1948 Riley RMA. I waited outside Woolworths for over twenty minutes for Fanny to come out; she never did. I believe she left by the back entrance, for some reason or other. I do not think I ever mentioned this to Uncle Phil. I was so young and she and he were famous, so I probably wondered if it was all my fault. It was the last time I saw Fanny, and also my uncle. He moved with my aunt to a serviced apartment in Bayswater shortly afterwards, where he died.'

It had always been a notion floating around in the collective Cradock mind that they could replace themselves in time: a sort of futuristic Fanny franchise. An idea to maintain the income, without physically doing all the work themselves. From the beginnings with Little Johnny Harper being trained up as an apprentice, through the steady stream of applicants willing to come and learn at the snappy heels in the Cradock household, the idea never really left them. Something always managed to get in the way, however; the young assistants did not seem to share the desire to be the 'new' Fanny (or Johnnie), choosing instead to spread their wings into the wider world of culinary wonder.

For the next venture, into yet another relatively unknown arena, Fanny would require the support of all her assistants, and more, to ensure its success. This was something bigger than her simply sitting down and bashing out words at her battered and bruised typewriter; bigger than weaving in secretive and illuminating biographical details, hidden in plain sight in books, magazines and newspapers; more than spending days on end perfecting a technique to beat eggs on screen, talking at the same time. If Fanny could not clone herself (just yet) and earn a decent living from her franchisees, she could at least trade on her own celebrity and culinary legacy, with over twenty years of food knowledge at her freshly scrubbed fingertips.

Fanny had an idea for something that would take her into the homes of those who watched her regularly on television and keep her there long after the set was switched off. Her cookbooks had been, and would continue to be, extremely popular; however, they at times failed visually to match the colourful persona and approach to presentation that she so encouraged on television, simply due to limitations in photography for cookbooks at that time. Imagine if there were a full-colour publication each and every week in which Fanny would take readers by the hand and lead them through her culinary mind, in all its glory: showing them how to begin to cook, begin to garnish, begin to present their creative work and slowly begin to climb the culinary ladder to success, just as Fanny had done herself? All with Fanny by their side, gently guiding them to improve and exceed even their own expectations? Surely it would be a dream come true…

One publishing company certainly felt so and put the plans in motion to make this multicoloured dream a reality. BPC Publishing Ltd, under the imprint of Purnell, had recently unleashed a raft of weekly magazine anthologies, or partworks, into the world, to which avid hobbyists and collectors would subscribe (hopefully), purchasing each weekly part in a given series on any number of topics. Whether it was subjects such as *Man, Myth and Magic*, *Discovering Art*, *Discovering Antiques* or *The History of the First World War*, these weekly magazines were popular, selling in large quantities in newsagents around the world. Purnell were a large company of around two thousand employees in the mid to late sixties, with some titles being printed in quantities of around four hundred thousand. The partworks produced by Purnell tapped into a new and lucrative market, hooking readers in with enticing initial editions that encouraged them to stay for the entire run, which at times could be as many as one hundred and twenty-eight parts, split into volumes of sixteen magazines. Collectors could purchase a binder in which to keep each volume, building up a library for each title to show off on shelves, and increasing revenue for titles with anything between six and eight volumes.

Purnell had dipped their toes into the world of food with the 1968 set, the *Cordon Bleu Cookery Course*. This partwork promised: 'Apart from going over the basic cooking techniques – and that includes knowing when to save time in the kitchen – we also give twenty or more varied recipes and suggested menus every week,' which readers and collectors lapped up. Purnell published seventy-two editions, in five volumes, each collected together in tastefully designed, finely grained, dark blue PVC box binders. Each week the magazine encouraged people to 'be better cooks' for themselves, their families, friends and indeed anyone that they could think of to invite round to show off to. Each edition was packed with gaudy colour images of each dish in its final presentation, as well as step-by-step picture tutorials on how to achieve the best results for each and every recipe.

The *Cordon Bleu Cookery Course* aimed to make cooking an adventure, under the expert guidance of Rosemary Hume and Muriel Downes from the Cordon Bleu Cookery School in London, where they had already turned thousands of students into Cordon Bleu cooks. Each weekly part had a cover price of four shillings and sixpence, roughly equivalent to around four pounds in today's money. For that price, readers received access to a range of around twenty recipes each week, expertly tested at the Cordon Bleu Cookery School, plus tips on techniques, terminology and menu-planning. Readers were additionally able to purchase specially selected items for their own kitchens, such as saucepan sets, at a special 'club' price, so long as they collected a certain number of tokens from successive parts. It was a merchandising dream.

The weekly set was illustrated throughout with lavish photography, with overblown piles of food in every conceivable colour nestling on covetable crockery, garnished within an inch of its life and set off with the odd bottle of wine and accompanying side dishes of equally colourful food. The *Cordon Bleu Cookery Course* had a revolving team of photographers ready to deal with each recipe. One of the team was a young photographer named Michael Leale, who hailed from Guernsey in the Channel Islands but who had found his way to the streets of London in the swinging sixties via a stint as photographer on his local newspaper. Michael would go on to take the cover shots for notable albums by the Kinks and Sandie Shaw; but for a while his work, and camera, focused on creating killer shots of food.

The collection was a first for Purnell in the sphere of food, and a successful first at that. The initial print runs sold extremely well, so well that a reprint of the entire series was scheduled for 1970. Purnell sensed that further titles relating to cookery and food would sell well, and approached Fanny to sound her out to perhaps produce her own version.

Fanny's imagination immediately went into hyperdrive; this could be her opportunity to show her lifetime's work on food in one, superbly colourful place. She would teach the nation to cook. Johnnie could include a section on wine. Young minds could be satisfied with recipes 'specially for small fry'. The legion of happy assistants could be gainfully employed testing, preparing and presenting the dishes each week, photographed at home in Fanny's kitchen at the Dower House. Fanny already had the best contact book in the business when it came to product placement, so featuring desirable items would be no problem at all. This would additionally allow Fanny to cut deals to sell equipment, gadgets and kitchen paraphernalia direct to her fans. Who would not wish to recreate 'Fanny's Dream Kitchen' in their own home?

Purnell were as excited as Fanny. To seal the deal, Fanny invited them to a special Christmas Cookery Show she had staged in 1969 to showcase what 'kitchen magic' the Cradock household could create as a weekly partwork. David White from BPC Publishing, who owned Purnell, was amazed not only at how much he was able to learn, but also by the 'extraordinarily intense response from the public, of all ages'. Profoundly impressed by the showcase, and immediately getting the appeal of the Cradock touch, which he described as 'gay devotion', he was keen to set the wheels of production turning. David himself was 'swept up in the crowd, like a fiesta', in awe of Fanny's pulling power, and could 'see the sales of the partwork soaring upwards' with Fanny, doing what she did best, getting peak reaction from the public. He knew the venture would be 'disgustingly commercial' following the 'glorious piece of market research' he and his 'publishing soul' had been witness to.

He commended all involved, praising the set-up with: 'Congratulations to all the Cradock team; they were all of them absolutely splendid, and came over as a team, each telling of what they know as a team. If we unobtrusively get that feeling into the partwork, the reader loyalties will run really deep.' He knew that Fanny was the star attraction, but that her supporting cast were vital to the success of the project.

Purnell duly commissioned *Fanny and Johnnie Cradock's Complete Cookery* (renamed the *Fanny and Johnnie Cradock Cookery Programme* before publication), scheduling an autumn 1970 publication date for the first of ninety-six issues, collected together in six volumes. They announced that the partwork would be heralded with a quarter of a million pounds' worth of promotion, presenting the famous Cradock team in their own home preparing thousands of recipes and passing on all their know-how in buying, preserving, storing, garnishing and presenting food.

Fanny and Johnnie starred in their own television commercial, pictured sitting at their kitchen table as Johnnie poured the wine and Fanny put the decorative finishing touches to a Sunday roast. Both were dressed in their finest seventies shades of brown, Fanny with elaborate choker-style necklace and Johnnie with his monocle, as they flicked through the first edition of the partwork and goaded the audience through the lens. 'Are you nervous cooking for your husband's boss?' enquired Fanny. 'Does your mother-in-law outshine you?' Johnnie insinuated, before Fanny delivered the killer blow: 'Would you like to impress that Mrs Jones next door?' Fanny assured any waverers that 'You can do it, with *Cradock Cookery*. Come and join Johnnie and me each week in our kitchen – we think you'll have just as much fun as we do!' Johnnie would not let things go, pitching in with 'Can you truss a chicken?' before they both raised a glass of (presumably) the finest red to the camera as a final incentive. Who could possibly resist?

The partwork began its two-year publication in 1970, published every Thursday, priced at four shillings and sixpence (also for sale in Canada, Australia, New Zealand and South Africa), styled in orange and brown with a now iconic photo of Fanny and Johnnie at work in their kitchen at the Dower House on the cover. Johnnie wears an orange shirt with brown cravat, while Fanny matches in a brown slip dress, a large bow made from the same material in the back of her hair, and with the same glittering gold necklace from the television advert completely covering her neck. Fanny is carving a roast bird as Johnnie looks lovingly on, perhaps at the bird rather than at Fanny. They are surrounded by mounds of green mashed potato, little tartlets filled with peas and garnished with tomatoes, copper pans and mounds of fresh produce. A typical day in their kitchen.

The first edition outlined their manifesto. Fanny and Johnnie wanted to share the secrets and skills that they had gained from a lifetime of discovery in cooking. They likened this to a bunch of 'culinary keys', of which there were ninety-six on their particular 'bunch'. Each week would represent a 'Key to Success' in one special aspect of cookery, garnishing and presentation. If readers were from the 'Great Cooking Army of women' who feed their husbands and families, without home help, then this was for them. If readers were enthusiastic cooks who longed to widen their experience and repertoire with so-called 'difficult dishes', then this was for them. If readers were cook-hostesses who had to cope single-handedly with entertaining, whether it be for 'his' business contacts, for good causes or for mutual friends, then this was for them. If readers were teenagers, then this adventure was for them. If readers were from the 'unfortunate brigade' who were overweight but believed that 'inside every fat person there is a thin person struggling to escape' then this was for them: an 'escape route for the overweight' Fanny described it as, admitting that both she and Johnnie had previously fallen into that category too.

Fanny would explode 'old fallacies' and 'culinary bogies', sharing only facts, enabling readers to produce proper results 'at speed' without the need for gadgets or special pieces of equipment, except of course those that had been specially selected for sale through the partwork. Fanny took a swipe at other 'cookery writers' who did not test their recipes before publication. Every recipe in the partwork would be tested, tested and tested again before it was shared. The assistants must have never stopped.

Part One is a guide to all things poultry, including pictorial instructions courtesy of young Peter on how to truss that bird Johnnie had referred to in the TV commercial with ease. Later, Fanny is shown instructing Peter in more advanced techniques. As it is the first issue, Fanny also shared some basic recipes for mayonnaise, soufflés, meringues and Swiss rolls – the first 'key' to be unlocked. Each recipe was accompanied by a great deal of narrative, making each part of the set a long, often amusing, always exciting read, all in Fanny's unique style. They included a short, but punchy, biography of their career to date, their love of Escoffier and their plans for the future, which seemed to include a book on flower decoration which never materialised. Johnnie wrote about wine, 'a joyous affair', and their friendship with Monsieur André Simon, the 'grand old man of the wine world' who was ninety-three at the time.

Readers were bombarded with many more ideas than they could possibly tackle. However, if they did attempt some of the recipes with success they could write and tell Fanny all about it, and she may award them a 'Golden Diploma' in return. Meantime, readers were encouraged to collect tokens towards 'bonus items' to purchase. If they saved hard and demonstrated their commitment to the *Cradock Cookery Programme*, at the end of the series they could purchase selected items designed to replicate Fanny's Dream Kitchen in their own homes, including a Parkinson Cowan gas cooker, chest freezers and even a dishwasher, all at specially reduced prices. For week one, 'club members' could send off for a Romertopf earthenware Roman pot to lock in all the natural vitamins, nutritional qualities and flavours of meat, poultry, fish, game and vegetables, just as the Romans themselves had allegedly done. Fanny received a commission on each sale. The 'small fry' were shown how to make ducks from leftover stuffing, swimming in a pool of gravy. All bases were covered.

This pattern continued as a template for each of the weekly parts. Each issue could be collected in a stylish (at the time) set of olive green, wipe-clean PVC binders, ideal for any potential kitchen mishaps along the way. Unlike the Cordon Bleu series, which had a team of photographers working to capture the finished dishes, Fanny worked with just one, Michael Leale. Michael was seconded to her from Purnell to capture her years and years of cooking knowledge, and above all, garnish and presentation, in colour for the very first time.

'They chose me generally because I work so quickly and get things right. I had photographed probably half of the Cordon Bleu Course, so they knew I could do it,' Michael recalls. 'When I left Guernsey, I was maybe nineteen or twenty, and to be honest I didn't even know who Fanny was. By the time we worked together, though, I certainly did. Fanny had a bit of a reputation, even at that time, for being quite difficult. I was young and naïve and thought I could handle her. Besides, I was freelance, and it was a job, and I only got paid when I was working. We got on all right, I think principally because from the start I let her know I was working *with* her and not *for* her and that made a big difference. She did treat her staff rather cruelly at times, she could be a bit of a witch. As I was working *with* her, we were on a more equal footing.'

For the next eighteen months, twice a week, Michael would drive to the Dower House to take pictures. 'It was all done in her house, with her china and whatever as props; mostly in her kitchen while everyone was cooking around me. She was involved in the styling; I would never have dreamed of using green food colouring in my mashed potatoes – quite frankly I was horrified. To this day, I am still a little embarrassed by it!' Fanny was very much responsible for the styling of each picture: she presented the dishes and chose what they were displayed on, and it was left up to Michael to deal with the lighting and make a composition out of it as best he could. 'It wasn't easy, dealing with choux pastry swans and all sorts of wonderful things,' he laughed.

All the work took place in the kitchen. Fanny and Johnnie were joined by their two young assistant cooks: 'I think they were Richard and Sally, but she had a couple of au pair boys, Frank and René, too; she always had a steady stream of young people in the kitchen – she liked young people around her that's for sure,' Michael thinks back. 'She was all right with me, but the tongue lashings she gave the others, and Johnnie too; I just stood back and kept my own counsel. It was not just once every now and again, it was quite often, which was difficult to be around.' Thankfully Michael was prepared for Fanny's reputation. 'She could also be quite mean; for example, we did a shoot of lots of different curry dishes, so it was decided a jug of beer would be quite good in the shot. Johnnie was sent to the cellar to get a bottle of ale, which was poured into a jug ready for the picture to be taken. Once we had got the shot we needed, Johnnie took the beer and poured it back into the bottle, ready to be tucked away again in the cellar!'

Michael recalled that Fanny also had a nice side to her character. For one issue of the partwork the entire team were shipped off to Portugal to take pictures in Pinto. 'I photographed the natives treading grapes – the girls hitched their skirts into their knickers and started treading the grapes,' Michael reminisced. 'We went to the Krug champagne vineyards en route – Fanny knew the owners – then straight across Spain to Portugal. When we arrived all they had to eat for lunch was *arroz de bacalhau* – salt cod and rice. Fanny pronounced it totally inedible, which it was; but rather than upset the owners, she shovelled handfuls of it into her handbag so as to pretend we had eaten it. The sight of Fanny getting great handfuls of this rice and fish and shoving it into her bag! It was quite something!'

Michael continued, 'It was one hell of a trip. We stayed a few days. Most nights after dinner we sat around a fire with Fanny telling ghost stories in the moonlight – she was really rather good at telling them. She was entertaining. For me, a humble boy from Guernsey, it was an experience and a half. I remember it all very fondly; it was special for me, so different and unique, really a *wow* time in my life. I felt like I was living it up with this television star; even if she was a bit odd, I was doing it!'

Michael remembers one particular time back at the Dower House when they were taking pictures for a whole edition of the partwork that would be devoted to 'parties'. 'She could be quite fruity at times as well. She once asked if I had ever put on a mink coat, which I had not. She went on to suggest that I should go upstairs and take off all my clothes, and wear the mink coat inside out to find the true meaning of sensuality… I did *not* do as I was told!'

Although sales were initially good, unfortunately they dwindled as the partwork progressed into 1971, resulting in the planned run of ninety-six being cut short at eighty. The series still managed to cover a wide range of topics including all the old Fanny favourites. New ideas such as foods from exotic parts of the world were showcased, there were ideas for wedding parties, and even instructions for how to make over your home to be (a little) like Fanny's were included. Fanny and Johnnie had expected that the 'disgustingly commercial' venture would alleviate their financial concerns not only for the time, but also as they progressed towards their aspirations of retirement, but it was not meant to be. The partwork remains one of Fanny's greatest legacies today, however, featuring her unique writing style, presentation ideas and foolproof recipes. Collectors covet the set, poring over the seventies styling and colourful culinary keys.

Work on the series lasted for a full eighteen months from start to finish. Michael was sorry that it came to an end prematurely. 'After the *Cordon Bleu Cookery Course*, which was modern, clean, and featured French cuisine, Fanny's version seemed strangely old-fashioned and a bit too fussy for the modern housewife. Fiddling about with green food colouring for your mashed potatoes was just not on. I felt at the time that the pictures were fussy; it was decoration for the sake of decoration, forgetting what it actually tasted like. That was Fanny all over. It was her stock-in-trade. She was the boss lady, most definitely, so we just did what she said.'

Never someone to dwell on the past longer than it deserved, Fanny's mind returned to the future. She gave an interview to *Woman* magazine in early 1973 in which she outlined her secret to a happy life. For Fanny, hard work was happiness, and she wasn't about to give it up, she assured. Working twelve-hour days, including weekends too, no one could accuse Fanny of shirking. The interview acknowledged that Fanny was seen by some as a forthright, forceful woman who 'must have enemies'. By this stage in her many careers, Fanny had plenty of those, leaving a trail of mistreated colleagues and acquaintances alike in her wake. Production teams at the BBC continued to find her difficult to deal with, and the insurance claims for lost or damaged items, such as make-up and kitchen utensils, continued to be submitted.

Most of all, Fanny told the interviewer, she had no time for people, especially women, with no self-discipline, particularly when it came to weight. Fanny told the interviewer that at one time she had been fourteen stone and nine pounds, which made her depressed. Depressed enough to concoct a rigorous diet which she claimed to have stuck to ever since, resisting all temptation to fly towards the biscuit barrel. Of course, she was fortunate to have Johnnie by her side, in the happiest of marriages.

Fanny vowed to go on until she dropped dead, even if Johnnie – whom she was 'dotty about' – went before her, which she suggested he more than likely would, being five years older than she. Sensing that the interviewer was about to ask when they would retire, Fanny cut in to say 'Never.' This was the public message; she would not do anything to diminish her pulling power, her bankable asset of celebrity, her draw to television producers and media outlets. However, behind closed doors back at the Dower House, quiet thoughts were slightly different.

Previous attempts to train people up to replace and represent Fanny and Johnnie, carrying on the Cradock name, flair and income, had fizzled out before they had taken off. Perhaps it was Fanny's focus on young men as apprentices, or perhaps they simply had not found the right faces to fit the particular mould they had cast. Perhaps Fanny needed to find someone more relatable, someone more down-to-earth (as she felt herself to be) and in need of the support and instruction that she herself had supposedly received at a young age.

Fanny thought that she may just have found that person in 1973 when Sara Barker entered her life. The story that Fanny spun, which may well have been true, was that Sara wrote to her at the *Daily Telegraph* telling her about her recent marriage to Paul, an art teacher, and confessing her love for the Bon Viveur recipes, which never failed. Inspired by Fanny, Sara wondered how she could learn further and practise her own cookery. Evening classes were not for her; she had a limited budget and worked as a secretary, so she had to make the household income work hard by making everything they ate herself. She never bought convenience food. She always bought the cheaper cuts of meat, fresh vegetables, fruits and cheese. She only had puddings on special occasions, to keep costs down.

If the story is correct, Fanny wrote straight back to Sara to invite her to come to the Dower House once a month to learn more about cookery directly from her and Johnnie. Sara naturally agreed, but only if she could bring her husband with her. In return all that Fanny asked was that she could write about it all in a monthly column in the *Daily Telegraph*. It all seemed perfect: a newly married young couple of hard-working people, keen as mustard to learn, and already huge fans of the approaches taken by Fanny.

Fanny described Sara as looking much younger than her twenty-six years, fair, with blue eyes and very pretty. She enjoyed sewing, gardening, reading and of course cooking. Paul, slightly younger at twenty-four, had put on around a stone in weight since their marriage the previous year, but Fanny thought he was still a slim young man. He liked painting watercolour landscapes, eating, and drinking wine. They could not have been more perfectly suited to be taken under the wing of Fanny and Johnnie.

Sara seemed to have the same culinary likes and dislikes as Fanny. She hated boiling vegetables, preferring them to be steamed; she detested malt vinegar, vanilla essence, table salt, and most of all margarine. Just like Fanny. Perfectly so. Sara had sadly lost her own mother, just a few days before the wedding, although she and Paul still talked fondly of her, which Fanny said she could relate to.

So, the monthly sessions began, all timed around Sara's job as a receptionist and her and Paul's joint venture to establish a home together, having just purchased a small cottage in need of some redecoration. 'We are really very lucky,' Sara told Fanny, 'but even so we have to watch every penny. Paul adores his tum, and I adore cooking; and whatever it is I may want to learn most from you, I must use this wonderful opportunity you and the *Daily Telegraph* are giving us to learn how to cook well and inexpensively.'

Sara was quick to learn. In the first month she mastered steamed vegetables, basic sauces, mayonnaise and a very basic soufflé, all with Fanny by her side to guide her and to answer any queries she may have. All these were printed up in the *Daily Telegraph*, alongside pictures of a beaming Sara 'obviously delighted' with the results. In the coming months Sara got to grips with poultry, pastry, omelettes, meringues, yeasted doughs and pancakes before tackling the more 'top-level' savoury mousses, the kind that Escoffier made. Sara seemed to share Fanny's love of colour, making green mayonnaise and bright pink veloutés.

As the months rolled by, Sara grew in confidence, requiring only a glance over the shoulder from Fanny now and again for reassurance as she skilfully attempted more involved procedures, fancy breads like lardy cake 'for picnics and parties', savarins and rich Christmas cakes. Sara proved to be a dab hand at icing, as well as Christmas decorations, which would no doubt prove to be useful in her future role as assistant on the *Cradock Cooks for Christmas* television series in 1975.

Sara's future as a replacement for Fanny did not materialise, but they remained close. Fanny referred to her and Paul as 'the children' and even tried to adopt them at one point. When the couple went on to have a son, Jonathan, Fanny was keen to pay for his education at Harrow, where Johnnie had been schooled. Sara and Fanny remained in contact throughout the next decade, although their relationship became strained, partly due to Fanny's exasperating behaviours. When Johnnie died in 1987, Sara and Paul were the executors of his will. This was to be the last contact with Fanny that they had, the friendship by now having broken down completely.

Leaving behind the prospect of replacing herself in the world of food, along with the disappointing success of the partwork, Fanny, with barely a glance backwards, moved on to something new. However, things were also changing at home, financially, and indeed throughout the country. The continent was changing; politics were changing; and this was to have a surprising effect on the fortunes of Fanny and Johnnie. The 1970s began with a Conservative government in place, and a committed celebration to join the European Community, with Britain joining the Common Market in 1973.

With nearly all their money tied up in the Dower House and appearances on television dwindling in regularity, Fanny looked to the future for a way to harness some income, using the talents she had at her fingertips. She seemed to write day and night: letters (not all of them nasty), ideas, treatments, articles – she was like a machine when it came to producing words. So, if her face did not seem to fit the ideal of what television moguls desired any longer, and she had exhausted her food repertoire and legacy, perhaps it was time to think of a new way to remain involved with television, without actually appearing on screen herself and without cooking or preparing food in any way.

Fanny's idea was for a soap opera. Not the kind of televised drama that was popular in Britain during the seventies, such as *Crossroads* or *Coronation Street*: her ideas were grander, more aspirational, more in tune with her life, or at least the life she had already been portraying for decades in front of, and behind, the cameras. Her idea was more along the lines of *Dallas* or *Dynasty*, years before either went into production, in terms of popularity and scale, mixed with *Downton Abbey* as a backdrop for the storyline. Fanny had no plans to star in the soap opera herself, merely to write it, at least at the time. Perhaps she may have written herself in as a guest star eventually, but for now her motivation was to stay firmly behind the typewriter.

Initially Fanny discussed the project with the BBC, who, surprisingly, seemed keen on the idea. However, they suggested to her that it would need to be written initially as a novel, before being adapted for the small screen in the way in which she envisaged. She wrote in her notes: 'If it has to be written as a novel first in order for it to sell for what I want, then so be it.' Not only was the idea grand, but Fanny's financial expectations for the work were larger than life, in the hope that it may solve the problems with money that she and Johnnie had encountered.

Early in March of 1974, work was well under way on what Fanny was now referring to as her 'saga' story. Fanny was concerned that Britain's changing views on European Union membership had already had an impact on the cost of food, with inflation rising, and that a change in government to Labour would result in a change in taxation, especially for high earners, like herself, living in the country. With her head down, she vowed to get her latest project off the ground and buck the trend.

Fanny was a lifelong friend of Dugald Malcolm, a diplomat with a background of education at Eton College and Oxford University, who was at that time the British Ambassador to Panama. She wrote to him outlining her ideas and excitement for the project, which had already expanded in her mind to a series of three books:

> Nearly finished Book 1 of the saga – it should run to 150,000 words. I've finally decided on calling it *The Lormes of Castle Rising*, with sub-titling of the three books as follows – 1) *The Casket* 2) *Pandora's Box* 3) *The Four Horsemen of the Apocalypse*. The BBC have asked for Book 1 to see if they can use it for a TV series which is heartening. It has also been asked for in the USA – and two more publishers have gotten in on the act, asking if I've finally settled on one, which I have not. I am also tying up the film and other rights before I let any of them get their tiny fingers on it now that first reactions have been so (surprisingly) good. In the event of people like the BBC being interested they will see that there could be three series, not just one. Finally, I shall write the first chapter of Book 2, will let the final choice of publisher have the manuscript and send it to 'Aunty' in whom I have great hopes. After all, it is better to travel hopefully.

It had long been an ambition of Fanny to be recognised as a writer in the United States, with all the success, and financial reward, that may have come with that. Sadly, it did not come soon enough to save Fanny and Johnnie from the financial situation in which they found themselves. Fearful of the descent into bankruptcy that had befallen her father, Fanny felt that she had no option other than to take matters into her own hands. For years, it had been suggested that the Cradocks had been involved in creative accounting; however, small duplications of expenses in their tax returns would no longer suffice. Fanny realised that in order to save the life that they had built up, they must sell the Dower House and seek a new home, in a country which would not seek to (as she clearly saw it) strip their wealth through heavy taxation.

Fanny and Johnnie were still filing reviews as Bon Viveur for the *Daily Telegraph* and somehow managed to convince the newspaper to support 'research trips' to potential locations to find a new home. After one such trip, Fanny wrote to Dugald's wife, Patricia, in May with a rundown of the news:

> We had a recent trip to Jersey, to look at options for living. We would rather starve. We've looked at the Isle of Man, Gibraltar, Switzerland, Normandy, even Tobago. If Labour are elected we shall be 'Gone with the Wind' with wealth taxes etc, taxes to the Government. We have no male domestic staff, Peter and Sally are with us and another Peter and a Gillian joining the cooking strength in July and August respectively. Both have been trained by us. We are busy, well and fighting fit – and planning hard. I have lashings of work, have finished the first 'saga' book, embarked on the second, am doing a film, lots of television and am really very lucky. Johnnie has nearly finished his new Wine book and the garden is looking lovely. We now sell surplus compost-grown fruit and veg and are doing a roaring cash trade to go in with our 'floorboards money!'

Fanny signed the letter 'Phyl' which was the name by which her closest friends still knew her, even if those neighbours in Watford purchasing the excess produce over the garden gate were buying genuine Fanny Cradock items. By June, the deal to sell the saga had been completed, and Fanny again wrote to Dugald with the update:

> Good news, sold the first volume of my saga at 40,000 words and went on to complete it at 170,000. Not happy with the publisher who offered, but agreed with WH Allen (who are very good). They have bought hardback and paper-back – I am expecting actual terms any minute. I have at least proved that I

> can still earn a living as a novelist if all else fails. WH Allen will give me a big launch party and seek to sell it on the American market. We are in the process of forming a little company with Andrew in Jersey in such a way as to channel funds away from the thieving claws of the mad bulls in current office in our Government.

Writing to Dugald's wife, Patricia, Fanny said, 'Meanwhile we have invested a pretty healthy sum in Jersey which yields us about eight thousand per annum of which, if we don't get at it to other places, will all go to the Government save about one thousand and three hundred pounds. Shocking isn't it when we have worked like slaves to earn it, paid our taxes on it and been prudent and saved?'

Coincidentally, Fanny had discovered a very attractive tax-loop for 'new authors' living and working in Ireland, which meant that earnings on any published works would be tax-free for ten years. Such an incentive was hard to pass by for Fanny, who conveniently had never published works of fiction under the name 'Fanny Cradock' and would therefore be eligible for the tax break, as a 'new' author. Suddenly Ireland was chosen as their new home. A suitable residence was found two miles north of the small historic town of Doneraile, in County Cork. Fanny wrote to Dugald to say, 'We have bought a darling house with seven acres and lovely grounds (all need re-landscaping) thirty miles from Cork in the heart of the most exquisite country. We are delicious at the prospect of being among people who still have good manners, and cannot wait impatiently for the day of departure.'

Doneraile also had proud literary connections, serving as a place to which well-respected authors went to write. Previous writers who hailed from the town included Patrick Augustine Sheehan and John B. Keane. Well within easy reach of Cork Airport, it enabled access to work opportunities back in Britain, and across Europe as Fanny continued to present *Nationwide* slots encouraging viewers to believe that eating and holidaying on the continent was for the best.

Fanny wrote again in July to Dugald to tell him of the move, saying, 'According to the financial boys we shall be alright if we do not work, but we are keeping jobs that we want and shedding the rest with alacrity.' The Dower House was advertised for sale in the 29th of August 1974 edition of *Country Life* magazine, then and now seen as the 'world's most celebrated magazine of the British way of life, its countryside and gardens'. The selling agents, Stimpson, Lock and Vince, who were established in Hertfordshire in 1903 (and are still selling homes today simply as Stimpsons), proudly announced the sale 'by direction of Fanny and Johnnie Cradock' to boost interest in the 'magnificent period residence dating from the 17th century in a tranquil setting a mile and a half from Watford town centre'.

The Grade II listed Dower House sold for around ninety thousand pounds, equivalent to just short of a million pounds in more recent terms, allowing Fanny and Johnnie to escape to Ireland. The Dower House went on to be sold for four million in 2009. Fanny wrote to the BBC to let them know their new address to send payments to, asking that the channel treat the information with the utmost confidentiality. The address was not to be given under any circumstances to anyone working in press or publicity as Fanny and Johnnie were hoping, they claimed, to carry on their work for many years to come and, according to their medical advisors, they would only be able to do so with a bit of privacy and peace. The letter was added to the front page of all Fanny's files at the BBC, marked as confidential, with a note asking for it always to be kept on the top of each file.

The first instalment of the Castle Rising saga was published in 1975 by WH Allen, now part of the Penguin Books empire, specialising in publishing 'engaging, provocative books that start conversations' and describing itself as 'home to some of the biggest thinkers of the past three centuries' without any mention of Fanny. *The Lormes of Castle Rising* was billed as the first in a 'remarkable trilogy' which charted the rise, decline and ultimately the fall of a great family, a family 'once powerful but in the end unable to survive the social and economic forces which transformed society in the twentieth century'. The blurb for the book promised an exciting and varied narrative, fine characterisation and an unerring sense of period detail and social history as it explored the subtle relationship that once existed between good employers and their employees, and the mutual loyalty and devotion that flowed between 'the strata of society not yet torn by class strife'.

Illustrated with a scene of a country shoot on the front, the back cover featured a large photograph of Fanny wearing a short, fashionable hairstyle, smiling sweetly to the camera with direct eye contact, revealing strings of pearls around her neck, wrapping herself tightly in a fur coat. This was her 'writer's look' to match the information that she had already written over eighty books, although this was noted to be her most ambitious and mature work to date.

Dedicated to Johnnie, 'because we can both echo Justin Aynthorp's "vale"… "je t'aime et je ne regrette rien"', Fanny attributed the dedication to 'Jill' which was Johnnie's pet name for her. Fanny thanked her colleagues at the *Daily Telegraph* information office for their 'infinite patience' in researching material for her over a period of three years to include in the book. Fanny claims to have begun writing the book in 1966 before returning to it in the early seventies to prepare it for publication. In the intervening years she had, she said, spent some time researching her own family history which she would then 'plagiarise' for use in the Lorme family. Many of the names used in the story originate from real-life family members and acquaintances. Justin was the name of her very first grandchild, Christopher's son with Nikki, who had relocated to Australia. Aynthorp was a close approximation of Apthorp, the family home in Leytonstone where she had lived as a small child. Castle Rising itself had a real location in Norfolk, which Fanny initially claimed not to realise.

The Lormes of Castle Rising sold well, paving the way for the other two planned books in the saga. It went on to win the Best Fiction Talking Book of the Year awarded by the National Listening Library. However, not all readers were enthusiastic about either the plotlines or the historical accuracy which Fanny claimed had been so carefully researched. Clarissa Dickson Wright, who became well known as a celebrity chef herself in the nineties as one half of the 'Two Fat Ladies', but was also a writer, businesswoman, barrister and owner of a cookbook shop in Edinburgh, said it was a 'dreadful book whose only claim to fame was that at various stages throughout the book she (Fanny Cradock) gave recipes, so you'd have "William the Conqueror came and dined at the Castle on Tripes à la Mode des Caen"; the recipes were the best bit of the book'. It was a technique that Clarissa also introduced to some of her own books, amusingly.

To conceal that they were living in Ireland while the books were published, Fanny gives her address, unnecessarily, in the foreword as Des Cotils, Jersey in the Channel Islands, presumably where the tax-haven company she had established was based. The first book trails the following two, given at the time to be *Shadows Over Castle Rising* and *The Castle Rising Smarties*. *Shadows over Castle Rising* followed in 1976, reviewed by the *Sunday Times* as 'a solid and entertaining account of a crucial period of social change'. The action had moved forward to the Edwardian age, ending with the First World War, this time with meticulous research (and 'infinite patience') by Mr Matthews from the London Library, one of the world's leading institutions, which counted Charles Dickens, Virginia Woolf, Agatha Christie and Harold Pinter as members. Fanny told readers that the character of the Dowager, Lady Aynthorp, was based upon her own Gran, and another character, Stephen, was based on a close relative whose identity Fanny would prefer not to disclose. The books were becoming more entwined with the fantasy of Fanny's family life as they proceeded, and readers bought into it.

The third, and final planned, instalment was renamed *War Comes to Castle Rising* before publication in 1977, dedicated to Sara, Paul and Jonathan, 'with love, because they are our continuation'. The opulent Edwardian era had drawn to a close, and the changes that the First World War had brought to Europe were being felt at Castle Rising, including devasting deaths. Continuing to sell well, in Britain and crucially for Fanny in America too, the books were still drawing mixed reviews. The *Yorkshire Post* said it was a 'very well and solidly researched' book; while another review said, 'If you haven't been following the Castle Rising saga since its Norman Conquest beginnings in the *Lormes of Castle Rising*, the familial relations in this third volume will be just about incomprehsible.'

Incomprehensible they may have been, but WH Allen were extremely pleased with sales of the three-part saga. So much so, that plans were put in place to extend the saga much further than Fanny had originally envisaged, to a series of ten books, one to be published each year of the ten-year tax-free window she was eligible for as a new writer. Locations shifted to London homes. Cover designs became more 1920s 'flapperish' in design. Fanny's back-cover photograph changed to a full-colour portrait taken by Allan Warren, showing a slightly older and more surprised Fanny in a green felt cloak trimmed with fox fur. The Lorme family themselves grew rapidly and became entwined in intrigue, ménages à trois, confidence tricks, lost fortunes and fabulous parties during the Roaring Twenties. Titles hinted at the drama contained within the pages of *Wind of Change at Castle Rising*, *Uneasy Peace at Castle Rising*, *Thunder Over Castle Rising*, *Gathering Clouds at Castle Rising*, *Fateful Years at Castle Rising* and *The Defence of Castle Rising*. After the Second World War, new relatives from America were discovered, who brought with them new challenges, dilemmas and plot twists such as 'who really owns Sue-Ellen's aeroplane factory?' The Lorme family saga was truly morphing into a modern-day soap opera; but the option to make a series for television or film, on either side of the Atlantic, never became reality.

Volume ten of the saga, *The Loneliness of Castle Rising*, was published in 1986 and would become the final book in the series, despite the plotlines becoming stuck in the postwar era. Fanny planned an eleventh, and final, part to the story, tentatively titled *Castle Rising Closes the Circle*, which would bring the 'extensive Castle Rising series with its extravagance of detail' to a close for its loyal readership. An initial edit of the completed manuscript threw up some discrepancies in detail and timing of events linked to the previous novels. Fanny paid little attention to the correct period details for the book, which was set in or around 1949. She made reference to characters wearing jeans, which did not become popular until the late 1950s and 1960s. Fanny mentioned bands such as the Beatles, who did not form or become famous until the 1960s. Some of the text alluded to Princess Margaret and Lord Snowdon, who in reality would not marry until 1960.

With a confusing narrative and inconsistency of detail, the project was called to a halt. The circle at Castle Rising was never closed.

However, WH Allen did publish one final title of fiction authored by Fanny Cradock. *The Windsor Secret* was held back for publication, allegedly, until 1986, following the death of Wallis Simpson, the Duchess of Windsor, in April. Previously, Fanny had hinted that Wallis and her husband, the Duke of Windsor, had been close friends of Fanny and Johnnie, even writing newspaper articles about their time spent together. The Duke had died in 1972 from cancer, and the Duchess spent the remainder of her life reclusively, frail and living with dementia. She lost the power of speech in 1980 and became bedridden until the end. Several other books about her life were penned during her final years, but kept back for publication until after her death, for fear of falling foul of libel laws and the accusations of invasion of privacy that an unauthorised book may have brought with it.

Fanny's book was the first to be launched onto bookshelves, having languished in the vaults, waiting patiently. The first edition, in hardback, was perhaps deliberately vague as to whether the story was fact or fiction, making no claims to either. When it was republished in paperback, this was rectified. Some felt the publication was in bad taste, a misjudgement professionally, but WH Allen were determined to cash in on the controversy. The entirely fictional story centres upon the question: 'What would have happened if Wallis Simpson, the twice-married American who stole King Edward's heart, had given birth to a son?' Fanny weaves a tale of a handful of loyal friends and servants who tried over the years to protect Edward and Wallis, two people passionately in love with each other, from the prying eyes of the public throughout the world. Drawing on all Fanny's own experiences of global travel, the story takes place in Italy, Geneva, London and Australia, involving political intrigue, public outcry and a dramatic conclusion.

In Fanny's story, the secret child is bundled off to live with a wealthy Englishwoman living in Australia, primarily to save the reputation of the King. The final chapter carries the subtitle 'Thy Seed, Thy Harvest', perhaps as a nod to the Frances Dale novel, *My Seed, Thy Harvest*, published decades earlier. Although Fanny worked hard to tangle together fact and fiction, supposedly using information shared directly to her by the Duke and Duchess, the book remained laborious to read, with clunky dialogue and strangulated description, in many ways in the same vein as the Castle Rising saga had become. Despite this it became a 'controversial bestseller' for WH Allen, with the *Daily Mail* calling it 'riveting'.

Fanny continued to write, with increasing confusion and lack of clarity which may have mirrored her own life, aiming to churn out yet more books. She planned a novel, *Paradise Regained*, that she hoped to publish under the pseudonym of either Peter Christopher or Christopher Peters, in a somewhat late homage to her two sons. Again, Fanny hoped that it would be considered as a television serial or soap opera, but the bizarre storyline failed to land, even as a novel. The plot was to revolve around a mysterious 'elixir' which had rejuvenating properties when injected, making users look younger and younger each day. The story would reveal the tiffs, twists, turns and tribulations involved in securing the secret recipe, and potentially bringing it to market, or alternatively (as British Intelligence preferred), making sure it never came up for sale.

A further planned script entitled *Over Our Shoulders* looked back at the reign of Queen Victoria, entangling royal history with food history, hoping to capitalise on the connections with the House of Windsor, but never amounted to anything in the end. Not all of Fanny's ideas were landing successfully, as they once had. The ideas themselves were not perhaps the problem, but rather the confusing, and increasingly erratic, execution of them.

End of the Big Time

FANNY AND JOHNNIE WERE SUCH recognisable faces in Britain at the beginning of the seventies that they were lampooned on television regularly, with the best comedians and impersonators trying their hardest to take them on. Ever since the days of Betty Marsden playing the thinly veiled character of gravel-voiced cook Fanny Haddock in the radio series *Beyond Our Ken* in the late fifties and early sixties, Fanny Cradock was ripe for a parody.

One of the most famous sketches on television featured on *The Benny Hill Show* in 1971, watched by a staggering twenty-one million viewers. The sketch was titled *Fun in the Kitchen with Johnny and Cranny Faddock*, with Benny Hill himself playing the character based on Fanny, although he made no real effort to resemble her other than wearing a dress, a pearl necklace and a brown wig. Bob Todd played a monocled Johnnie in a suit, assistant to 'Cranny' and partial to a swig or two of booze. The scene was played out in a kitchen similar in style to the Dower House, complete with green patterned tiles, gas cooker and a selection of equipment which could have easily been purchased directly from the partwork.

Reviews were favourable, noting that Benny had captured most of the mannerisms of the famous 'queen of the kitchen' while cracking some corny jokes about 'Freud Chicken'. It illustrated that Fanny and Johnnie were at a level in their career where they were laughed at, fondly, and the subject of much discussion, even on other people's prime-time television shows.

However, they liked to keep the celebrity spotlight on themselves too, frequently appearing on entertainment shows when they could. Whether it was a blindfolded panel, including a giddy Kenneth Williams, clearly a fan of Fanny, attempting to guess Fanny's identity despite (or perhaps as a result of) her terrible French accent on the game show *What's My Line?*, or appearing on *The Generation Game* to judge rival families as they recreated the giant mincemeat pies Fanny favoured so much, Fanny and Johnnie were game for a laugh.

The real Fanny and Johnnie were often featured alongside one another. One such appearance on the comedy game show *Celebrity Squares* on ITV, hosted by Bob Monkhouse, led to some controversy for the couple. Various guest celebrities took part in each episode, each sitting in a different square on the set, with contestants choosing celebrities to answer questions and hoping to get a straight line of three correct 'celebrity squares' to win. Comedians tended to excel on the show, with slick ad-libbed jokes thrown in to keep the viewers entertained. For Fanny and Johnnie, off-the-cuff comedy did not come easily, but the show's producers insisted that the stars were not primed beforehand. Some viewers were not convinced. Fanny and Johnnie sat together in one square and were singled out as likely candidates who had rehearsed their quips.

In a less humorous turn, and feeling certain that their time as television cooks was about to be 'up', the Cradocks took the opportunity to take part in a radio broadcast to announce yet another new career that they were about to launch: faith healing. Previously Fanny had been asked about her belief in faith healers when she appeared on the *Parkinson* chat show, hosted by the popular Michael Parkinson, in 1972 but was somewhat reticent to discuss it at that time.

Michael Parkinson had asked Fanny about her psychic abilities in a roundabout way, and she talked freely about knowing that her first husband, Sidney, would be killed at a young age, leaving her with her son, Peter. She said that she and Sidney had talked about it as a sort of premonition; however, it was still a shock when 'I heard on the Wednesday that I was going to have a baby and he died on the Friday.' Michael followed up the conversation by asking about her interest in faith healing, as she 'admitted' that she had been interested in it. Fanny tensed up on screen, merely saying that 'it has been achieved' before elaborating that she had received and experienced faith healing for a 'serious illness' before stuttering out the single word, 'cancer'. Michael asked if she had been cured; Fanny replied, 'Yes, and my doctors will confirm it...' before declaring the subject not suitable for 'chatsies' and asking the host to move the conversation on.

The cancer that Fanny referred to was bowel cancer, which she had been diagnosed with in 1966 and which she had spent the intervening years denying or covering up with various fabricated stories. Even at the time, she was not keen for the real story to be told. She had been due to record some talks for BBC *Woman's Hour* to coincide with the publication of the booklet *Come For a Meal.* Fanny cancelled, rearranged and cancelled the recordings so often around this time that irritation at the BBC was high. Fanny had until then not given a reason for her apparent unprofessionalism. In early 1967, Fanny's then secretary, Shirley Trigg, wrote to the BBC to give full details of Fanny's condition, supported by doctors' notes.

Rumours were flying round the press about Fanny's condition, many of them seemingly fuelled by Fanny herself; and the BBC were rightly concerned at the possibility that she was attempting to cover something up. A similarly high-profile press story had circulated following their boating accident in Cannes, France, in which the Cradocks' three-thousand-pound cabin cruiser, the four-berth Francoise II, had allegedly blown up, resulting in Fanny being badly burnt and subsequently having to take a rest from planned work. Fanny planned to sue the boat's builders, the Bletchley Boat Company, for upwards of ten thousand pounds in 'special damages to include lost contracts for film, television, commercials and demonstrations'. The company would deny negligence.

The BBC seemed to think she was trying to wriggle out of a commitment, and the truth seemed to genuinely affect them. The 'official' press release, put out by Fanny herself, let the public know that Fanny had had an operation to remove a sinus[24] which had been lying over the base of her spine. The press release, without any hint of irony, details Johnnie's attempts to keep the (untrue) story, and particularly the details of the operation, out of the press so as to avoid any further upset to Fanny, and so not revealing the true story. Attributed to her 'typical femininity', Fanny had reportedly said, 'It's disgustingly unattractive to have lumps dug out of one's behind and I had hoped to keep it a secret.' Instead, the release gave details of

[24] A medical term for an infected tract leading from a deep-seated infection, not to be confused with the more familiar definition referring to the cavities in the bones of the skull.

potential hazards that may have resulted from the operation – damage to the spinal nerve causing paralysis; possible incontinence as the 'sinus' had been close to the bladder; the possibility of a growth being discovered – but that 'mercifully' none of these hazards had occurred. Fanny, it said, had made a 'record recovery' and would be heading abroad to recuperate before returning to record more television programmes.

Shirley Trigg wrote that she and other Cradock staff were under strict instructions to shield Fanny from any potential stress and strain that work may cause, until she had been given the 'green light' to return. Fanny being Fanny, however, had sought special dispensation to work on a few special television programmes, with a nurse in attendance, on her return from Morocco. Shirley thanked all at the BBC for being so understanding of the current situation. The BBC had no option but to cancel the contract for the *Woman's Hour* programme which had been previously issued to Fanny. Like all her contracts, it was for a single programme; and as she, despite their efforts to pause and rearrange, was unlikely to be able to make it at all, the programme would go ahead without her. And without payment.

Peter Botterill, working at that time at Langton House in Shooters Hill as one of the trainees, recalls Fanny telling him of her upcoming cancer treatment. She claimed to feel that it had been caused by a nasty tumble outside the *Daily Telegraph* offices, which had ended up with her damaging her coccyx bone, just a few weeks before the cancer was diagnosed. She told Peter: 'One cannot sit back and die, you have to pull yourself up and get on with it.' Peter does recall that Fanny paid a visit to a faith healer, Ted Fricker, ahead of her appointments at hospital. Ted would later write a book, *God is My Witness*, about his 'gifts' and the celebrities he had helped, including film star Christopher Lee and pop singer Tom Jones, who had been cured of pre-performance laryngitis through laying on of hands.

On the day of the operation, Fanny continued to work until the very last minute; deadlines had to be met. Peter remembers Fanny seeming very positive and calm, which was unusual for her. Johnnie was worried, naturally, but remained supportive throughout. Following the operation, Fanny had to wear a colostomy bag, which must have been concerning for her. However, she told Peter that the surgeon had arranged for a smaller than usual bag to be made, which Fanny would be able to wear under her stage and television clothes, for which she was extremely grateful, allowing her to return to work more quickly as well as disguise the true nature of her operation.

Fanny made contact with her son, Christopher, following the operation, asking to see him and his wife, Jane, dramatically fearing that she could die. Peter recalls that Johnnie made the telephone call to Christopher. Jane remembers that they did visit, and once it was clear that she wasn't going to die, Fanny pushed them away again. The last thing Jane said to Fanny as they walked out of the house was a prophetic, 'One day, Fanny, you are going to be a very sad old lady.'

By 1975, it seemed she was willing to go public with the BBC Radio 4 feature *Will the Real Fanny Cradock Please Stand Up?* On the programme, Fanny attributed the faith healing to Johnnie's hands. 'Johnnie is a superb healer and has healed a lot of sick people,' she told the interviewer, opening up about their own work as faith healers publicly for the first time. Fanny said that she too had been helping Johnnie by diagnosing sickness in others. However, she still did not disclose the true nature of her cancer ordeal, hidden under piles of publicity for years, only now being discussed openly. Fanny said that her cancer had been of the cervix. 'I was given six months to live,' she said; 'I was healed.'

Discussing their proposed new career as faith healers, without any hesitation, Fanny expanded. 'At the moment we do not intend to do more than we already have on our plate until we have pulled out of television... I don't think that will be very long off now.'

In the interview, unusually, the Cradocks freely admitted to be living in County Cork in Ireland, where they had cooked up the idea of a new career in faith healing. Johnnie explained, 'Our work is merely a laying on of hands. We get help from higher beings of higher intelligence. We do not do the healing. We are merely the instruments – like a machine that transmits the power. I merely put somebody on the couch and I almost have other people standing around me to give me some extra power. Having discovered what we think is wrong with them we then proceed to work on the appropriate parts of the body.' Johnnie concluded that: 'There again we say that we are guided. We try to make our minds more or less of a blank and we do as we are told.'

Fanny had been linked to spirituality in the press throughout her career, often making the linkages herself as in the case of press releases stating that she had dictated entire novels from those in the afterlife. The year before the interview about faith healing, an article appeared in the *Sunday People* about famous people, including disc jockeys Noel Edmonds and Pete Murray, who had seen ghosts, as part of a series exploring connections between stars and spirituality, which was popular at the time.

Fanny was also interviewed for the piece. Fanny told the interviewer that her first husband, Sidney, a fighter pilot, had materialised in their cottage two days following his death during the war. 'I saw him,' she said, 'from his toes to the top of his nose. Then I later found that the top of his head had been blown off. He spoke to me and I spoke to him. He told me that the baby I was carrying would be a boy and that I would one day be famous.' The interviewer noted that psychologists believed that people were particularly receptive to seeing ghostly spirits when they were in a highly emotional state, or when they were ill.

'She really was in tune with all that,' remembers her assistant Wendy Colvin. 'When I worked for her, I really wanted a child but could not get pregnant. Fanny said I should drink some of the "special punch" recipe she had, which she claimed Henry the Eighth had given his wife Catherine in her dotage. Anyway, she had the recipe from somewhere, but she would not give it to anyone. She was a bit like a witch. She gave me the punch, and sure enough I became pregnant. The night I went into hospital, she phoned to say, "You are going into hospital tonight, everything will be fine, and I will be the godmother." She was right.'

Wendy considered it further: 'We had a connection. I would know as soon as I arrived at her home what sort of mood she was in. It was in the ambience of the house, even before she would come down. Sometimes, I would do things that she had told me to do "mentally", not physically. Other people wondered how I knew what she wanted, but she had "asked" me, even though technically she had not. She did get into my mind a lot. There was something very spooky about her. That was real.'

Fanny returned to the topic of faith healing and her cancer in an interview with *Woman's Own* magazine in 1979. The resulting article, 'Faith Healing Cured Me', outlined how a doctor had described Fanny's cancer, which she still insisted had been cervical, to have been 'hopeless', confirming her 'worst fears' that it had taken hold of her. She told how she was determined not to give up, despite refusing conventional treatment. She claimed not to be able to afford the publicity that a hospital stay would attract. Instead, she visited a faith healer once a week, with regular top-ups from Johnnie at home. After six months, Fanny was given the all-clear by her astonished doctor.

The 'planned' career in faith healing never really seemed to take off following the flurry of publicity and broadcasts surrounding it; but it did cement in the popular imagination the power of Fanny and Johnnie as 'celebrities' who could count on their fame to earn a possible fortune, instead of seeing them 'just' as cookery experts. Fanny too, it would seem, was beginning to see the potential to remain in the public mind without the bother of weekly television programmes. An opportunity to be forever cast in the minds of almost everyone who can recall the name 'Fanny Cradock' was just around the corner, which would allow her to do just that, while at the same time continuing to work on her novels, tax-free.

Esther Rantzen was putting together a new show for the BBC which would feature ordinary people taking on extraordinary tasks, attempting to turn a 'hobby' into a 'profession' with the help of those already in *The Big Time*. It was decided that one edition of *The Big Time* would feature an amateur cook being given their dream job: to cook for a Foyles Literary Lunch, given for former Prime Minister Edward Heath at the Dorchester Hotel in London. That amateur cook was Gwen Troake, whom Esther had first met on the televised Cook of the Realm competition a few years earlier, with Fanny as a judge.

Esther remembered Fanny well, from that time but also as the resident cook on *Nationwide*. 'I remember walking through the studio and hearing her shouting at the researcher, who was actually the producer, and shouting at her student assistant; I was surprised. I hadn't heard such bullying going on. I couldn't understand why the director let her get away with it. There were limits to how bullying she could be to the researcher. It stuck in my mind; she was a very popular chef on television, the best-known cook in the land. So, when we decided to do the programme with Gwen Troake, who was so delightful – a farmer's wife from Devon with a voice like clotted cream, so lovely, so sweet – I immediately thought, well, the most celebrated cook in the land should be Fanny. We always tried to get the best for *The Big Time*. Fanny made a huge impression. She was clearly a dragon lady; viewers like a bit of danger on television, and Fanny was always a danger. I was not aware of how much…'

If Esther had an inkling of what was to transpire, Gwen was apparently not aware of what she was getting into. 'Fanny made some conditions,' remembers Esther. 'She would only do it if she got first-class fare to and from Ireland, and the best accommodation in London. She and I had a phone conversation prior to it; I explained Gwen's menu and thought she maybe needed a little help with the pudding. Fanny was renowned for spun sugar, she would spin it at the slightest opportunity, so she thought a little pastry yacht like *Morning Cloud* with spun sugar would be a graceful tribute.[25] She told me the ingredients, we bought them. Then the day dawned…'

On the day of filming, the scene was set for Fanny to introduce a more suitable idea for Gwen's banquet menu. 'We did not realise it was going to be solid gold,' Esther recalls. 'Every time a delectable dish arrived, Fanny would look at it and say it looked absolutely divine, before adding: "Of course, I could never eat anything like that myself…" The conversation was quite social, anyway, cheerful, until the crew wanted to know where to set up. So I said to Fanny, "Erm, well now, the camera crew is here, and we need to agree where to film you making the dessert?" Fanny said, "I will not touch the food; my minimum fee for a demonstration on *Nationwide* is two hundred guineas," which had not been part of the agreement for *The Big Time*. My face fell. So I said, "But I've bought all the ingredients…" She said, "Well, I will not touch the food." I asked if we could arrange it around her – set up the food around her. Thankfully, she agreed.'

Gwen herself was not present through any of this discussion. The scene was agreed: Fanny was going to taste Gwen's pudding and suggest an alternative. 'Fanny, sat next to Gwen, leant round to speak directly to the director to say, "Darling, no tighter than this," showing how loose she wanted the shot to be. No close-up. The director said nothing but bowed to her.'

As the scene played out, Fanny pretended not to know what a bramble was, and scoffed at every part of the menu Gwen had prepared. 'Every time Gwen suggested her menu, Fanny pretended to be sick,' Esther remembers. 'Every time Fanny pretended to be sick, the cameraman zoomed right in on her mouth. Everything Gwen said went down in such a bad way. My view was that Fanny had been so bad-tempered with us all that she thought she was being sweet and kindly, mentoring Gwen helpfully. She had no idea how patronising and bullying she sounded.'

The scene ended, and in due course Esther joined the film editor in the cutting room. 'We tried to edit it; we absolutely could not,' Esther laughed. 'It was like some great battle – Waterloo or Trafalgar – everything depended on what had just happened, the rage of the situation; so in the end we could

---

[25] *Morning Cloud* was the name of the yacht belonging to Edward Heath, a keen sailor.

not shorten it. So, we left it as it was. Then all hell broke out. The pages of the *Radio Times* became incandescent; the British public rose up. I had no idea this would happen. You could not have constructed the scene between Gwen and Fanny, and actually we didn't predict it.'

Reflecting on it over forty years later, Esther said, 'I have always felt rather guilty about it, because we made the programme as well as we could and, you know, I think it was a triumph for Gwen that the banquet should be successful. I had absolutely no intention of destroying Fanny's television career, and I suppose these days she would quickly hire a PR company who would blame us for exaggerating it, but we did not – all we did was film it! Fanny really made the show. What a double act!'

The Big Time was originally broadcast on Thursday the 11th of November 1976, at nine twenty-five in the evening. Newspapers that day mentioned the programme in their listings; *The Big Time* was recommended viewing each week, and although it was listed as 'Gwen Troake's Banquet', neither the *Daily Express* nor the *Daily Mail* made mention that Fanny Cradock would be appearing. The *Radio Times* in its own listing referred to Fanny alongside many other experts whom Gwen had always admired, who would guide her towards *The Big Time*. It seemed that no one, not least the BBC publicity department, was prepared for the impact the show would have.

In the days following the broadcast, newspapers did not comment upon or react to the programme with any significance. Most newspapers made no mention of it at all. The *Daily Mail* highlighted the Gwen Troake chapter of *The Big Time* as having 'made the artificial format worthwhile'. Gwen herself was singled out to be a seemingly nice person and a 'true poetess of the carbohydrates'. The reviewer recognised Fanny's horrified reaction to Gwen's menu choices; however, the story was reported very matter-of-factly.

In the following weeks, newspapers were full of supposed scandals which had been seen on television. A young Pauline Quirke began her own television show, broadcast on ITV from December 1976, called *Pauline's Quirks*, which drew gasps from audiences, according to the press reports, who spotted a poster on her bedroom wall with the words 'Get 'Em Off' written on it. This was deemed to be shocking and gained a fair bit of negative press coverage. On the 1st of December 1976 the punk band the Sex Pistols famously swore on live television during an interview with Bill Grundy, which ended his career and ensured their notoriety. The newspapers at the time were full of reports of this scandalous story. Fanny pulling a face at the thought of Gwen Troake's pudding was not, at least initially, added to the list of shocking moments to be broadcast in those weeks.

Early in December 1976, a few weeks after the show had been broadcast, the *Radio Times* printed some letters from viewers who were unhappy at the way that Fanny had addressed Gwen Troake on screen. Seven letters were published, but later reports claimed that hundreds had been written, under headings such as 'Oh Fanny, How Could You?' and 'Apologise, Mrs Cradock!' Viewers seemed upset to see Fanny, who they admitted had been asked for her honest opinion, displaying arrogance and bad manners towards Gwen Troake. One viewer called for Gwen Troake's coffee pudding to be tipped over Fanny's head.

Fanny was given right of reply in the *Radio Times*, and had this to say:

> I was horrified to hear that viewers found me condescending, and if I gave the impression, I must apologise most sincerely. To be truthful, I was genuinely astonished that the programme compilers showed someone who seemed to have no concept of making a menu and whose palate was so extraordinary that she seemed incapable of appreciating how sorry a combination of her rich duck dish and the subsequent very sickly pudding would be.
>
> If my inward bewilderment registered as condescension, I am very cross with myself. What I was feeling was pity for an obviously very nice person who was clearly out of her depth, and also how unfair it was for her to be catapulted into the world of professional cookery; but condescending, no.
>
> I have always tried very hard to make my cookery television appearances as close to sharing things with my friends in my kitchen as I could. Will you please convey my chagrin to the viewers who have always been so kind and generous to me.

The *Radio Times* printed Fanny's letter alongside Gwen's recipe for the coffee cream pudding.

A fortnight later the *Daily Express* published a story, written by William Hickey under the headline 'Why Gwen is throwing the book at Fanny', in which Esther Rantzen tells of the 'considerable bad feeling' that had been aroused at the BBC following *The Big Time* episode featuring Gwen and Fanny. The report suggested that Fanny had been paid one hundred pounds to 'supervise' the episode, which had left viewers unhappy. The apology letter, labelled an 'unfeeling jibe', the report said, had made matters worse instead of better. The report quoted Gwen Troake as saying, 'My personal opinion is that she (Cradock) wanted to steal the show and get her own menu on to it.'

The Big Time episode 'Gwen Troake's Banquet' was repeated on BBC1 the following year, again in a prime-time slot of nine twenty-five in the evening. The show was highlighted in the *Daily Express* as 'Tonight's Choice' for viewing, saying that it deserved to be renamed 'The Battle of the Coffee Cream Pud' and should not be missed. It recounted for viewers that the episode featured Gwen, a Devon farmer's wife, who dreamed of catering for a banquet in a large hotel, and that Esther Rantzen had granted her wish. It went on to outline that Fanny had quashed her dream, making withering comments about her pudding and in return revealing more about herself in the process. 'What Mrs Cradock reveals about herself is much more delicious to savour than any of her recipes could ever be.'

The *Daily Express* recommended viewers to watch the programme, possibly again, as Gwen sat calmly listening to Fanny's horror and childish manners, which had originally entertained millions of viewers. Viewers gasped as Fanny told Gwen, 'You could kill pigs with that menu. Do you have any friends in Devon, dear? Living?' She said that the coffee cream dessert was 'too sickly', adding: 'Think of the poor stomach.' Gwen, the paper said, had won the admiration of people all over the nation, and had spent the intervening year collecting together her own recipes for publication in a book which was 'out now!'

Published in 1977 by Macdonald and Jane's (previously publishers of *The Hardy Boys* series of books among others, and now owned by Time Warner) as *Gwen Troake's Country Cookbook*, the book compiled many recipes which Gwen had already published in magazines such as *Woman's Realm* and *Woman* as well as on wrappers of Wonderbread. Esther Rantzen supplied a glowing foreword detailing their history together from the Cook of the Realm in 1972, ending in the 'explosive confrontation' with Fanny in *The Big Time*. Esther insisted that the real star of the show was of course Gwen and her recipes, all of which were featured in the book, including three now reinstated for '*The Big Time* Menu for a Foyles Literary Lunch at the Dorchester': Seafood Admiral, followed by Roast Duckling with Bramble Sauce; ending with a Coffee Cream Pudding – which Gwen herself noted was a lovely creamy pudding that Mr Heath did not get, but her family and friends loved, especially with fruit, fresh or tinned. The book is filled with 'family favourites' from Devon, loved by her husband Dudley and daughters Teresa and Janet, winning recipes from the Cook of the Realm competition and even one Gwen had included in a sandwich competition, which she of course won.

Gwen Troake sadly died not long after the cookbook was published, but it would not be the last time her family would hit the headlines in Britain. Gwen's granddaughter, Jo Yeates, daughter of Teresa, a landscape architect from Hampshire, went missing following a night out in Bristol with friends in December 2010. The case gathered a great deal of publicity at the time, and intensive police enquiry. Sadly, her strangled body was discovered on Christmas Day that year, launching a murder investigation. Initially, her landlord, Christopher Jefferies, was the number one suspect, but he was later released without charge. Several British newspapers were found guilty of printing details of the case which could have prejudiced the trial, leading to a successful libel action by Mr Jefferies. The horrific case captured the public attention for several months to come before Vincent Tabak, a Dutch engineer, was found guilty of the murder.

In more recent years, especially following her own death, the 'Gwen Troake incident' has often been described as bringing about the end of Fanny's television career, with claims that the BBC were horrified by her behaviour and cancelled her contract. Like much of the furore surrounding *The Big Time*, it appears that this may have been merely fluff and fodder for the publicity machine. Fanny never held a contract with the BBC for longer than any particular show or appearance. Contracts in her BBC file were occasionally marked as 'cancelled' if, for example, the shooting of a piece to camera for the *Nationwide* programme needed to be rescheduled or if, like her appearance on *Woman's Hour* to discuss the *Come For a Meal* booklet, it had to be abandoned altogether. These cancellation notices were simply indications to the accounts department at the BBC not to process a particular payment. There was, and had never been, an overall contract to cancel.

Fanny had spent most of the 1970s attempting to cut herself free from the shackles, as she saw them, of appearing regularly on television. She attempted to replace it with acts of notoriety and celebrity which instead would bring her more lucrative, and less intensive, work opportunities. Perhaps she herself was pleased ultimately with the reaction garnered from *The Big Time* appearance, which ensured at least that she would be forever remembered, featured on clip-shows in the future and lampooned generally for her rudeness, harsh personality and thoughtlessness towards poor Gwen Troake.

Fanny really did not make many more appearances on television during the seventies, except for the occasional slot on game shows such as *Those Wonderful TV Times* on ITV, hosted by Norman Vaughan. The show delved into the archives of ITV's history, asking two panels of guests, including Joan Bakewell, Alan Freeman, Shirley Anne Field and David Jacobs, alongside Fanny, some very difficult questions about the clips they viewed. Fanny can be seen cheerfully, and not very subtly, reading notes on her lap as she answers everything correctly. Perhaps those rumours which dogged her on *Celebrity Squares* and other game shows were true after all.

Regardless, the plans that Fanny made throughout the seventies to 'retire' from the screen and to focus on an equally lucrative career writing and generally being a 'celebrity' for hire appeared to have worked. For now.

Return to the Screen

Fanny and Johnnie had an eventful few years in the late seventies, off the screens and away (mostly) from the headlines. Spotting what she thought was the death notice for her second husband, Arthur (the third, Greg Holden-Dye, had died in 1974), in a newspaper in 1977, Fanny assumed that she was at last free to legally marry Johnnie. A low-key ceremony was arranged at Guildford registry office for the 7th of May 1977, with only a few specially selected invitees to witness the occasion.

The marriage certificate was as much a work of fiction as any of Fanny's novels. Fanny gave the name Phyllis Chapman and her age to be fifty-five, shaving a full thirteen years from the truth. Fanny was recorded as a widow, which she believed to be true, and living in Chiddingford, Surrey, although both she and Johnnie were still in Doneraile, Ireland at the time. She gave no profession. Fanny's father is given the name Arthur Pechey, an approximation of reality, and is at least listed truthfully as an author and deceased. Johnnie is recorded as being a retired major (he had been retired from the Territorial Army Reserve Officers for Royal Artillery in 1954, with permission granted to retain the title of Major), ten years older than Fanny at sixty-five. In just two weeks following the wedding he would actually be seventy-three. He too provided a false address, in the London Borough of Beckenham, where indeed he had once lived.

The marriage must have been a strange event, for everyone. Fanny and Johnnie had been living together as a supposedly married couple for almost forty years and would certainly be recognisable to the registrars conducting the ceremony and signing the legal documents. The marriage was witnessed by Fanny's assistant, Alison Leach, and Johnnie's sister Dorothy, who was apparently 'totally mystified' by the whole affair. However, possibly the most bizarre twist was yet to come. The death notice that Johnnie had read in *The Times* actually related to a very different Arthur Chapman. Fanny was now in the position of having committed bigamy for the second time, the Arthur Chapman whom she married in 1928 being very much still alive.

The truth was 'exposed' in the *Daily Express* a couple of years later, by which time Arthur had actually died, so there was no retribution to be sought. Fanny and Johnnie were married, legally, and morally, finally.

Life in Ireland had not gone according to plan either. Barely welcomed into the level of society that they had expected to be, and following an alleged death threat by IRA sympathisers involving 'You're next' being daubed on their front door, Fanny and Johnnie reluctantly moved on. The Channel Island of Guernsey was to become home for the next six years or so.

With a population of around fifty thousand at the time, the small island was not a place to live incognito. Guernsey restricted who could reside on the island, assessed through wealth. However, it did offer the relatively low rate of twenty per cent income tax, which appealed to Fanny. The prospect of living tax-free in Ireland had not become the reality that Fanny had expected; she was stung by the Inland Revenue while in England hosting a launch party for a book. Settling in the southern province of St Martin in Guernsey, they at least were able to make it some kind of home in the sun.

Fanny gave an interview to *Punch* magazine, the weekly publication famous for its humour and satire, shortly after the exhaustive move. Fanny claimed that many of their valuable items and pieces of furniture had been damaged beyond repair during transit. Alabaster tables had been 'smashed to smithereens' seemingly by the removal company carelessly stacking two stone pineapples on top. Historical antiquities had been 'crushed to powder'. All of Johnnie's silk shirts, which he needed to wear when in London, had disappeared. Indeed, Fanny was still compiling a final inventory of the damaged and missing items at the time of the interview, presumably for a hefty insurance claim.

Fanny relayed information about Johnnie's health, which wasn't great. Like many other eighty-year-olds he had suffered incredible pain in his hips, requiring an operation. He was walking again, but only with the aid of a stick. He spent most of his time seated, which Fanny thought would not be at all suitable for any appearances on television. Johnnie's sight had gone completely in the eye that had been affected by iritis, but he was not in any pain as a result. Fanny told the interviewer that he had been cured of all pain by a faith healer.

Fanny felt the lifestyle in Guernsey would be of benefit to them both, despite the twenty per cent taxation, living life as they had 'in a sandstorm' for the past six months. She was sure that the sun would recharge her, telling the interviewer that both she and Johnnie loved nothing more than to bask in its rays, lying almost motionless on the south-facing terrace (the garden was yet to be tamed), which was so unlike Fanny's normal life, only venturing indoors now and again to fill their glasses.

Although they remained in Guernsey for six years, most of their time spent there was uneventful. Michael Leale, the photographer from the early seventies partwork, who hailed from Guernsey himself, remembers that neither Fanny nor Johnnie did much to find favour with the locals. 'She upset the natives no end by being Fanny. She'd go into the Post Office and see a queue, where she was expected to stand at the back. She would say, loudly, "Don't you know who I am?", all that sort of thing. That did not go down well in Guernsey; they are rather blunt over there.'

Fanny was also infamous for her poor driving abilities. However, she continued to get behind the wheel on an island where speeding was neither tolerated nor required. Fanny was fined five pounds not long after they arrived on Guernsey for failing to give way. She insisted that the driver of the car that she collided with was going at 'maniacal speed', refusing to accept photographic proof of the incident claiming that 'the camera can lie easily'.

With the end of the self-imposed 'ten-year break' from television, Fanny's mind was beginning to whirr back into action, just as the bank balances began to finally dwindle. Fully aware that not only was she now older, but also that television had changed so much in the intervening years, especially cooking on television, she knew that she had to come up with a new concept to excite the executives. The answer appeared to be her own legacy. Surely as the premier television cook 'back in the day', with all her experience, television companies would be foolish to ignore her, never mind not commission her programmes?

With the audience perception following *The Big Time* adventure, Fanny realised, at least to some extent, that re-establishing that legacy would require an uphill struggle. It was one that she was prepared to work for. In 1981, Fanny and Johnnie published a bizarre book of reminiscences, a not-quite-follow-up to their autobiography but almost heading in that direction. *Time to Remember*, subtitled *A Cook for All Seasons*, was published by Webb & Bower in association with the *Daily Telegraph*. As a publisher, Webb & Bower specialised in collaborations, releasing titles ranging from those which focused on 'Edwardian Ladies' to books about modern-day royalty in association with Debrett's, themselves a publisher specialising in etiquette and behaviour.

The book promised to give 'behind-the-scenes glimpses into the kitchens, both the famous and the not so famous, as the couple remember their colourful and exotic lives and indulge in shameless name-dropping and mouth-watering descriptions of the many meals they have cooked and eaten'. Readers would be disappointed as they turned the pages to read, or try to read, the rambling chapters divided into each month of the calendar, without much (or any) reference to that month in the narrative. The book dripped with hidden, and confused, detail, and certainly delivered on the promise of name-dropping. However, most of the names would not be familiar to anyone reading, being mostly acquaintances from various trips across Europe during their heyday.

The book is written collectively, but it is never too clear who was writing. Whereas previous books, even if credited to both Fanny and Johnnie, were clearly written by Fanny and in the first person, this volume is from the perspective of 'we'. Both Fanny and Johnnie are mentioned throughout in the third person, making the narrative even more confusing to follow. Each chapter is littered with elaborate recipes and menus, meals that they shared or created as they travelled through life. It is difficult not to read each monthly instalment as a work of part fact, part fiction, with some truths woven into the fantasies of idyllic family life. Fanny even claims to have been born on the Channel Islands, perhaps only to ensure that her residence in Guernsey was not threatened.

During the 'September' chapter, Fanny mentions a family punch which was a brew that she claimed an alleged ancestor, Catherine Parr, had given to Henry VIII in his dotage, with remarkable results. Fanny said that in her family, the punch was known as 'nine months to the day', so potent was it in ensuring a pregnancy. Sadly, a recipe for the less aphrodisiacal-sounding 'Mum's Very Un-Cornish Pasty' is given instead.

Time to Remember did not, surprisingly, fly high in the bestseller list. Undaunted, Fanny continued to work on an idea that she hoped would re-establish her in the dual realm of television and cookbook sales. She developed a format for a television series which, although it sounded bizarre, was also ahead of its time. *My Aunt Fanny*, as the title suggested, would feature Fanny in various kitchens with a young relative who was struggling to learn to cook alone. The helpful figure of Aunt Fanny, who of course would be Fanny herself, would teach and demonstrate the fine art of cuisine from the basics up. It had always been Fanny's belief that simply presenting a cookery show 'straight', without an angle, a hook, made it simply like a demonstration by the Women's Institute: suitable for the small-scale local venue, but not dazzling on screen as television cookery needed to be.

Fanny planned a four-part cookbook to accompany the series, which gave an outline of her plans for individual episodes. Part One would feature recipes on *Cooking for One* in recognition of Britain's changing society in the eighties. The second volume would expand on the basics learnt in Part One, developing and extending the themes and recipes. Fanny was keen to ensure that the keynote would be 'simplicity, economy, lack of fuss and above all, nothing piss-elegant'. The third instalment would focus on *The Family Cook*, with Fanny cooking up meals for all kinds of 'families' including babies, children, 'the occasional old person', long journeys, holidays abroad (presumably self-catering) and parties. The very final volume of the book, and the concluding episodes of the television series, would be elevated to a 'grander level' for *The Ambitious Cook and Hostess*. In an attempt to update her tried and tested theme, Fanny gave an example. She would support a wife whose husband was an MP who had a flat in London, which he would require to be at through the working week. Naturally, the flat would have its own deep-freeze, allowing the wife to prepare 'ambitious' meals in advance, ready for him to defrost and heat after a hard day at the House of Commons.

Fanny's attempt to update what she had been essentially doing on screen for years did not provoke the reaction that she had hoped for among television producers and commissioners. Undeterred, Fanny continued to compile the books, which would assemble almost her entire repertoire of recipes, again, and include some new ideas and twists, to be published by WH Allen, as a series of three books under the collective banner of *A Lifetime in the Kitchen* in 1985.

To promote the books, Fanny accepted an invitation to cook, and be interviewed, on the ITV breakfast television programme TV-am, presented by Anne Diamond and Nick Owen. TV-am had had a rocky start a few years earlier, troubled by changes in management and presenters, and dogged by major financial cutbacks hampering its operations. By 1985 things had begun to calm down a little. The format of the show was a mixture of news, current affairs, 'showbiz', health and fitness, and cookery. Not only had television changed in the 'missing' ten years of Fanny's self-imposed exile, but in particular television cooking had.

TV-am had regular cookery slots, and additionally invited in guest presenters to cover holidays, for special occasions or any gaps, sometimes just for fun. John Eley, an English Anglican priest known professionally as the Cooking Canon, was the first regular cooking expert to appear as part of the programme, making a switch from rival channel BBC, where he had appeared as a chef on *Pebble Mill at One*. The Cooking Canon was replaced by Rustie Lee, who joined the show as the in-house cook as a fresh face to the screen, famous for her hearty laugh and love of Caribbean cooking. She rapidly became incredibly popular both as a presenter and as a personality, chuckling her way through each food segment, often accompanied by celebrity guests such as comedian Les Dawson and actor Kenneth Williams.

Fanny was joined in the TV-am kitchen by regular host Nick Owen, who interviewed her while she cooked. This was not something Fanny had been accustomed to; normally she would talk directly to the audience through the camera lens. Other people in the kitchen set-up were generally there to support Fanny as assistants, to fetch and carry, to clear up. This was a new environment for her, pushing her out of her comfort zone a little, and it showed.

Fanny appeared heavily made-up, and remarkably fresh-faced, dressed in a massive cream blouse with wide shoulder pads and matching skirt, set off with strings of pearls of various sizes. Her hair was lighter and blonder than it had been in the seventies. Copper pans and cabbage-leaf dishes sat on the worktop around her, suggesting her retro-ness and history. She didn't miss a beat, however, when Nick asked her what she was going to cook, ever thinking of promotion, telling him: 'Something from the new book, the one I haven't written yet…' as she pointed to a shelf, which presumably contained the newly published *A Lifetime in the Kitchen*, explaining that the three volumes only constituted one book.

She insisted on talking while she worked, so began by showing a packet of Greek filo pastry (which had allegedly been in her freezer for six months) to the 'frustrated housewives' out there who may not have heard about it before, and certainly could not make it for themselves. She likened it to millefeuille, wafer-thin and normally layered up with confectioner's custard. Her recipe would only take seven minutes, she boasted, as she pushed sheets of filo into a flan dish, before adding banana slices (which had been sitting in a bowl, doused with lemon juice), strangely using a cake slice to transfer them from bowl to dish.

Becoming frustrated with the inefficiency of the cake slice, Fanny accelerated the proceedings by grabbing handfuls of banana, plonking them into the dish and covering them with soft brown sugar. 'I've gone right off using white sugar whenever I can possibly avoid it,' she informed Nick. She topped the flan with a large pile of dry, screwed-up filo: 'You can hear it crinkling!' Nick looked on, bewildered. Fanny gave the oven temperature in both gas and electric measurements, before adding, typically on-brand, '... but I don't use electricity and I hate it!' Fanny brushed on melted butter (which Nick had to prompt her to identify), and looked around in a mild panic before sprinkling more sugar on top. She said the finished dish could be served with cream either as a pudding or a cake.

Nick, still seeming uncertain of what to say, remarked, 'Very sweet, I should think, isn't it...?' Fanny raised her head and looked daggers at him, declaring 'No!' and telling him she has used the juice of two lemons with the bananas. 'For balance?' suggested Nick helpfully, but an increasingly flustered Fanny said, 'No, to keep them from turning colour!' She then went on to describe how she was putting together a new little book, for after 'this huge one', describing all the techniques that housewives thought impossible and proving that they could in fact do them.

It is clear that Fanny had rehearsed her lines very carefully, but was beginning to stumble over them, confusing sections of the recipe and planned connections to highlight. She appeared to have some difficulty walking towards the (electric) oven to put the finished flan in, having recently undergone an operation on her hip, and removing the cooked one, clearly made entirely differently from the dish she had just demonstrated. 'It's gone red?!' Nick exclaimed in astonishment, before Fanny explained she had made this one the previous July, with raspberries she had frozen. She flinched upon accidentally touching the hot dish, but continued regardless to cover it thickly in icing sugar, which Nick had apparently never seen in his life. 'It is now ready to eat!' Fanny pronounced. Nick looked not at all convinced. The audience at home could almost be heard declaring their confusion.

Nick remembers the day very vividly, perhaps for all the wrong reasons. Following the cookery slot, Fanny joined fellow guest Pamela Stephenson, the actress and comedian famous for her appearances on *Not The Nine O'Clock News* in the UK and *Saturday Night Live* in America, who later became a psychologist and wife of Billy Connolly, on the sofa for what was planned to be a cosy chat to end the programme.

Pamela Stephenson had campaigned in the past against the use of food colourings and other additives in food especially targeted towards children. However, it was not Fanny's excessive use of blue and green hues in her cooking which tipped Pamela over the edge that day. Perhaps it was the prospect of publicity; and she seized the opportunity, leaving Fanny stunned into silence, no doubt reflecting just how much television, and life, had changed. While eating some of Fanny's filo flan, Pamela decided to take the opportunity to ambush Nick, attempting to rub some of the pudding into his hair, to distract him while trying to tear his trousers off.

'That day, Fanny was looking horrified at what happened,' Nick recalls. 'I got a lovely letter from her afterwards; she was horrified about what had gone on. It was difficult for me personally: I had had a back operation the week before and I could hardly move, and as soon as I rang my specialist, she had seen the headlines in the tabloids – me being assaulted by Pamela Stephenson – so I was back in hospital for more work. My main memory was that Fanny was on the sofa with Pamela Stephenson that day. Fanny was open-mouthed. She wrote me a letter to apologise; it was very sweet of her. She was nice to others in the industry, I found. I never met Johnnie, I don't think; he wasn't there that day.'

Nick does not really remember much about the cookery slot with Fanny. 'Food was not really my forte then. My role was just to say, "Mmm, that is nice," or throw in an occasional line. I sort of remember her glory days; I did not know her outside of the interview. She was a lot older than me; I was about thirty-five and she was about seventy-five then. She hoped it would be a resurgence of her television career, appearing on TV-am, but she had a reputation of being difficult to work with; but I found her fine. I approached her with some trepidation, I enjoyed interviewing her. She was spikey – she knew what she wanted to say, very forthright.'

Fanny never returned to TV-am to cook, or indeed to any other television studio, again. Instead of an opportunity to reintroduce herself to a new audience of cooking fanatics – exploiting her legacy, continuing to showcase new products but this time with a twist of history and experience – this was to be the final time she would cook anything on television. It did make headlines, but for Pamela Stephenson. Not the blaze of glory she envisaged; not the beginning of a new series linked to *A Lifetime in the Kitchen*; not the start of a new concept in cooking, *Aunt Fanny*. Instead a confusing, sad and unsatisfactory end to a cooking career that had begun on television thirty years previously. Not the legacy Fanny had in mind.

Fanny and Johnnie had left Guernsey behind and moved back to England to begin their re-entry into the 'cooking classes' their legacy would surely afford them, settling into a charming salmon-pink four-bedroom detached period property dating from the mid-eighteenth century, Orchard House, in Little Bentley near to Colchester in Essex. It was extremely private, with no immediate neighbours, had only a small kitchen but ample entertaining space, should they have required it, and a manageable garden.

The new home soon became a 'pigsty' according to Fanny, with many of the boxes shipped over from Guernsey remaining exactly where the removal men had left them. The same removal men had packed things ready for the move, so Fanny and Johnnie really had no idea where anything was to be found, never mind the ability or motivation to do anything about it. Fanny complained that 'dailies seem as rare as gold dust here too' which only compounded the mess and disorganisation. However, Fanny and Johnnie seemed happy in their new home, saying to friends, 'By comparison with bloody Guernsey it's heaven now.'

Colchester was within easy reach of London, so Fanny and Johnnie expected to be travelling into the city regularly for television appearances, book signings, celebrity parties and the other fabulous invitations that would come their way. In the event, they were few and far between.

Then the phone did ring. It was an eager young researcher keen to make her mark in a new role at the BBC, researching and booking guests for the *Wogan* chat show. Presented by popular host Terry Wogan, originally from Ireland but who worked for the BBC for the majority of his career, the show was broadcast live from BBC Television Centre in Shepherd's Bush in London. In 1986, the show was at the height of a popular and sustained run which ended in 1992.

Diana Henry, now an award-winning food writer, remembers her first encounter with Fanny. 'I had just started as a researcher on the *Wogan* show, and it was my very first job. She was at the top of the list I had given in when I went for my interview there, and they thought, yeah, whatever happened to Fanny Cradock, that would be great. So, we got hold of her and it was all kind of fine, she wanted to meet and everything. I do not think at that time she was getting much attention. She had disappeared for a long time. I do not really think she liked that. She asked me to come and meet her and Johnnie for lunch, somewhere near Colchester.'

By the time Diana arrived at the agreed time of two o'clock, Fanny and Johnnie had already had their lunch. 'They did that starry thing of eating, then I would arrive and pay the bill. I wouldn't do it.' Diana was defiant, although this left her in the tricky position of having to win Fanny round. 'It was really uncomfortable. It was my first interview and my first proper job. So, it was difficult, but you know how you kind of have to work with people to pull them round – I eventually did. She was one of the most difficult people I ever had to interview, and she was also the first.'

Diana had previously been a bit of a fan, but was shocked by the person she met that day. 'Their car was covered in dog hair. It was awful. That was the thing about Fanny, unfortunately: everything was on the surface – underneath they really were not so great at all. She was really awful to Johnnie; she did treat him really badly. I said to her, what was Johnnie's role? Was he a sidekick, or worse? She treated him like old boots. She replied, "I do not. You will have to take that back." Fanny was friends with Barbara Cartland, but she was horrible about her. Fanny did not have a good word to say about anyone. But the more you asked her about herself – I would not say she began to defrost, but she became slightly easier to deal with. She worked from a position of hostility and anger as far as I could see. I mean, I was tense the whole time. When I got back on the train, I was relieved. She was not what I expected at all.'

Fanny made a list of demands before she would agree to appear on the *Wogan* show. 'She was totally all about attention and money,' Diana recalls, 'how much she could get, and about her own appearance. When she eventually came on *Wogan* then, she had to have better treatment than other people. She was one of those people. She had to have her hair done in Harrods – only Harrods would do. So, she had it done at the salon. We had her picked up. She did not want her make-up done by the make-up girls.

When she arrived, she had so much make-up on; her make-up was really thick and dense – it was extreme, over the top, she looked like a doll. The make-up was so bad it was already on her clothes. I was worried that on screen it would be obvious.'

Fanny also insisted that she would cook something for Terry; being Fanny Cradock, she could not come along without bringing anything to eat. 'We did not know how to put what she had made on the set because it was awful. It was a raspberry tart, but she had not used any pastry, she used filo. A round of filo sort of folded over at the edges, and she had put raspberries in that. They were old and tired, leeching everywhere. I had to go out and get more raspberries. We thought we would stick with the tart case because we could not do much about that: she would have noticed if we had changed it. We put many more raspberries on it than she had, put a little dusting of icing sugar on it and make it look as good as possible.'

The disguise seemed to work. 'I was excited to meet her, but she was not what you expected a cook to be: she was not giving, she was not kind, she was not any of those things. Perhaps she was insecure. Sometimes you warm to people after a while; you did not with her. She was difficult from beginning to end.'

Fanny seemed to love being back in the limelight. She wore a bright blue and white outfit, her hair blonder than it had been. In between questions from Terry, Fanny turned to the audience for approval and reassurance, ultimately looking very pleased with herself to 'be back' on television. Diana recalls, 'She was lovely to Terry, that was different. She was terribly grand, and very kind of giving commands to everyone else, all the floor managers, that kind of thing. There were two sides to her. She built up to the performance.'

While the interview was happening, Diana and the rest of the production crew watched from the green room. 'I was thinking, "This is good for me!" so I have to acknowledge that. I thought maybe I had got her at the wrong time of her life, that she would make herself look dreadful, but she was not that stupid. So, she was able to pull it off. She did a very good interview. She was not an easy guest at all. I will never forget that first interview.'

Fanny hoped that the appearance would stimulate a return to television for her. Diana was not convinced. 'She was too much of a horror to make a comeback, she was too bad, it would not have been tolerated. It was obvious you could not work with her; maybe that was the reason no one made a series with her.'

Following the appearance on *Wogan*, Fanny returned home to Colchester hopeful that the offers would come flooding in. Instead, Johnnie's health deteriorated once again. He was this time diagnosed with lung cancer, at the age of eighty-two, a devasting blow for them both. His illness took hold, requiring an admission to Basingstoke General Hospital, in January of 1987, for several weeks. Fanny made excuse after excuse for not visiting, leaving Johnnie to assume that she had abandoned him there. Friends knew that Fanny did not like death and was frightened of illness, but the surgeon attending to Johnnie phoned Fanny warning that, if she did not visit, she may never see her husband alive again. Fanny eventually turned up, very briefly, in a wheelchair that she did not require, causing a scene and generally antagonising everyone.

Fanny did not appear to be handling the news at all well; her behaviour was becoming more and more bizarre and difficult to predict. Out of the blue, she called her literary agent to let her know, incorrectly, that Johnnie had died. During Johnnie's hospitalisation, Fanny often stayed with friends, rather than returning alone to the isolated house in Colchester, whether she was visiting Johnnie or not. On two separate occasions the home in Little Bentley was raided by thieves who reportedly emptied the place of anything that seemed valuable. With most of their possessions still packed in boxes, and the house left unattended for long periods, this would have been an easy target.

Following a police chase, some of the stolen property was recovered, found abandoned in an estate car. Some items, which Fanny and Johnnie had collected over their lifetime of travel, were never to be seen again. A young local antique dealer, Peter Head, who was just twenty-five at the time, and his pregnant girlfriend, Amanda Graham, a few years younger, were arrested following the discovery of the stolen items in their abandoned car. Their home was searched and several larger items, including a Chinese chest, a table and some silver candlesticks, were recovered.

At the trial, Mr Head claimed to have bought the items from a local market trader for two hundred and seventy-five pounds, although the entire contents of the house, which had all been taken, were valued at fifty thousand pounds. Fanny provided an inventory of missing items, which included her mink coats, a one-hundred-piece set of Crown Derby tableware engraved with Bon Viveur initials, clocks, and Georgian saucepans, many of which were never to be seen again. Fanny arrived at the trial at Chelmsford

Crown Court to give evidence by chauffeur-driven car, clashing with court officials as she tried to take her dog, Mia, into the proceedings. She told of her trauma resulting from the raids, compounded, she said, by her constant vigil at the bedside of her dying husband.

The antique dealer was eventually acquitted of the two burglaries, cleared outright of the first burglary and found not guilty of the second. However, he was found guilty of dishonestly handling items stolen in the raids, and was sentenced to two and a half years in jail. Fanny later received an insurance payout of eighty thousand pounds, but was not awarded any compensation for the ordeal.

Traumatised by the raids, Fanny rarely returned to Orchard House. However, the show must go on. Fanny was booked to appear on the short-lived *Pamela Armstrong* show on BBC Two: an afternoon magazine, broadcast live, which promised to 'entertain every weekday with thirty minutes of conversation, music and a look at the unexpected side of life'. The show had been running for a few months by the time Fanny was booked to appear at the Pebble Mill Studios in Birmingham on the 29th of January 1987. While Fanny waited for the show to begin, Pamela Armstrong walked on to the set to wish her luck, presumably hoping to put her at her ease ahead of the live broadcast. It had the opposite effect. Fanny, who had previously reacted badly to being addressed in an overfamiliar way by people she did not know, even if they themselves were television personalities, reportedly 'stormed off' the set, refusing to take her seat for the interview. Fanny left the studio, leaving a gaping hole in that day's schedule.

The next day, Johnnie died in Basingstoke General Hospital, reportedly with a half-drunk bottle of (doctor-approved) claret by his bed. The following day, Fanny appeared at the hospital and demanded that his large overcoat be returned to her, along with his signet ring. Staff were panicked in their search for the personal items, until it was discovered that Fanny had removed them on her previous, brief visit.

Fanny refused to attend Johnnie's funeral, held at Aldershot Crematorium, claiming that women in her family were always spared the pain. His death was barely marked in the press. Fanny was beginning to show increased signs of pain, after discovering that her expensive hip operation had failed, and would need to be repeated on the National Health Service. The thought filled Fanny with dread. She wrote to friends saying, 'The very thought of the lack of privacy, filthy food and curious people drowns me in misery.'

Fanny did keep all the cards that family, friends and well-wishers sent with flowers after reading Johnnie's death notice in the *Telegraph*. 'Ann' wrote that, 'You will never know how much I learnt from both of you during my time at the Dower House – both in the culinary sense and in a growing and getting ready for the world outside sense.' 'Yvonne', recalling their first television appearance together at the Royal Albert Hall, found words hard to write, but comforted Fanny with: 'Your life's companion – what an adjustment for you, and in a new environment into the bargain.' 'Joan' chose the following words of comfort: 'You know and I know that words don't matter; you know that I am thinking of you both a great deal of the day; and I know enough of you to know that life will adjust itself in whatever way you need it to.'

Alan Whicker, the British journalist, television presenter and broadcaster famous for his travel series *Whicker's World* on television, who was clearly a personal friend of the couple, wrote to Fanny to pass on his upset at hearing the news of Johnnie. 'He was a lovely man,' he wrote, 'and much appreciated his good fortune in sharing his life with you. You filled his life wonderfully. You are one of those dauntless women with such a force that not even this grievous blow will deflect you from living to the best of your ability and to others' enormous satisfaction.'

Fanny's own tribute to her husband was left on a simple card signed 'Jill', the name Johnnie called her in private. The brief message read, 'Not the extinguishing of the light, but the putting out of the lamp because the dawn has come.'

Fanny was the sole beneficiary of Johnnie's will in which he gave 'all my estate to my wife Phyllis Nan Sortain Cradock absolutely'. Fanny would receive a widow's pension; and also, unfortunately, inherit some income tax liabilities which had remained unpaid from 1984. The slight increase in her pension would not cover the much greater premium on her car insurance; this had risen to one hundred and thirteen pounds a month by 1988 and, as her financial advisor wrote to inform her, was 'because of your unfortunate accident history'.

Three months later, Fanny was preparing for what would become her very final public appearance on television. She had been invited to be a guest on *The Last Resort*, a popular, alternative, late-night chat and comedy show hosted by Jonathan Ross on Channel Four. The show featured a house band, magicians, and interval acts as well as the other guests who that night were

Lulu, David Cassidy and Eric Idle with Lloyd Cole providing the music. The show was fast-paced, with each guest having only ten minutes at most in which to plug their latest book/tour/record and engage in some witty repartee with the host. All in front of a studio audience, and broadcast live. The 'anything could happen' feeling was part of the audience attraction.

Fanny was trailed as a special guest throughout the show, eventually appearing around thirty minutes in. Jonathan introduced her as 'the most famous' of all television cooks who was 'celebrated for taking cordon bleu out of the kitchen and into the living room, where it belongs'. Fanny was seated at a nearby table, with a glass of champagne close to hand, blowing kisses to the audience. She had updated her look, wearing a colourful, wildly patterned eighties dress in yellow, green and blue, with her favourite elaborate gold necklace covering her entire décolletage. She wore vivid red tights and looked quite striking with her blonde hair, still unmistakeably Fanny.

Jonathan looked slightly uncomfortable as he offered to top up Fanny's glass of champagne. He then asked her if she would like a cigarette, letting the audience know that she wanted to be asked this. Fanny claimed that he 'Must be raving mad!' before launching into a story about how she gave up smoking, after previously having gone through fifty a day, following a trip to France. She had since had the greatest possible contempt for those without willpower who cannot. The audience laughed along with Fanny and her story, while Jonathan smirked at her. She appeared to be lapping up the attention.

Jonathan then asked her what she did with the unsmoked cigarettes: 'Are they still lying around?' Fanny snorted that this was a silly question. The audience seemed to agree as Fanny looked slightly confused, taking a sip of champagne to revive herself, giving a cheeky look to the audience. She then began to deliver the same line again about giving up smoking and willpower, seemingly unaware that she had already said it.

It is clear as the discussion progresses that the 'script' had been rehearsed, but that Fanny was not coping well with any variances from it. Off-the-cuff was no longer her forte, if indeed it had ever been. The audience seemed to be behind her, willing her along, but Jonathan laughed at her, sneering at her responses, blowing raspberries to the audience and generally grappling to steer the interview back on track. 'My life is flashing before my eyes…' he said as he addressed the camera. He attempted to return to the prepared line of questioning; however, Fanny was already lost.

Fanny took a deep breath, a huge gulp of air; and, visibly upset, told the audience that she would never cook on television again. Choking back tears, with the audience waiting on her every word, she said, 'Because Johnnie is no longer with us, all right?' Quick as a flash, she returned to the previous conversation, but the look of upset on her face did not diminish. She became angry with the inane questions from the host, much to the amusement of the audience, retorting that 'I am so much better without you!', pointing to Jonathan. Her answers to his follow-up questions were brief as she tried, unsuccessfully, to compose herself.

As the interview came to an end, Jonathan asked her if she would come back to the show one day. Fanny slowly said, 'Ye-e-es,' although her face said clearly 'no' as she took a sip of champagne and looked to the audience knowingly. They erupted into cheers and claps, with Fanny waving wildly to them. The show moved on, introducing Lloyd Cole who would sing his latest hit record. Fanny could be seen in the background being helped off the set. Her final television appearance.

Shortly after this, Fanny moved to a new home again, settling in a petite, warden-controlled flat in the small town of Stockbridge, Hampshire, close to Southampton. While there, Fanny gave one final interview for *Woman's Own* magazine, primarily because her lifelong friend, royal biographer Douglas Keay, whom she knew from her days on the ITV show *Late Extra* in 1960, would be conducting the interview. The piece appeared without much fanfare in June of 1988, with no mention of it even on the cover of the magazine. Instead, readers were tempted in with tales of Jan Francis and Paul Nicholas being 'just good friends' (as the name of their hit comedy show suggested); Jimmy Connors telling the truth about his tennis, his money and his loneliness; Michael Douglas convincing readers he could change the way they looked; and a graphic picture of what the AIDS virus looked like, introducing the idea that everyone should be tested.

Hidden away on pages thirty-two and thirty-three, Fanny's final words are printed, alongside a large current photograph of an updated Fanny with ginger hair, wearing a bright orange twinset and pearls with wide shoulder pads, and with her nails painted to match. The headline claimed, 'I've had my cake and I've eaten it', setting the scene for a reflective interview with Fanny. Douglas noted that Fanny and Johnnie were the 'greatest double act to ever hit the kitchen' and that this was the first interview Fanny had given since Johnnie had died.

Fanny turned up at the interview in a car driven by a policeman. The reasons she gave were long and complicated, but involved her having driven in a straight line round a bend a few days earlier and being stopped by the police. 'Not one of our local force,' Fanny claimed, 'who are darlings.' Fanny had promised to take her insurance documents into her local station prior to the interview, and the kindly police officer had helped her search her flat for them.

Fanny was walking with a stick by this time, slightly lame and recovering from her hip operation. However, the famous Fanny Cradock wit and charm were still evident. 'Being dull is an insult to God!' she told Douglas, as she took off her mink coat to reveal a white cardigan over a plain brown dress. Douglas noted she was well preserved, to which Fanny retorted, 'Nivea!' The article retold Fanny's history, perhaps for a new audience, from birth to broadcast, ending in Johnnie's death after forty-nine 'wonderful, wonderful years together'.

Douglas wondered if those that remembered Johnnie would assume that Fanny had made his life a misery. 'But it was all an act darling,' she told him, her eyes misting over. 'We used to practise beforehand. We were devoted to each other. And now that he is gone, I don't want to live. I walk with memories and they're so painful. Everybody thinks I ran Johnnie. But it's just not true. I did every single thing I wanted to do, but when it came to the really major things Johnnie put his foot down. Otherwise I wouldn't have loved him. We had terrible, flaming rows and then we'd go to bed and that was the lovely part.'

Fanny felt, and indeed hoped, that their paths would cross again, in the afterlife. 'But I do talk to Johnnie every night,' she admitted. 'I have one photograph of him, in uniform, in an old leather frame. And one day I put on his glasses, because they're stronger than mine, and I looked at the photograph and it was alive. So now I look at it every morning and it gets me going for the day.' Fanny was devastated, and it had taken her over a year to come to some kind of terms. A lifelong believer in reincarnation, she lived her days 'keeping my covenant with the Almighty. I've had my cake and eaten it. And I mustn't grumble.'

Fanny also lamented on her own personality, from the viewpoint of her older, wiser and more lonely self. 'It's my greatest fault,' she told Douglas, referring to her snobbery. 'I think I should have been more dignified, and I would have more friends now if I had been more restrained.'

Ending more positively, Fanny insisted that she was still writing. She told Douglas that she was currently preparing the final chapters of part twelve of the Lormes family saga, perhaps forgetting that the eleventh instalment had never been published. Fanny told Douglas that she was no longer wealthy, but hoped that she had enough to 'see her out'.

Evangeline Evans remembers the time well. 'When Johnnie died, she completely fell apart. Tenniel, my husband, buried him. Johnnie was a gentle man. Not a drunk: I never saw him drunk. He looked dopey, was quiet, he was a wise man. He probably really loved Fanny; they lived this extraordinary, pretend life together.'

Evangeline continued, somewhat uncomfortably, 'At some point she moved to a sheltered flat in Stockbridge in Hampshire. Fanny suggested that we should come for lunch, but "Don't bring anything." Knowing her well, we brought the lunch anyway. The flat had a large living room with a fridge against one of the walls. Fanny said to my husband, "Tenniel darling, in that fridge there are some very delicious things I have made, please go and get them." When he opened the fridge door, a black cloud of flies flew out. Tenniel shut the door again and made up some lie about the food; we were so used to doing so. Fanny really was not herself. She was cared for, in a way, but really in a bad way. She went downhill very fast. She then went out of our lives. She became so dotty. We were busy. There was a long bit when we did not see her towards the end.'

She stayed in Stockbridge for a year, before moving again to a flat in Chichester, near Bognor Regis on the south coast of England. She remained there for three years before moving to a care home in Hailsham, East Sussex, further along the south coast near to Eastbourne. Fanny had been discovered living at the Chichester flat in what could only be described as squalor and confusion by an old friend, Phil Bradford, on a chance visit in 1991. He found her surrounded by pills, leaving him in no doubt that, hit hard by Johnnie's death and desiring to join him, she was contemplating suicide. Phil arranged for other friends, Rosemary Bromley and Christopher Dorman, to have Power of Attorney from the 24th of July that year. Subsequently they arranged for Fanny to move to the care home in Hailsham, close to where Phil lived with his partner, Terry Hibbert.

Friends seemed grateful that Phil and Terry had rescued Fanny in those final years. 'They got to know her when they ran a restaurant in Old Church Street, Chelsea,' recalled Evangeline Evans. 'They saved her life. They were marvellous. Two very nice men; we were never friends, but we met them and liked them very much. They were the ones who really saved her from total destruction.'

This is where Fanny would spend her final days. In seclusion, but comfortable. With dignity. Fanny died two days after Christmas in 1994 aged eighty-five, almost eight years after Johnnie. Fanny's will left fifty thousand pounds to Phil and Terry, along with the furs she had promised to other friends, and which had supposedly been stolen from Orchard House. The remainder of her estate, one hundred and fifty thousand pounds, went to the Help a Child to See charity.

Tenniel Evans conducted the funeral, held at Eastbourne Crematorium in the south of England, as he had for Johnnie too. Plans were made for Fanny and Johnnie's ashes to be reunited under a rose shrub in the crematorium garden. Tenniel's wife, Evangeline, shudders when she thinks back: 'I don't remember all that much about the funeral; I was so shocked and saddened by the bleakness of it all, I really did not take it in. We bought a terrible bunch of flowers at Victoria Station on the way down – they were the only flowers that were there. Only one of Fanny's sons, Christopher, was at the funeral. It was tragic: there were only about ten of us there. She had deteriorated. She had made hideous mistakes along the line; she was very ruthless. She'd antagonised so many people. She was impossible. The only way we coped with her was knowing she was impossible. We loved her in spite of that – accepting the impossibility. If you ever fought against her, you were lost.'

Evangeline, however, has fond memories. 'She was a strange person. She antagonised a lot of people but was always faithful to Tenniel and me. One night, she appeared as we were having supper; there was Fanny saying, "I've left Johnnie." I remember saying to her, "Oh darling, you only have a small suitcase?" She clearly had not intended to leave him for terribly long. She spent five quite extraordinary days with us.'

Evangeline wonders if there was more to Fanny at the end than she was able, at the time, to pinpoint. 'Was it dementia? We did not know about things like that then. Knowing what one knows now about mental illness, she must have had dementia. I remember one time the police called to say they had a Mrs Cradock with them: she had been driving the wrong way up the motorway on her way to see us. She was a terrible, terrifying driver. She honked at everybody to get out of the way. They were enquiring if this was right; were we expecting her? Fanny arrived eventually in her dressing gown. The way she deteriorated was really quite sad.'

Evangeline and Tenniel were her friends throughout, even when Fanny had made traditional friendship quite difficult. 'They never dropped us; maybe we were too dull. She did ring up one day, saying, "Darling, I am making my will; if I leave you my furs, will you wear them?" I always wanted a mackintosh lined with fur, so of course I said I would wear them. "I am leaving you my coats," she told me. She didn't. She left them to one of those darling couple of boys at the end.'

Trying to sum up Fanny some twenty-five years after her death, Evangeline said, 'It is difficult to find good things to say, because she was so artificial. She was just somebody making her way in the world, doing her damnedest to be glamorous and live life with a bit of colour. After the war, lots of women didn't have cooks; that's when Fanny really saw her moment. Whoopee, here is a way I can get in with something. She made herself into a cook. If she was telling the truth about her background she would not have been anywhere near a kitchen.'

Fanny's son Christopher and his family all attended the funeral. 'The children met up, which was nice,' Jane recalls. 'We took our two; the children were there (Peter, her other son, was not) so at least the kids met up. The funeral was not well attended, there were not all that many people there. She had been exiled from the celebrity scene by then anyway.'

Jane remembered that Peter had not been at all bothered about being in touch with Fanny. 'He had been in touch with Christopher, but not with Fanny again; he wanted nothing to do with her. Peter was eighteen months older than Christopher. He had been through the same things with her. Pamela was working with Fanny, they got together, then they were both cast out, exactly the same.'

Jane had not seen Fanny either during her final years. 'I did not know her through her worst years. Once Johnnie died, she went downhill. She must have been absolutely horrendous, knowing what she was like before. Johnnie kept her under control in a sense. Once on her own she would be a nightmare. I do not know what sort of state she was in at that stage. She could have been heading for dementia. Fanny with dementia would have been an absolute nightmare! The last time I saw her I was pregnant with my son; he's now fifty.'

Initially, very little about Fanny's death was reported in the press. There was no one to file the press release, a role Fanny had taken on for herself for most of her life. However, little by little, press reports began to emerge, many of which would preserve in aspic her image and reputation. Prue Leith, at that time owner of Leith's Restaurant in West London, was reported as saying: 'She was infinitely watchable, whatever you thought of the mad way she did it all. And she cooked wearing all those extraordinary clothes and diamonds. She was the Keith Floyd of her day, but I have never found a recipe of hers that worked.'

More recently, Prue reflected: 'I never met her; by the time I was on the scene, she was still on television, so very occasionally I would see her. She did demonstrations, she was amazing. My memory of her was very bossy, with everyone around on the set, in an extremely brisk way – sometimes people say the same about me. I did find her manner unattractive, but you can't help admiring her. She really knew what she was doing.'

Comparing her programmes to those shown today, Prue states, 'It is not the sort of cooking I would recommend today; it's out of fashion, green potatoes and all that. She did it with great speed and talent. I am full of admiration for her. She was a teacher, she wanted people to learn how to do it. She knew how to do it. She was like a dragon teacher at school: frightening, but you remembered what she taught you. She was entertaining, but it was not her object. She was entertaining, naturally. She was refreshing, she admitted there was a camera there, she spoke to the audience. She was very natural. She has become a kind of joke, we are all guilty of laughing along, but she is more than a joke. She was not a joke at the time, she was a forthright, knowledgeable schoolteacher.'

Keith Floyd, celebrating his fifty-first birthday at the time she died, said: 'She was first-class. I was probably about ten when I first saw her on black-and-white television. It was compulsive.'

Gyles Brandreth remembers both Fanny and Johnnie positively. 'They were lovely, very kind to the staff. Michèle even went on to work with Fanny, to do a book about cookery. She was amusing. The stories that she bullied people were not true, she was very considerate. She was wonderful! We were very close; she made me the hero of one of her Lormes novels, I was the romantic lead. There is nothing ill that we can say of her. When she died, after a documentary about Fanny had aired, I wrote to *The Times* to say how easy it was to bring someone down. It was sad.'

John Diamond, husband of Nigella Lawson and columnist for *The Times*, wrote a respectful retrospective of her life, and her place within the pioneers of television cooks, for the newspaper towards the end of the year. He wrote that: 'We watched her because she wore too much make-up and shouted at Johnny (sic) and at us. But she also had one extra ingredient to her cooking which (Philip) Harben left out: gentle snobbery.' He concluded his piece by saying: 'But now, as then, people who want to learn to cook buy books or take lessons or cling to their mothers' apron-strings. Television cooking, as Fanny recognised all those years ago, is for people who would rather just watch.'

And they did.

Bibliography and Appearances

A comprehensive list of all appearances by Fanny Cradock across BBC television and radio can be found on the BBC Genome website (www.genome.ch.bbc.co.uk) which is fantastic. Appearances on Independent Television are somewhat more difficult to search; however, a comprehensive list is available online at:

www.fannycradock.com/fanny-cradock-on-screen.html

Fanny herself often found it difficult to keep track of an accurate list of her many publications. The author has compiled a (hopefully) comprehensive list, which is available for the first time, here and online at:

www.fannycradock.com/fanny-cradock-in-print.html

Should anyone be aware of any missing publications or TV or radio appearances, please do get in touch.

Body, A. & Bon Viveur, 1967 *The Book of Foil Cookery.* London: Spectator Publications Ltd
Bon Viveur, 1951 *In Quest of Pleasure.* London: H. A. & W. L. Pitkin Ltd
Bon Viveur, 1951 *Eating in England's Inns.* London: H. A. & W. L. Pitkin Ltd

Bon Viveur, 1951 *In Search of a Holiday Hotel.* London: H. A. & W. L. Pitkin Ltd

Bon Viveur, 1951 *Eating Out in London.* London: H. A. & W. L. Pitkin Ltd

Bon Viveur, 1952 *Around Britain with Bon Viveur.* London: John Lehman

Bon Viveur, 1952 *New Dishes from the Daily Telegraph.* London: H. A. & W. L. Pitkin Ltd

Bon Viveur, 1954 *Holiday in Barcelona and the Balearics.* London: Frederick Muller Ltd

Bon Viveur, 1954 *Holiday in Holland.* London: Frederick Muller Ltd

Bon Viveur, 1954 *Bon Viveur's London.* London: Andrew Dakers Ltd

Bon Viveur, 1954 *Bon Viveur in London.* London: H. A. & W. L. Pitkin Ltd

Bon Viveur, 1954 *ABC of Wine Drinking.* London: Frederick Muller Ltd

Bon Viveur, 1954 *Definitely Different – Daily Telegraph Recipe Book.* Andover: The Chapel River Press

Bon Viveur, 1955 *Inside Information – the experts' advice from the Daily Telegraph.* London: Daily Telegraph

Bon Viveur, 1955 *Cooking with Bon Viveur.* London: Museum Press Ltd

Bon Viveur, 1955 *Holiday in Sweden.* London: Frederick Muller Ltd

Bon Viveur, 1955 *Holiday in Belgium.* London: Frederick Muller Ltd

Bon Viveur, 1955 *Bon Viveur's London and the British Isles.* London: Andrew Dakers Ltd

Bon Viveur, *1955* *Holiday in Denmark.* London: Frederick Muller Ltd

Bon Viveur, 1956 *Holiday in the Touraine.* London: Frederick Muller Ltd

Bon Viveur, 1956 *Holiday in the Austrian Tyrol.* London: Frederick Muller Ltd

Bon Viveur, 1956 *Bon Viveur Recipes – A Daily Mail Publication.* London: Daily Mail

Bon Viveur, 1958 *The Bon Viveur Request Cook Book.* London: Museum Press Ltd

Bon Viveur, 1959 *Mr Therm's Encyclopedia of Vegetable Cookery Vol 1 – Cabbages and Things.* London: Butler & Tanner Ltd

Bon Viveur, 1959 *Mr Therm's Encyclopedia of Vegetable Cookery Vol 2 – Veg and Vim.* London: Butler & Tanner Ltd

Bon Viveur, 1959 *Wining and Dining in France.* London: Putnam

Bon Viveur, 1960 *Holiday on the French Riveria.* London: Frederick Muller Ltd

Bon Viveur, 1963 *Natural and Pure Olive Oil – Book of Recipes.* London: International Olive Oil Council
Bon Viveur, 1964 *Bon Viveur Guide to Holiday in Europe.* London: Andrew Dakers Ltd
Bon Viveur, 1964 *The Daily Telegraph Cook's Book.* London: Daily Telegraph
Bon Viveur, 1967 *The Daily Telegraph Sociable Cook's Book.* London: Daily Telegraph
Bon Viveur, 1973 *Modest but Delicious.* London: Arlington Books Ltd
Bon Viveur, 1974 *Lessons For A Cook.* London: Daily Telegraph
Bon Viveur, 1975 *Pasta Cookery.* London: Daily Telegraph
Bon Viveur, 1975 *365 Puddings.* London: Daily Telegraph
Bon Viveur, 1977 *365 Soups.* London: Daily Telegraph
Cowell, F. and Cradock, F., 1965 *Everyday Cookery: A Recipe Supplement to Woman's Hour Talks.* BBC Pamphlets Paper 13
Cradock, F., 1960 *Something's Burning.* London: Putnam
Cradock, F., 1962 *Cooking with Can and Pack.* London: Museum Press Ltd
Cradock, F., 1965 *Fun with Cookery.* London: Edmund Ward Publishers Ltd
Cradock, F., 1965 *Home Cooking.* London: BBC Publications
Cradock, F., 1966 *Adventurous Cooking.* London: BBC Publications
Cradock, F., 1966 *Come For A Meal – Woman's Hour Cookery Book.* London: BBC Publications
Cradock, F., 1967 *Eight Special Menus.* London: Mendham Bros Ltd
Cradock, F., 1967 *Problem Cooking.* London: BBC Publications
Cradock, F., 1968 *Ten Classic Dishes.* London: BBC Publications
Cradock, F., 1968 *Colourful Cookery.* London: BBC Publications
Cradock, F., 1969 *Giving A Dinner Party.* London: BBC Publications
Cradock, F., 1970 *Fanny Cradock Invites.* London: BBC Publications
Cradock, F., 1972 *Nationwide Cookbook.* London: BBC Publications
Cradock, F., 1973 *Common Market Cookery – France.* London: BBC Publications
Cradock, F., 1974 *Common Market Cookery – Italy.* London: BBC Publications
Cradock, F., *1975 Fanny Cradock's Christmas Cookery.* London: Wolfe Publishing Ltd

Cradock, F., 1975 *The Lormes of Castle Rising.* London: WH Allen
Cradock, F., 1976 *The Sherlock Holmes Cookbook.* London: WH Allen
Cradock, F., 1976 *Shadows Over Castle Rising.* London: WH Allen
Cradock, F., 1977 *War Comes to Castle Rising.* London: WH Allen
Cradock, F., 1978 *Wind of Change at Castle Rising.* London: WH Allen
Cradock, F., 1979 *Uneasy Peace at Castle Rising.* London: WH Allen
Cradock, F., 1980 *Thunder Over Castle Rising.* London: WH Allen
Cradock, F., 1981 *Gathering Clouds at Castle Rising.* London: WH Allen
Cradock, F., 1982 *Fateful Years at Castle Rising.* London: WH Allen
Cradock, F., 1984 *The Defence of Castle Rising.* London: WH Allen
Cradock, F., 1986 *The Loneliness of Castle Rising.* London: WH Allen
Cradock, F., 1986 *The Windsor Secret.* London: WH Allen
Cradock, F. & Cradock, J., 1959 *Happy Cooking Children Vol 1 – Beginning to Cook.* London: Putnam
Cradock, F. & Cradock, J., 1959 *Happy Cooking Children Vol 2 – Children's Outdoor Cookery.* London: Putnam
Cradock, F. & Cradock, J., 1959 *Happy Cooking Children Vol 3 – The Young Chef.* London: Putnam
Cradock, F. & Cradock, J., 1959 *Happy Cooking Children Vol 4 – Children's Party Cookery.* London: Putnam
Cradock, F. & Cradock, J., 1968 *Coping with Christmas.* London: Fontana
Cradock, F. & Cradock, J., *1970 The Cook Hostess' Book.* London: Collins
Cradock, F. & Cradock, J., 1970-1971 *Cradock Cookery Programme Weekly Partwork Vol. 1-80.* London: Purnell
Cradock, F. & Cradock, J., 1970 *Cradock Cookery Programme Weekly (Compiling Parts 1 – 16).* London: Purnell
Cradock, F. & Cradock, J., 1971 *Kitchen Diary 1972.* London: Queen Anne Press
Cradock, F. & Cradock, J., 1978 *Fanny and Johnnie Cradock's Freezer Book.* London: WH Allen
Cradock, F. & Cradock, J., 1978 *Cooking is Fun.* London: WH Allen
Cradock, F. & Cradock, J., 1979 *A Cook's Essential Alphabet.* London: WH Allen
Cradock, F. & Cradock, J., 1981 *Time to Remember – A Cook for All Seasons.* Exeter: Webb & Bower Ltd

Cradock, F. & Cradock, J., 1985 *A Lifetime in the Kitchen – Volume 1 – For Beginner Cooks.* London: WH Allen
Cradock, F. & Cradock, J., 1985 *A Lifetime in the Kitchen – Volume 2 – Family Cooking.* London: WH Allen
Cradock, F. & Cradock, J., 1985 *A Lifetime in the Kitchen – Volume 3 – For Ambitious Cooks.* London: WH Allen
Cradock, J., 1975 *Wines for Today.* London: Frederick Muller Ltd
Cradock, P., 1949 *Gateway to Remembrance.* London: Andrew Dakers Ltd
Cradock, P., 1951 *The Eternal Echo.* London: Andrew Dakers Ltd
Dale, F., 1942 *The Scorpion's Suicide.* London: Hurst & Blackett
Dale, F., 1944 *Women Must Wait.* London: Hurst & Blackett
Dale, F., 1944 *The Rags of Time.* London: Hurst & Blackett
Dale, F., 1945 *The Land is in Good Heart.* London: Hurst & Blackett
Dale, F., 1945 *When Michael Was Three.* London: Hutchinson's Books for Young People
Dale, F., 1947 *When Michael Was Six.* London: Hutchinson's Books for Young People
Dale, F., 1946 *My Seed, Thy Harvest.* London: Hurst & Blackett
Dale, F., 1947 *Always – The Enchanted Land.* London: Hutchinson's Books for Young People
Dale, F., 1948 *O Daughter of Babylon.* London: Hurst & Blackett
Dale, F., 1948 *The Dryad and the Toad.* London: Hutchinson's Books for Young People
Dale, F., 1949 *The Echo In The Cup.* London: Hurst & Blackett
Dale, F., 1949 *The Practical Cook.* London: John Lehman Ltd
Dale, F., 1950 *The Story of Joseph and the Pharaohs.* London: Hodder & Stoughton Ltd
Dale, F. 1950 *Brigadier Gooseyplum Goes to War.* London: Hodder & Stoughton Ltd
Dale, F., 1950 *The Shadow of Heaven.* London: Hurst & Blackett
Dale, F., 1950 *The Gooseyplums By The Sea.* London: Hodder & Stoughton Ltd
Dale, F., 1950 *Dark Reflection.* London: Hurst & Blackett
Dale, F., 1950 *Gooseyplums of Duckpond in the Dip.* London: Hodder & Stoughton Ltd

Dale, F., 1950 *Bon Voyage – How To Enjoy Your Holiday In Europe By Car.* London: John Lehman Ltd

Dale, F., 1951 *Daily Express Enjoyable Cookery*. London: Daily Express

Dale, F., 1952 *The Ambitious Cook.* London: John Lehman Ltd

Dale, F., 1952 *Fish Knight and Sea Maiden.* London: Hodder & Stoughton Ltd

Glasse, H., (Introduction by Cradock, F.) 1971 *The Art of Cookery Made Plain and Easy.* London: S. R. Publishers Ltd

Gouffe, J., (Introduction by Cradock, F.) 1973 *The Royal Cookery Book.* Wakefield: E. P. Publishers Ltd

Leigh, S., 1947 *Naughty Red Lion, Beware.* London: Hodder & Stoughton

Sources

MANY, MANY SOURCES have been investigated and interrogated during the research for this book. In addition to the staggering number of publications from Fanny Cradock herself (listed in the previous Bibliography section and owned by the author) the following publications and sources have been particularly crucial.

Bateman, M., 1967 *Cooking People.* London: Leslie Frewin
Dickson-Wright, C., 1999 *Food: What We Eat and How We Eat.* London: Ebury Press
Ellis, C., 2007 *Fabulous Fanny Cradock: TV's Outrageous Queen of Cuisine.* Stroud: Sutton Publishing
La Rue, D., 1987 *From Drag to Riches.* London: Viking
Patten, M., 1992 *What's Cooking? Recipes of a Lifetime.* London: Hawker
Various, 1961 *Gilbert Harding by His Friends.* London: Andre Deutsch

The many books of Fanny's father, published as Valentine and Mark Cross by Ward, Lock & Co.

Online resources:

The genealogy websites www.ancestry.co.uk, www.scotlandspeople.gov.uk and www.findmypast.co.uk
The British Newspaper Archive www.britishnewspaperarchive.co.uk

BBC Genome website www.genome.ch.bbc.co.uk
The TV Times Project www.bufvc.ac.uk/tvandradio/tvtip/
ITV Archive www.itvarchive.com
BBC Archive www.bbc.co.uk/archive and across social media
Peter Botterill blog www.peterbotterillfannysboy.blogspot.com

Physical resources (various dates and years):

Woman magazine
Woman's Own magazine
The Listener magazine
Radio Times
TV Times
Punch magazine
The Spectator
Daily Mail
Daily Telegraph
Daily Express

References and Acknowledgements

THE AUTHOR AND THE PUBLISHER would like to thank:

Chris Duffy, The Auchtermuchty Food Museum for such generous access to the Fanny Cradock Personal Archive.

Hannah Ratford at the BBC Written Archives Centre, Caversham, for access to the 'Fanny Files' and for making me keep my notes organised.

Staff at the National Library of Scotland, especially in the Reading Room on George IV Bridge, Edinburgh, for patience and sheer brute strength in wheeling trolleyloads of resources (especially *The Listener*, *Radio Times*, *Woman* and *Woman's Own* magazines and various newspaper collections) around so that they could be accessed.

The British Film Institute (BFI) for access to rare and otherwise unavailable footage. And to the Moving Image Archive in Glasgow for viewing facilities.

To Phil Lyon, Ana Tominc and the Gastronomy team at Queen Margaret University, Edinburgh, for encouraging me to write my master's dissertation on Fanny Cradock in the first place.

To everyone who has ever uploaded clips of Fanny Cradock to YouTube, I am eternally grateful, with special mention for Fanny-fan, Lewis Pringle.

To all the social media followers on Twitter, Instagram and Facebook who have shared memories, reactions and clues which have helped to track down vital information – thank you all.

Mostly, the most enormous thanks go to all those who knew Fanny personally, professionally and otherwise up-until-now privately, who gave time to be interviewed. So, many special thanks to:

Sir David Attenborough
Gyles Brandreth
Jane Chapman
Wendy Colvin
Evangeline Evans
Diana Henry
Charles Kenyon
Graham Kerr
Michael Leale
Prue Leith
Nick Owen
Nicholas Parsons
Dame Esther Rantzen